MW01622879

Betrock's

LANDSCAPE PALMS

Betrock's

LANDSCAPE PALMS

Alan W. Meerow

Betrock Information Systems, Inc.
Hollywood, Florida

First Edition 2006

Published by
Betrock Information Systems, Inc.
7770 Davie Road Extension
Hollywood, Florida 33024-2516

Portions of this book were originally published in a slightly different form as **Betrock's GUIDE TO LANDSCAPE PALMS**.

Library of Congress Cataloging-in-Publication Date
Meerow, Alan W., 2006
Betrock's LANDSCAPE PALMS / Alan W. Meerow
Library of Congress 2005938136
ISBN 0-9629761-7-2

Front and back cover design by Bette Betrock and Catherine Galletta
Front and back cover photography by Cornelia Bularca
Inside front and inside back cover photograph by Irv Betrock
Page layout and design by Donna Kurtzer

Printed in the United States of America

Areca vestiaria
Photo credit: Geoff Stein

Contents

Acknowledgements .... *vii*
Preface .... *ix*
Introduction *1*

Section I

An Introduction to the Palm Family *5*
How Palms Grow *7*
Classification of the Palm Family *10*
International Palm Society *11*

Section II

Encyclopedia of Landscape Palms *13*

Section III

Use and Care of Landscape Palms *153*
Propagation of Palms *154*
Transplanting of Palms *156*
Landscape Use and Care of Palms *158*
Cold Protection and Treating Cold-Damaged Palms *159*
Fertilizing Palms *160*
Insect Pests of Landscape Palms *163*
Disease Problems of Landscape Palms *165*

Section IV

Europe-USDA Plant Hardiness Zone Map *172*
USDA Plant Hardiness Zone Map *173*
Landscape Characteristics Tables *174*
General Index *183*
Glossary *189*
A Selected Palm Bibliography *190*
About the Author *191*

Washingtonia robusta

Acknowledgements

Numerous colleagues, students, teachers and friends have helped make this book a reality through their enthusiasm, dedication, and love of palms. My former colleagues at the Fort Lauderdale Research and Education Center, Drs. Timothy K. Broschat, Henry Donselman, Monica Elliot, Robin Giblin-Davis, Nigel Harrison and Forrest W. Howard have enlightened all palm horticulturists with myriad developments in the science of palm horticulture. Donald R. Hodel aided in the accuracy of the information on Chamaedorea. Chuck Hubbuch and Nancy Edmundson reviewed the manuscript in its first edition. In addition, the following people, directly or indirectly, have enriched my own experience of palms and, as a consequence, the value of this book: Dr. Bill Baker, Dr. Michael Balick, David Bar-Zvi, Dr. Byron and Libby Besse, Dr. Ann Chase, Murray and Deborah Corman, Paul Craft, John DeMott, Dr. John Dransfield, Don Evans, Dr. Jack Fisher, Martin Gibbons, Dr. William Hahn, Dr. Andrew Henderson, C. Way and Geri Hoyt, Dearmand Hull, Danilo Viana Lima, Dr. Harri Lorenzi, David McLean, Jack Miller, Dr. Larry Noblick, Chris Oppenheimer, David Pais, Ron and Charlotte Schaff, Jeff and Larry Searle, Dr. Gary Simone, Toby Spanner, Bill Theobold, Dr. P. B. Tomlinson, Dr. Natalie Uhl and Dr. Scott Zona. However, all opinions and subjective commentary expressed within these pages are my own and should not be laid at the feet of these individuals.

I am indebted to Geoff Stein for allowing the use of many of his fine photographs. I also thank the following individuals who provided photographs in this book: Timothy K. Broschat, James DeFilipis, Martin Gibbons, Robin Giblin-Davis, Nigel Harrison, Don Hodel, Chuck Hubbuch, Byron R. Keith, Michael Richards, Jr. and Toby Spanner. My sincerest appreciation to Irv and Bette Betrock, Denis Bedu and Donna Kurtzer, of Betrock Information Systems, for their patience and diligence in welcoming this revised edition of our successful project into the world. In 1992, we turned an idea into a reality, one that we now have made even better. I dedicate this book to my wife Linda and my children, Sara, Andrew, and Erica, who put up with my many long nights in front of a computer screen.

Livistona saribus

Preface

At the Royal Botanic Gardens, Kew in London, where I work, I am able to escape to the steamy tropics of the famous Palm House at a moment's notice, even on the chilliest Winter day, and enjoy the lush and diverse palm collection that thrives in that magnificent Victorian conservatory. However, I cannot help feeling envious of those who live in warmer countries where palms feature not as mere botanic garden subjects, but throughout the horticultural landscape. No matter how familiar I have become with commonly cultivated species, such as Dypsis lutescens *or* Roystonea regia, *they never fail to thrill me. Palms provide drama, strong architecture and glamour to even the most mundane of horticultural design schemes, and in creative hands they can work real magic. Their merits extend beyond their aesthetic properties, however. Many palms are remarkably adaptable to a range of cultivation conditions and the ease with which large specimens of some species may be transplanted means that they may be used for instant effect. It is hardly surprising that the landscape industry cannot get enough of the palm family!*

In revising the ever-popular **Betrock's Guide to Landscape Palms**, *Alan Meerow has done a great service to palm growers and the landscape industry. Unlike other palm guides which provide information on so wide a range of species that it can be difficult to distinguish the readily available and easily grown from rarities best reserved for the enthusiast, Dr. Meerow's book focuses on the most important landscape species. He has also thrown in a few for good measure, such as Satakentia liukiuensis, that are more unusual, but have the potential to become increasingly popular. He has gone to great efforts to make the text accessible to all by describing the horticultural and botanical properties of each species in easy bullet-point form and straightforward language. A concise section on the structure and classification of palms will help the reader to navigate the terminological labyrinth that can be so off-putting to the non-botanist. The book also includes a valuable discussion of the cultivation, pests and diseases of landscape species.*

As a recent recipient of the Peter H. Raven Award for Scientific Outreach from the American Society of Plant Taxonomists, there can be no better qualified person than Alan Meerow to write such a thoughtfully designed and informative book. In **Betrock's Landscape Palms**, *Dr. Meerow has combined his skills as a professional botanist with his talent for supporting the public understanding of science in horticulture. There is no doubt that this new edition will be invaluable to experienced palm growers and inspirational to new generations of enthusiasts.*

William J. Baker, Ph.D.
Head of Palm Research
Royal Botanic Gardens, Kew

Hyophorbe verschaffeltii

Introduction

Palms are the universal symbol of the tropics. As exotic and inextricably related to pleasure as this mystique may be, it belies the importance of this family of plants that Linnaeus called "Principes," the princes of the plant kingdom. Palms are second only to the grasses or grains in economic importance. The palm family, consisting of over 2500 species arrayed among 200 genera, is known to botanists as the Arecaceae, though the old name Palmae is still sometimes used in horticulture. Over 90% of the diversity within the family is contained within the world's tropics, and the utility of many palms in human industry at both the subsistence and world market levels makes the Arecaceae the third most economically important family of plants after the grasses and the legumes. Throughout the world's tropics, palms have figured in local and national economies for centuries, even millenia. For some species in fact, virtually every part of the plant has found some use by people: leaves for thatch and fiber, food and oil from the fruits and seed, sugar and intoxicants from the sap, and even trunks for construction. Certain Amazon tribes revere a particular palm as the "giver of all life," so dependent are they on the sustenance provided by that plant.

As landscape plants, palms are prized for their unique architecture and the intricate texture and form of their leaves and stems. Their beauty, durability, and variety rank them among the most highly valued of all landscape plants in subtropical and tropical regions.

With but a few exceptions, the 126 species covered in detail within these pages represent the most popular and available palms for landscape use in regions of the United States where palms can be grown outdoors. It is intended, however, that this book be useful anywhere in the world where palms are used as exterior or, in some cases, interior landscape plants. A few of the palms treated are not yet widely offered in nurseries but have proven themselves well worth wider cultivation. It is not intended as a complete guide to myriad species of palms available to the collector, but as a sourcebook for the novice and landscape professional alike.

How to Use This Book

This book is divided into four parts. The first section provides some background about the palm family. The second section of the book is an encyclopedia of 126 cultivated palm species arranged alphabetically by scientific name. Each species treated is illustrated with at least one color photograph. The text that accompanies the photos follows a structured format that remains constant throughout the book and which is designed to present descriptive and cultural information about each palm in a simple, easily accessible manner. Overly technical language has been kept to a minimum. Any botanical terminology used in the text is defined in the glossary located in Section IV. The third section of the book provides information on the cultivation of landscape palms including fertilization, transplanting, landscape use and maintenance, pests, diseases and other problems encountered by palms. The fourth section consists of lists of palms with particular landscape tolerances and an index to all the palms treated arranged alphabetically by common names and incorrect scientific name (synonyms). This should allow the reader to locate a species within the text even if he or she knows only a common name or incorrect scientific name for it.

Data referring to landscape tolerances such as drought tolerance, light requirements, etc. are based on expectations for the species in a warm, subtropical or tropical humid climate. In locations such as California, many of the palms listed as highly drought tolerant will require supplemental irrigation during that state's long, rainless summer season. Likewise, some of the palms whose light requirements are listed as "moderate" (a number of *Chamaedorea* spp., for example), are able to withstand full sun in coastal California's cool climate.

The following are brief explanatory notes about the data fields used throughout the encyclopedia:

Scientific Name: The universally accepted botanical name (genus and species) for the palm. Phonetic pronunciation is given in parentheses, with the accented syllable in capital letters.

Common Name: One or more widely used vernacular names for the palm.

Classification: The subdivision of the palm family to which the particular species belongs (see "Classification of the Palm Family," page 10). The first name is the subfamily and the second is the tribe. These are provided for the reader with interest in knowing to which other palms a particular species is related.

Origin: The part of the world to which the particular species is native.

Hardiness: The range of climate zones in which the palm can be grown successfully, based on the USDA Plant Hardiness Zone Map (see page 173). It should be kept in mind that during unusually severe winters, some species normally suitable for a particular zone may be injured or even killed. Actual temperatures where damage has occurred or for which survival has been recorded are also included. When a zone appears in parentheses, it indicates that the species may survive with protection in that zone. This book is oriented towards palm selection for USDA Hardiness Zones 10-11, where the greatest diversity of palms can be grown. For a much larger selection of palms suitable for USDA Zones 6-9, I refer the reader to the companion volume *Betrock's Cold Hardy Palms*.

Height: The average expected height or height range that the species can be expected to reach. However, the actual height that the palm will achieve will vary due to environmental and cultural conditions.

Growth Rate: The relative rate of growth of the species. Slow indicates annual growth of less than 1 foot (0.3 m). Moderate refers to annual growth of 1-3 feet (0.3-0.9 m). Fast indicates yearly growth increments of more than 3 feet (0.9 m). Again, the actual growth rate exhibited will vary depending on the conditions received in cultivation.

Horticultural Characteristics

Salt Tolerance: The palm's relative tolerance of salt, whether from spray received by the leaves or saline water in the root zone. Low indicates that the palm is largely intolerant of salt on the roots or leaves; moderate refers to palms that will require protection from direct spray and intensely saline water but can tolerant mildly brackish water and some incidental spray; high indicates a palm that can be planted in exposed seaside locations.

Drought Tolerance: The palm's relative ability to persist and grow without supplementary irrigation once established. Low indicates that the palm will require regular irrigation during periods of no rainfall; moderate refers to a palm that will require occasional irrigation during dry periods; high refers to a palm that can survive periods of drought without supplemental irrigation. Keep in mind that these ratings are oriented towards climates with rainfall distributed throughout the year and average humidity levels above 40% RH. Unless a palm is noted as particularly well-adapted to semi-arid regions, one should expect that the palm will be less drought tolerant than listed in such areas.

Soil Preferences: The type of soil most suitable to the palm. Acid refers to soils with a pH of less than 7.0; alkaline refers to a soil with a pH higher than 7.0; well-drained refers to a soil that does not remain water-logged; widely adaptable indicates a palm with a broad tolerance of soil types.

Light Requirements: The relative light exposures suitable for the palm. Low refers to deep shade (less than 500 foot candles); moderate signifies part shade (500-5000 foot candles); high refers to full sun (light intensities of 5000 foot candles). Light tolerance may increase for some species when planted in climates where high temperatures remain moderate.

Nutritional Requirements: The relative nutrient need of the palm. Low signifies a palm that requires no supplementary fertilization under typical landscape conditions; moderate indicates a palm requiring periodic light fertilization for good growth; high refers to palms that must receive regular fertilization in order to prosper.

Uses: The way in which the palm can be used in the landscape.

Propagation: The way in which the palm is increased. For most palms, seed is the only means of propagation, and germination times are indicated if known, as well as type of germination (see glossary).

Human Hazards: If present, indicates whether the palm presents any danger of injury, either due to spines or teeth present on some of its parts, or the presence of a skin irritant in the fruit or any other allergenic properties that may be encountered.

Pest Problems: Insect or mites that frequently attack the palm.

Disease Problems: Common diseases or other disorders that affect the palm.

Cultivars: Named cultivated varieties of the palm that are available in addition to the "typical" form. Most cultivated palms do not have recognized cultivars.

Comments: Miscellaneous biological and cultural information about the palm.

Morphology (Identification Characteristics)

Habit: Whether the palm is solitary (single-stemmed) or clustering (multiple-stemmed) and the number of leaves usually found in the canopy.
Stem: Salient identifying characteristics of the palm stem.
Leaf: A description of leaf shape and form (see glossary, page 188).
Foliage Color: A description of leaf color.
Leaf Size: Dimensions of the palm leaf.
Petiole: Size and description of the leaf stem.
Crownshaft: This field is present only when a true crownshaft formed by tightly sheathing leaf bases is present, and describes its distinctive features.
Inflorescence: A description of the form, position and size of the flowerstalks.
Gender: How sex is expressed in the flowers of the species. Some palms have bisexual flowers (male and female sex organs in the same flower); some have separate male and female flowers on the same flowerstalk (monoecious); and others have separate male and female plants (dioecious).
Flower Color: Color of the flowers.
Fruit Size: Size of the fruit.
Fruit Color: Color of the fruit.
Fruit: If this is present, the fruit contains calcium oxylate crystals that irritate the skin if the ripe fruit is handled without protection. If the fruit is edible, this field is present as well.

Throughout this book, all measurements have been converted from the U. S. System of Measurements to the Metric System. A conversion table follows.

Metric Conversion Table

Inch	Cm	Inch	Cm	Feet	Meters	Feet	Meters
1/8	0.3	6	15	1/4	0.08	9	2.7
1/4	0.6	7	17.5	1/3	0.1	10	3.0
1/3	0.8	8	20	1/2	0.15	12	3.6
1/2	1.25	9	22.5	1	0.3	15	4.5
3/4	1.9	10	25	1 1/2	0.5	18	5.4
1	2.5	12	30	2	0.6	20	6.0
1 1/4	3.1	15	37.5	2 1/2	0.8	25	7.5
1 1/2	3.75	18	45	3	0.9	30	9.0
1 3/4	4.4	20	50	4	1.2	35	10.5
2	5.0	24	60	5	1.5	40	12
3	7.5	30	75	6	1.8	50	15
4	10	32	80	7	2.1	75	22.5
5	12.5	36	90	8	2.4	100	30

With this guide, horticulturists everywhere should be able to fine-tune their selection of landscape palms to effectively match any site and climatic conditions. It is to palm enthusiasts everywhere, whether lifelong or recently converted, for whom the palm family truly represents (as the great L. H. Bailey said) "the big game of the plant world," that this book is dedicated.

Livistona rotundifolia
Photo credit: Geoff Stein

Section I

An Introduction to the Palm Family

Howea forsteriana

An Introduction to the Palm Family

Palms, despite the lofty heights that many may reach, are different from typical broad-leaved trees in profound ways that have significant consequences in horticulture. Palms are members of a large and natural group of the flowering plants known as the monocots. This group includes the lilies, grasses, irises, orchids and bromeliads. Most monocot families consist of primarily herbaceous plants; that is, low-growing, soft-tissued plants. Relatively few other monocots attain the size of many palms. This is largely due to certain constraints placed on the development of the monocot stem, which in turn distinguish them from the other flowering plants (known as dicots). All of our favorite flowering trees and shrubs, and most of our shade trees, are dicots. Oaks, maples, azaleas, roses and most garden annuals are dicots.

Dicots have a developmental feature that virtually all monocots lack. Within the stems of woody dicots, the water and food conducting tissue occurs in complete, concentric rings. In monocots, these same vascular tissues occur in bundles scattered throughout the internal tissue of the stem, rather than in complete rings. In dicots, a specialized layer of cells called the vascular cambium is formed between the water conducting rings (xylem) and the food conducting rings (phloem). The vascular cambium produces new rings of xylem towards the inside of the stem, and new rings of phloem towards the outside. For the vast majority of monocots, including all palms, no vascular cambium exists.

Woody dicots, blessed by nature with a vascular cambium, are capable of what plant scientists call secondary growth. This means that a dicot tree stem is always producing new vascular tissue and increasing in diameter as it ages. The vascular cambium also allows a dicot tree to repair injuries to its stem fairly efficiently, and horticulturists to successfully graft stems or buds of one species or variety onto the stem of another closely related species. This ability to produce secondary growth is evident in the pattern of growth rings that can be seen in a cross-section of a woody dicot stem.

Unlike an oak tree or an apple tree, palms are essentially incapable of secondary growth and do not produce annual growth rings. Once a palm stem achieves its maximum girth at a given point on the stem, it is largely incapable of increasing its stem diameter (though some palm stems continue to swell through other means). Furthermore, the bundles of conducting tissue within the palm stem must last the entire life of the palm. Once a palm stem achieves its maximum diameter, not one single additional vascular bundle will be added to the internal tissue of the stem! Palms are also not able to repair their vascular bundles if damage is received to the stem. And, not surprisingly, it is impossible to graft one part of a palm to another. Most importantly of all, the future of a palm stem rides upon the continued health of a single actively growing bud or "palm heart" with little or no ability to regenerate itself. Very few palms have the ability to branch on their aerial stems. Thus, if the palm heart is killed, the entire palm (if solitary) or the palm stem (if clustering) is doomed to eventual death.

With this in mind, it becomes all the more remarkable that palms have been able to reach such scales of height as they are indeed capable. P. B. Tomlinson of the National Tropical Botanical Garden, who has studied the structural biology of palms in detail, likens their stems (fibrous vascular bundles scattered in pithy stem tissue) to steel-reinforced concrete, a telling analogy indeed!

How Palms Grow

Unlike broad-leaved trees, palms complete their thickening growth or increase in diameter before elongating. This is most evident in those palms that do not develop a conspicuous aerial trunk for a number of years (*Sabal* spp., for example), but is true for all palm species. During this "establishment phase," as Tomlinson has called it, the palm is particularly sensitive to growth checks or less than optimal conditions.

Root system. Typical of all monocots, the functioning root system of a palm develops from the stem. Very shortly after seed germination, the seedling root of a palm ceases to function and is replaced by roots produced from a specialized area of the stem called the root initiation zone. It is during the establishment phase of its growth that a young palm fully develops this initiation zone at the base of the stem. Such roots, originating from the stem, are called adventitious, in contrast to the underground root systems of dicots which develop sequentially from a perennial seedling root. Again, unlike dicots, palm roots emerge from the stem at maximum thickness; they are incapable of secondary growth. They can branch, however, to three levels. The third rank of root branches are the thinnest and function primarily in absorption of water and nutrients. Palm roots do not produce root hairs. Palm roots are capable of significant lateral growth; roots of some palms have been measured well over a hundred feet from the parent trunk. On some palms the root initiation zone extends for some distance above ground level on the trunk. Most extreme in this regard are the "stilt-root" palms of tropical rain forests that produce long, thick support roots from as high as 6-10' (1.8-3 m) above the trunk base. Extensions of the root initiation zone can also be seen on those date palm species that produce a mass of aerial roots stubs at the trunk base.

Palm stems. The stems or trunks of palms are as diverse as the palms themselves, varying in thickness, shape, surface features and habit (Fig. 1.1). Though none are treated in this book, a sizable group of palms even grow as high-climbing vines into the canopies of rain forest trees. Many palm stems remain covered with the remains of old leaf bases for many years (Fig. 1.2); others shed their dead leaves very readily. For the first years of a palm's life, the stem consists of little more than overlapping leaf bases shielding the all important bud or palm heart. Some palm trunks swell noticeably at the base as they develop with age; others develop conspicuous bulges further up on the stem. Most tall growing palms eventually produce a clear trunk, usually gray or brown, sometimes green. The trunks of some palms are conspicuously spiny (Fig. 1.3); these spines are often the remains of fibers that occurred within the tissue of the leaf bases. The scars left behind by fallen leaves frequently create a distinctive pattern on the trunk. These may appears as rings, or, if the leaves incompletely sheath the trunk, variously shaped scars. The point on the stem at which a leaf scar occurs (or where a leaf is still attached) is called a node. Very few palms are capable of branching on their aerial stems in the normal course of their growth; occasionally an aberrant individual of an otherwise non-branching species will produce a branched head.

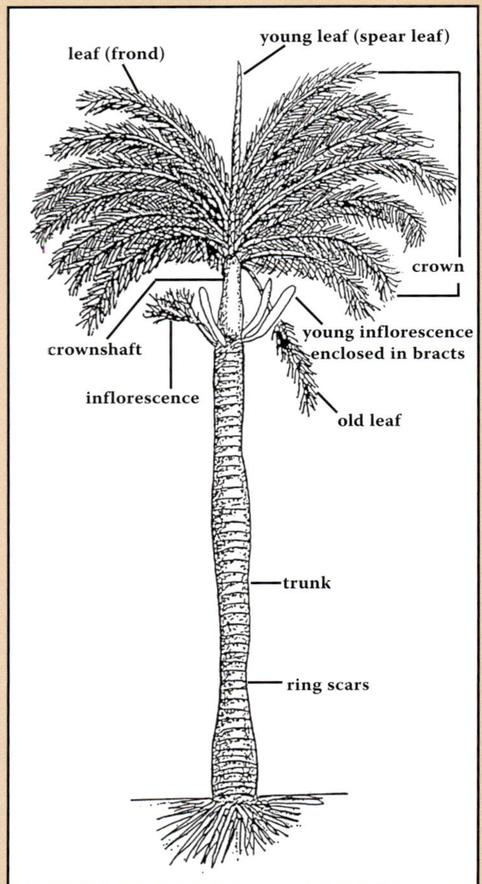

Fig. 1.1. Structure of a representative palm

Palm leaves. The leaves of palms are the largest such organs in the plant kingdom. All palm leaves consist of three main parts (Figs. 1.4-1.7): the blade, the petiole or leaf stem, and the leaf base. The leaf base is basically that part of the petiole that sheathes the stem. On many palms, the base remains attached to the trunk or stem for some time after the blade and the petiole drop off. In some cases, the pattern of leaf base stubs is a distinctive feature of the palm's appearance. The tubular leaf bases of some feather-leaved palms sheath each other so tightly around the stem that they form a conspicuous neck-like structure called a crownshaft (Fig. 1.8). Often waxy and smooth, and sometimes beautifully colored, the crownshaft is usually a structure of singular beauty. The leaf stem or petiole can be short or long; in a few species it is apparently obsolete. The petiole of a number of palm species is toothed along the margins (Fig. 1.9), ferociously so in some.

Fig. 1.2. Stem of pindo palm (*Butia capitata*) with intact leaf bases

Palm leaf blades basically fall into three main classes, palmate or costapalmate (the fan palms), pinnate or bipinnate leaves (the feather palms), or entire leaves. The fan palms are classified as either palmate (Fig. 1.4) or costapalmate (Fig. 1.5). Fan palm leaves are circular or shaped like an out-stretched hand. They are divided shallowly or deeply into a variable number of segments which are often split at the tips themselves. Palmate and costapalmate leaves are similar in appearance except for the extension of the leaf stem (petiole) into the blade of the costapalmate leaf. This extension is sometimes referred to as the costa. Costapalmate leaves are often twisted or folded sharply along or at the tip of the costa. Many fan palms have an additional feature called the hastula (Fig. 1.10) that is sometimes useful in identifying the species. The hastula is a small, thin, more-or-less rounded protuberance of tissue located at the point where the petiole meets the blade. Hastulas are most frequently located on the upper surface of the leaf; a few fan palms have them on both surfaces. It is blunt or pointed at the tip, and its function is unknown.

Feather palm leaves consist of a network of individual leaflets arrayed along an extension of the leaf stem called the rachis. Pinnately compound (Fig. 1.6) palm leaves are

Fig. 1.3. The spines on the stems of *Zombia antillarum* are the remains of leaf base fibers

feather leaves that are only once-compound; that is, there is only a single series of leaflets. The leaflets may be numerous or few, narrow or broad, pointed at the tip or blunt and toothed. They can be regularly arranged along the rachis or attached in groups of several. Bipinnately compound palm leaves (Fig. 1.7) are twice-compound; that is, the primary leaflets themselves consist of system of smaller secondary leaflets. Bipinnately compound leaves are very rare in the palm family, occurring in only a single genus, *Caryota* (the fishtail palms).

Entire-leaved palms have neither segments nor leaflets. Instead, the leaf consists of an unsplit (or at most two-lobed, called bifid) blade, longer than it is wide. The first leaves of most palm seedlings are entire or bifid, regardless of what type of mature leaf occurs on the palm.

Induplicate vs. reduplicate leaves. An important feature of palm leaves that has significance in the taxonomy and identification of the major groups within the family is the way in which the leaf segments (fan palms) or leaflets (feather palms) are folded around the main vein or midrib. Palms in which the leaflets or segments are folded upward, forming a "V", are called induplicate (Fig. 1.11). Palms in which the leaflets or segments are folded downward, forming an inverted "V", are termed reduplicate (Fig. 1.12). Most of the fan palms have induplicate leaves, while the majority of the feather palms have reduplicate leaves. The best place to look to determine which type of folding characterizes a particular species is right at the point where the leaflet attaches to the rachis (feather palms) or, on fan palms, the point where the segments first split from the rest of the leaf.

Palm flowers. The individual flowers of a palm are generally quite small and inconspicuous, but are usually borne in such numbers on the flowerstalk or inflorescence that they collectively are showy (Figs. 1.13-1.16). The inflorescences of palms are frequently quite long and much-branched, but on some species they are short and spike-like (unbranched). On palms with crownshafts, the flowerstalks are always produced from the trunk below the crownshaft, and thus below all the leaves as well. On palms without crownshafts, the infloresences emerge from among the leaves. On a few palms whose stems flower once (*Corypha* spp. and *Nannorrhops ritchiana*), the flowerstalks are held above the leaves. Some palm flowerstalks are backed by a large, boat-like bract or spathe (Fig. 1.14) that may persist even in fruit.

Fig. 1.8. The crownshaft of royal palm (*Roystonea regia*)

The parts of the simplest palm flowers occur in three's or multiples thereof; however, there is an enormous amount of variation in flower structure throughout the family. Likewise, palms vary greatly in the gender allocation of their flowers. Some have bisexual flowers with both functional male and female reproductive organs. Many palms have separate male and female flowers on the same plant, usually on the same inflorescence. Other palm species produce separate male and female plants altogether, with flowers of only one sex occurring on any one particular plant. All date palms (*Phoenix* spp.) fit in this third category. The small size and fairly bland coloration of most palm flowers led botanists to conclude that most palms were pollinated by wind. It is now known that, in fact, most palms are insect pollinated.

Palm fruits and seeds. In contrast to the often diminutive flowers, the fruits (and seed as well) of many palm species are fairly large and conspicuous (Figs. 1.17-1.20). In fact, the largest seed of any plant known on the face of the earth belongs to a palm, the double coconut (*Lodoicea maldavica*). The majority of palm fruits are classified as drupes. A drupe is defined as a fleshy, one-seeded fruit that does not open or split at maturity. Some palm fruits qualify as berries. A number of palm fruits contain more than one seed, but the majority carry only one seed within. The fruits of most palms have a fleshy or fibrous outer wall that is frequently attractively colored. For more than a few species, the display afforded by the ripe fruits is much more conspicuous than that of the flowers! The seed within a palm fruit is protected by a bony or fibrous coat. The seed coat of some species bears interesting patterns of ornamentation or sculpturing on its surface. Most of the volume of the seed is taken up by the nutritive tissue called endosperm that feeds the developing seedling. The actual embryo of a palm is quite small, and is located in a small chamber at one end of the seed (Fig 1.21).

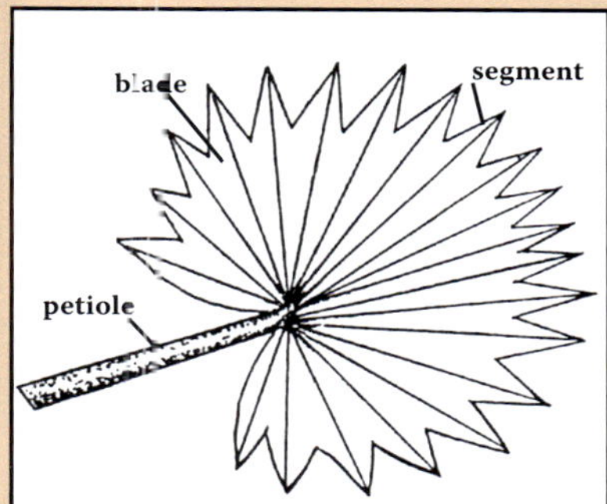

Fig. 1.4. Palmate or fan leaf

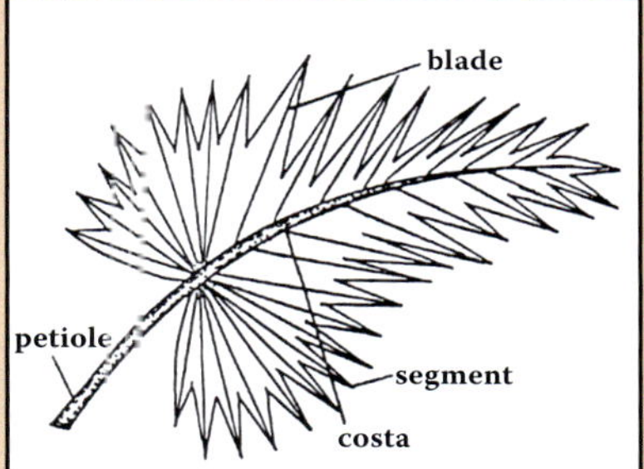

Fig. 1.5. Costapalmate leaf

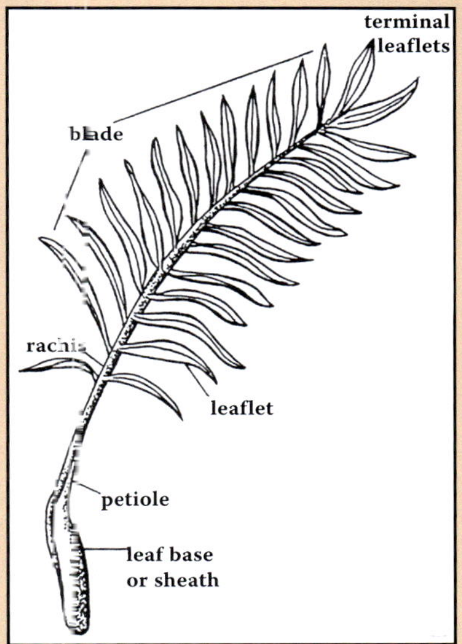

Fig. 1.6. Pinnate or feather leaf

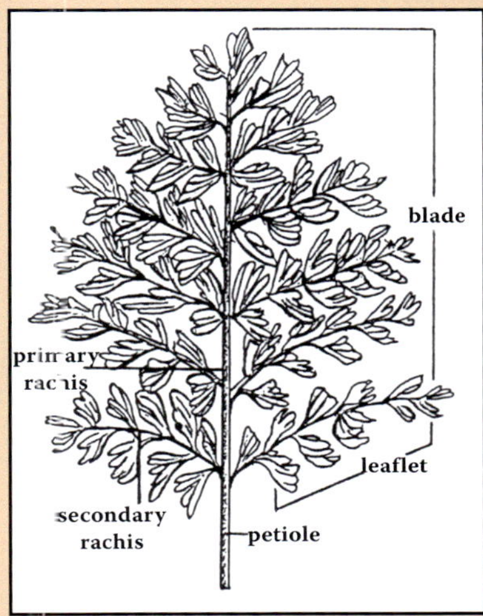

Fig. 1.7. Bipinnate leaf

Fig. 1.9. The leaf stem of *Livistona saribus* is armed with large, sharp

Seed germination. The way palm seeds germinate falls into one of two categories. In palms with remote germination (Fig. 1.22), the seedling axis develops at some distance from the actual seed. The first structure to emerge from the seed is called the cotyledonary petiole. It resembles, and many people mistake it for, the first seedling root. The cotyledonary petiole grows downward into the soil (sometimes very deeply) and swells at its base. From this swelling emerges the first seedling root (radicle) and seedling shoot (plumule). The actual cotyledon or seed leaf remains inside the seed functioning as an absorptive organ called the haustorium. The haustorium transfers nutrients from the endosperm to the young seedling. In palm seeds with remote germination, the radicle persists for some time and produces lateral roots. The seeds of date palms (*Phoenix* spp.) have remote germination.

The other main class of palm seed germination is called adjacent germination (Fig. 1.23). In these seeds, only a small portion of the cotyledon emerges from the seed. It appears as a swollen body abutting the seed surface and is called the "button." The radicle and plumule emerge from the bottom and top of the button. In palms with adjacent germination, the first seedling root or radicle is usually narrow, very short-lived, and is quickly replaced by roots formed at the seedling stem base (adventitious roots). As with remote germination, a haustorium remains inside the seed absorbing food from the endosperm. An example of a palm with adjacent germination is the pindo palm (*Butia capitata*).

Fig. 1.10. Hastula on the leaf of *Livistona chinensis*

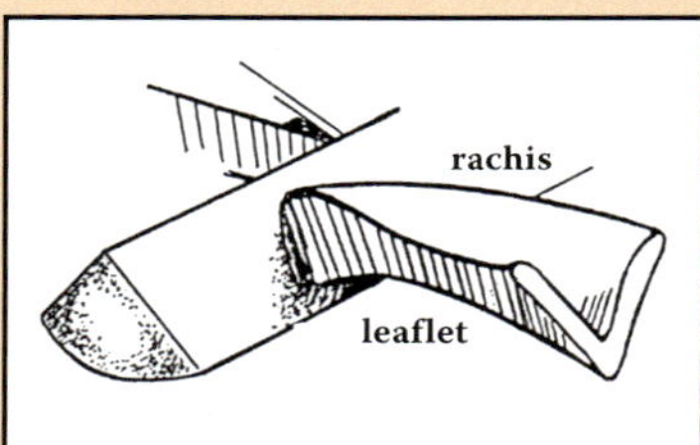

Fig. 1.11. Induplicate

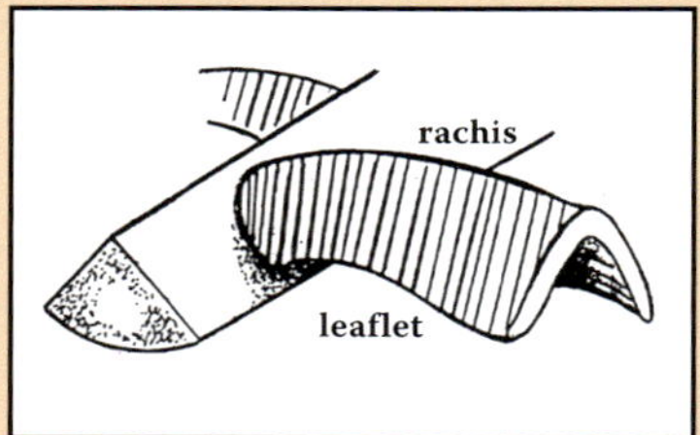

Fig. 1.12. Reduplicate

Classification of the Palm Family

The palm family, consisting of about 2500 species, is known to botanists as the Palmae or the Arecaceae. That branch of botany devoted to formulating the classification of plants is called taxonomy. Relative to many other large and economically important plant families, the Arecaceae has not been well studied taxonomically, largely due to the difficulty in preparing dried field specimens of palms, and the fact that well over 90% of the palm family's diversity is found in the tropics. In 1987, a landmark occurred in the taxonomic history of the palm family with the publication of *Genera Palmarum* by Drs. Natalie Uhl of Cornell University's Bailey Hortorium and John Dransfield of the Royal Botanic Gardens at

Fig. 1.13. Males flowers of pygmy date palm (*Phoenix roebelenii*)

Fig. 1.14. The flowerstems of *Butia yatay* are backed by a conspicuous bract or spathe

Fig. 1.15. Male flowers of European fan palm (*Chamaerops humilis*)

Fig. 1.16. Flowers of foxtail palm (*Wodyetia bifurcata*)

Fig. 1.17. Fruits of royal palm (*Roystonea regia*)

Fig. 1.18. Fruits of Chinese fan palm (*Livistona chinensis*)

Fig. 1.19. Fruits of bamboo palm (*Chamedorea microspadix*)

Kew. Inspired by years of work at the Bailey Hortorium by the late Harold Moore, *Genera Palmarum* presented the first complete, modern system of classification for the palm family through the rank of genus (a group of related species believed to be of common ancestry and defined by certain important shared characteristics that sets them apart from other species groups).

Uhl and Dransfield recognized six subfamilies in the palms, each in turn divided further into tribes and, in some cases, subtribes. These are: *Coryphoideae* (3 tribes), *Calamoideae* (2 tribes), *Nypoideae* (only one species), *Ceroxyloideae* (3 tribes), *Arecoideae* (6 tribes), and *Phytelephantoideae*. These six subfamilies basically represent six major lines of evolution. A revised classification is forthcoming, and will result in some changes, including a reduction to only five subfamilies. In the treatment of each palm species in Section II, the subfamily and tribe are provided in case the reader is interested in knowing to what other palms the hardy ones are related.

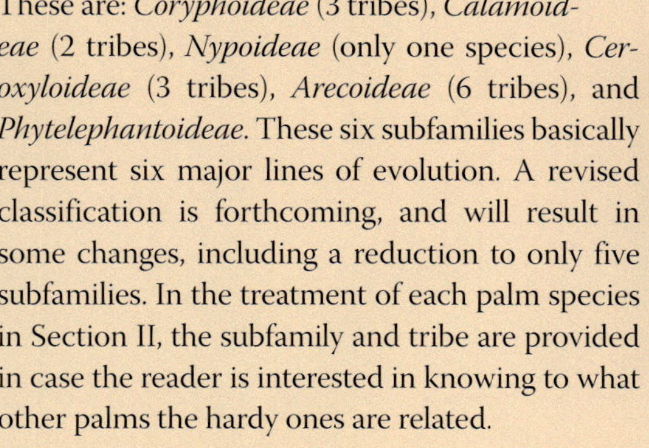

Fig. 1.20. The large fruits of coconut (*Cocos nucifera*)

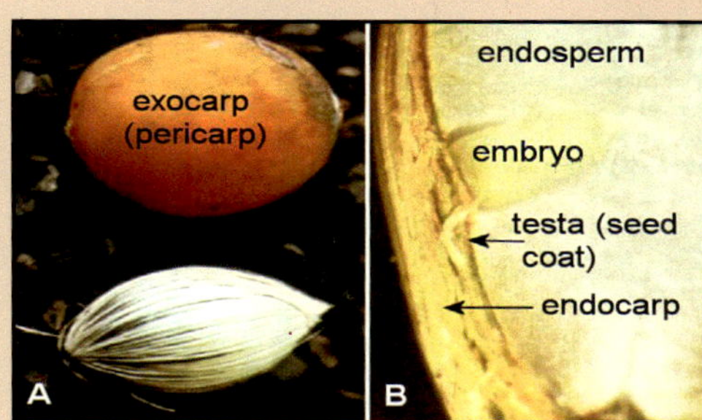

Fig. 1.21. Queen palm (*Syagrus romanzoffiana*) fruit and seed. A. Ripe fruit (top), seed cleaned to fruit endocarp (below). B. Cross-section through seeds of areca palm (*Dypsis lutescens*)

Conservation of Palms

No horticulturist working in the tropics or subtropics can afford to be indifferent to the loss of biodiversity that is currently taking place throughout the world's tropics. Palms are first and foremost a tropical plant family, and numerous species are known only from single populations or inhabit restricted ranges of distribution. In the past, palms were sometimes spared from destruction because the fibrous trunks would very quickly dull the blades of axes, but in these days of chainsaws and forest burning, rain forest palms are as easily reduced to ash and charred stumps as any other tree.

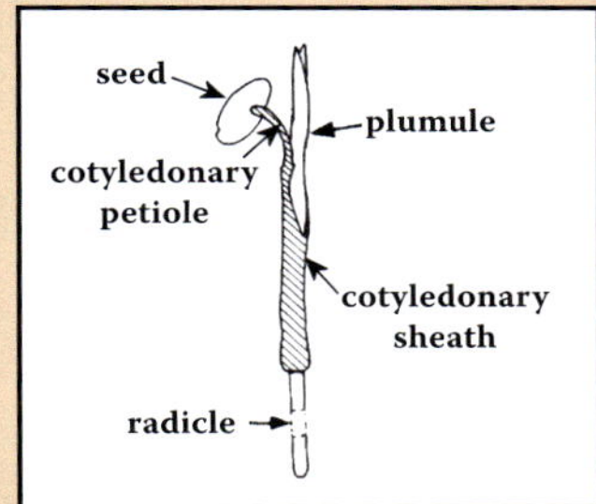

Fig. 1.22. Remote germination

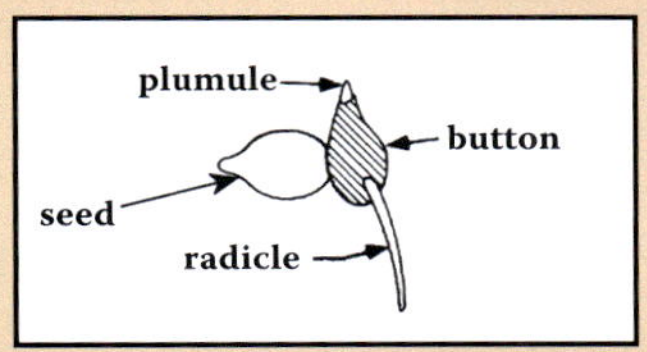

Fig. 1.23. Adjacent germination

Fortunately, horticulture can help in the preservation of many rare palms that might otherwise disappear off the face of the earth. A number of palm species are now represented in cultivation by more individuals than ever existed in the wild. Nonetheless, over zealous collection of seeds or plants from the wild can also place pressure on rare palms. Within the world of palm horticulture, horror stories circulate about rare palms being cut down in order that their seed crop could be collected and sold. Palm horticulturists need to become more sensitive to the source of the palms in commerce. One should not purchase rare palms grown from wild-collected seed unless you know for a fact that the seeds were harvested in a sustainable manner.

The International Palm Society

The International Palm Society is a not-for-profit organization devoted to the support of palm research, education, conservation, and cultivation. The Society has a number of local chapters in the United States and abroad, publishes a high quality and informative quarterly journal called "Palms," and holds a biennial meeting in various locations around the world that draws members internationally. For membership information write to: International Palm Society, P. O. Box 1897, Lawrence KS 66044-8897, USA or visit the IPS web site at http://www.palms.org/.

References: Tomlinson, P. B. 1990. *The Structural Biology of Palms.* Clarendon Press, Oxford
Uhl, N. W. and J. Dransfield. 1987. *Genera Palmarum.* Allen Press, Lawrence, KS.

Cocos nucifera 'Dwarf Golden Malayan'
Photo credit: Byron Keith

Section II

Encyclopedia of Landscape Palms

Scientific Name: *Acoelorrhaphe wrightii* (a-see'-lo-RAY-fe RYT-ee-eye)

Common Name(s): paurotis palm, Everglades palm, silver saw palm, hairy tom palmetto, guano, preto, tasiste, tique

Classification: Coryphoideae - Corypheae
Height: 20' (6.1 m) typical, but up to 40' (12.2 m)
Growth Rate: Slow

Origin: Florida and Caribbean region
USDA Hardiness Zone: 9A-11; variable leaf damage at 22° F (-5.6° C); root hardy to at least 18° F (-7.8° C)

Stem detail

Horticultural Characteristics

Salt Tolerance: Moderate; will tolerate periodically brackish water
Drought Tolerance: Moderate, but prefers moist soil
Soil Requirements: Widely adaptable, but avoid highly alkaline soils
Light Requirements: Moderate; high
Nutritional Requirements: Moderate
Uses: Multi-trunked specimen tree
Propagation: Seed, germinating in two to three months; remote germination; division
Human Hazards: Sharp teeth on petiole
Pest Problems: None reported
Disease Problems: Manganese deficiency, ganoderma, stigmina leaf spot, graphiola false smut
Cultivars: None are formally recognized. A population in western Cuba with gray-green leaves reportedly grows in dry, oak-cactus scrub, but has not been introduced into the U. S.

Morphology (Identifying Characteristics)

Habit: Clustering; each stem bearing 20-30 leaves
Trunk or Stem: Slender; persistent leaf bases and fiber
Leaf: Palmate, induplicate; divided to more than 1/2 into many narrow segments
Foliage Color: Green; silvery-green below
Leaf Size: 3' (.9 m) wide; segments 1" (2.5 cm) wide
Petiole: 3' (.9 m) long, armed with marginal teeth
Crownshaft: None
Inflorescence: From among the leaves; branched; 3-4' (.9-1.2 m) long
Gender: Bisexual flowers
Flower Color: White
Fruit Size: 1/2" (1.3 cm)
Fruit Color: Black

Comments: The paurotis palm is a distinctive part of the Florida Everglades flora where it frequently forms dense stands at the border of tree islands. It is one of the few cultivated palms that will tolerate poorly drained sites in the landscape. It prefers relatively moist soils; on drier soils growth will be particularly slow. On high pH soils, paurotis palms will manifest manganese deficiency ("frizzletop") unless fertilized regularly with manganese sulfate or a complete fertilizer containing manganese. The paurotis palm will, in time, form a large cluster that restricts its use to sites where such spread will not be a problem.

Scientific Name: *Acrocomia aculeata* (ak-ro-KO-mee-a a-kyoo-lee-AHT-a)

Common Name(s): macaw palm, gru-gru, macamba, mbocaya, mucaja, coyol palm

Classification: Arecoideae - Cocoeae
Height: 15-35' (4.6-10.7 m)
Growth Rate: Slow

Origin: Mexico and the West Indies, Central America, South America except Peru and Ecuador
USDA Hardiness Zone: 9B-11, but some forms hardy only to 10A; may be injured below 25° F (-3.9° C)

Geoff Stein

Horticultural Characteristics

Salt Tolerance: Moderate
Drought Tolerance: High
Soil Requirements: Widely adaptable
Light Requirements: High
Nutritional Requirements: Moderate
Uses: Specimen tree
Propagation: Seed, germinating in four to six months after scarification; adjacent germination
Human Hazards: Spiny
Pest Problems: None reported
Disease Problems: Ganoderma

Morphology (Identifying Characteristics)

Habit: Solitary; canopy of 20-30 leaves
Trunk or Stem: Smooth, spiny (especially when young), closely ringed, sometimes bulging towards middle
Leaf: Pinnately compound, reduplicate; over 300 leaflets that spread in different planes
Foliage Color: Gray-green to blue-green with whitish hairs on underside of leaflets
Leaf Size: 10-12' (3-3.7 m) long; leaflets about 3' (.9 m) long, 2" (5 cm) wide
Petiole: Armed with marginal spines, 3' (.9 m) long
Crownshaft: None
Inflorescence: 5-7' (1.5-2.1 m) long with a large, persistent woody spathe
Gender: Separate male and female flowers on same inflorescence
Flower Color: Yellow
Fruit Size: 2" (1.3 cm)
Fruit Color: Yellowish-green to brown

Comments: Despite the vicious spines on the trunk and leaf stalks (though some forms are less armed than others), the macaw palm makes a striking landscape specimen where space allows. In aspect, it suggests a very robust, spiny queen palm. These palms are natives of open, dry and often rocky areas throughout their range, occurring on well-drained sandy soils. Consequently, they are well adapted to seasonally dry tropical areas, but look better in cultivation if not allowed to become too drought-stressed. Local people use the pith from the stems as a source of starch for themselves and their livestock. An alcoholic beverage is often fermented from the pith as well. Twine is prepared from the leaflets, and the seed is a source of good quality palm oil. At one time, many *Acrocomia* species were recognized; most are now considered to be mere variants of *A. aculeata*, and the broad range of the species is in part likely the result of human introduction. Some of the forms are not as hardy as others. Those populations once referred to as *A. totai* from Argentina and Paraguay are probably among the most cold resistant.

Scientific Name: *Adonidia merrillii* (ad-o-NID-ee-a mer-RIL-lee-eye)

Common Name(s): Manila palm, adonidia, Christmas palm, dwarf royal palm

Classification: Arecoideae - Areceae
Height: 15' (4.6 m), occasionally to 25' (7.6 m)
Growth Rate: Moderate

Origin: Philippines
USDA Hardiness Zone: 10B-11; may be damaged at 32° F (0° C), possibly killed at 26° F (-3.3° C)

Fruit detail

Horticultural Characteristics 

Salt Tolerance: Moderate
Drought Tolerance: Moderate
Soil Requirements: Widely adaptable
Light Requirements: Moderate; high
Nutritional Requirements: Moderate
Uses: Small specimen tree, large containers, interiorscape
Propagation: Seed, germinating in one to two months; adjacent germination
Human Hazards: None
Pest Problems: None reported
Disease Problems: Highly susceptible to lethal yellowing ("veitchia decline")

Morphology (Identifying Characteristics)

Habit: Solitary, canopy of 9-15 leaves
Trunk or Stem: Slender, dark to light gray, smooth or slightly rough, closely ringed, swollen at base
Leaf: Pinnately compound, reduplicate, stiffly arching; with 100 jagged tipped leaflets held in several planes near base
Foliage Color: Bright green
Leaf Size: 4-6' (1.2-1.8 m) long; leaflets 1.5-2.5' (46-76 cm) long, 2" (5 cm) wide
Petiole: Short, 8-10" (20-25 cm) long, smooth, unarmed
Crownshaft: Short and thick, bright green with fine white scales
Inflorescence: About 2' (60 cm) long, borne below the crownshaft, much-branched, white
Gender: Separate male and female flowers on the same inflorescence
Flower Color: White
Fruit Size: 1.25" (3.2 cm)
Fruit Color: Red, glossy

Comments: Long known as *Veitchia merrillii*, Christmas palm has been returned to the genus *Adonidia* within which it is the sole recognized species. Though not as fast growing as the related genus *Veitchia*, adonidia has long been the most popular, due to its neat and formal appearance and since its small size lends itself to wide use, even in the smallest residential yards. Several plants are often grown close together as a single, multi-stemmed specimen. It has also been grown for interior use, having less of a tendency to stretch under shade conditions than the faster and taller growing *Veitchia* species. The showy fruit display of this palm coincides with Christmas time. Unfortunately, high susceptibility to lethal yellowing now limits its use to areas free of the disease. However, it could be argued that seedlings grown from local seed sources in Florida may represent a more resistant gene pool, since they are adonidias that have never succumbed to the disease.

Scientific Name: *Aiphanes aculeata* (EYE-fa-neez a-kyoo-lee-AHT-a)

Common Name(s): macaw palm, ruffle palm, coyure palm

Classificaton: Arecoideae - Cocoeae
Height: 20-30' (6-9 m)
Growth Rate: Moderate to fast

Origin: Northern South America
USDA Hardiness Zone: 10B-11; seriously damaged at 26° F (-3.3° C)

Geoff Stein

Horticultural Characteristics

Salt Tolerance: Low
Drought Tolerance: Low to moderate
Soil Requirements: Prefers deep, moist soil
Light Requirements: Low when young, moderate to high with age
Nutritional Requirements: Moderate
Uses: Specimen
Propagation: Seed, germinating in a few weeks if fresh; adjacent germination
Human Hazards: Long, stiff spines on trunk and leaves
Pest Problems: None reported
Disease Problems: None reported

Morphology (Identifying Characteristics)

Habit: Solitary with crown of 10-15 drooping leaves
Trunk or Stem: Slender, 4-6" (10-15 cm) diameter, heavily armed with long, black spines
Leaf: Pinnately compound, 50-80 spiny, wedge-shaped leaflets, irregularly-grouped, reduplicate
Foliage Color: Dark green, glossy
Leaf Size: 3-6' (.9-1.8 m) long; leaflets 1.5-2' (46-60 cm) long
Petiole: 2-3' (60-91 cm) long, quickly drooping, spiny
Crownshaft: None
Inflorescence: 2-3' (60-91 cm) long, borne among the leaves
Gender: Separate male and female flowers on the same inflorescence
Flower Color: Off-white
Fruit Size: Globose, 3/4" (1.9 cm) diameter
Fruit Color: Bright orange-red

Comments: The ruffled, "fishtail" leaves that droop to form a long skirt make an interesting contrast with other foliage. The black spines on trunk, both leaf surfaces, petioles and flower stalks are attractive but place limits on where the palm may safely be used.

Scientific Name: *Allagoptera arenaria* (al-la-GAHP-tah-rah ar-e-NAHR-ee-a)

Common Name(s): seashore palm, restinga palm, caxando, coco da praia

Classification: Arecoideae - Cocoeae
Height: 4-8' (1.2-2.4 m)
Growth Rate: Slow

Origin: Brazil
USDA Hardiness Zone: 9B-11 (9A with protection); little to no damage at 25° F (-3.9° C); may survive 20° F (-6.7° C)

Fruit spike

Horticultural Characteristics

Salt Tolerance: High
Drought Tolerance: High
Soil Requirements: Widely adaptable
Light Requirements: High
Nutritional Requirements: Low
Uses: Seaside landscapes; shrub
Propagation: Seeds germinating erratically for up to two years, adjacent germination, cracking endocarp may speed germination; may not retain viability for long
Human Hazards: None
Pest Problems: None reported
Disease Problems: Slight susceptibility to lethal yellowing

Morphology (Identifying Characteristics)

Habit: Clustering (with time); each stem bearing 16-20 leaves
Trunk or Stem: Trunkless
Leaf: Pinnately compound, reduplicate; about 40 leaflets in radiating groups of three that give a plume-like appearance
Foliage Color: Green above, silvery below
Leaf Size: 3-4' (.9-1.2 m) long; leaflets about 10" (25 cm) long, 1/2-3/4" (1.3-2.4 cm) wide
Petiole: 1-1.5' (30-45 cm) long; unarmed
Crownshaft: None
Inflorescence: Short, unbranched, dense spike with a woody spathe
Gender: Male and female flowers on the same inflorescence
Flower Color: Greenish-yellow
Fruit Size: 1/2-1" (1.3-2.5 cm)
Fruit Color: Yellowish-green

Comments: In its native habitat in coastal eastern Brazil, the seashore palm grows on primary dunes where constant salt exposure is assured. This fact alone makes it an extremely valuable addition to the landscape palm inventory. It may, in fact, be the most salt tolerant palm of all. This shrubby palm slowly forms a short mound of graceful, plume-like leaves that can be massed effectively or used as a single accent with other extremely salt tolerant plants. The leaflets are situated on the rachis in groups of three, with each radiating outward in a different direction, thus lending the leaves a full, foxtail-like quality. The silvery undersides of the leaves are eye-catching in even the slightest sea breeze. The unusual spike-like inflorescences are usually lost among the clusters of leaves. In inland areas, seashore palm does equally well, where its adaptation to beachfront soils allow it to thrive with negligible supplementary fertilization. Seashore palm is hardier than queen palm (*Syagrus romanzoffiana*), and should be trialed further north along the coast of Florida and California. Its habitat preference has also led to the loss of many populations of the palm due to rapid coastal development in Brazil. Though slow-growing, the seashore palm is attractive even when quite young. Its slight susceptibility to lethal yellowing should not be an issue outside of USDA Hardiness Zones 10-11.

Scientific Name: *Archontophoenix alexandrae* (ahr-kont-o-FEE-nix a-lek-ZAN-dree)

Common Name(s): Alexandra palm, King Alexander palm, King palm

Classification: Arecoideae - Areceae
Height: 40' (12 m)
Growth Rate: Moderate

Origin: Australia
USDA Hardiness Zone: 10B-11; severely damaged or killed at 26° F (-3.3° C)

Flower detail

Horticultural Characteristics

Salt Tolerance: Low
Drought Tolerance: Moderate
Soil Requirements: Widely adaptable
Light Requirements: Moderate; high
Nutritional Requirements: Moderate
Uses: Specimen tree
Propagation: Seed, germinating in six weeks to three months; best sown fresh; adjacent germination
Human Hazards: None
Pest Problems: None reported
Disease Problems: Transplant shock if poorly handled, phytophthora bud rot, fungal leaf spots
Cultivars: 'Kuranda' has a broader trunk than typical forms

Morphology (Identifying Characteristics)

Habit: Solitary; canopy of 8-12 leaves
Trunk or Stem: Light gray; ridged leaf scars, swollen base
Leaf: Pinnately compound, reduplicate; 100 or more leaflets
Foliage Color: Light green above, grayish-white below
Leaf Size: 6-10' (1.8-3 m) long, leaflets about 3' (.9 m) long, 2" (5 cm) wide
Petiole: Short, 6-12" (15-30.5 cm) long, unarmed
Crownshaft: Smooth; variable in color, from light green to purplish or dull red
Inflorescence: Short, wih numerous pendant branches
Gender: Separate male and female flowers on the same inflorescence
Flower Color: White
Fruit Size: 1/2" (1.3 cm)
Fruit Color: Red

Comments: The Alexandra palm makes a stately accent in the landscape and works well as a single specimen or a group of several. It is sometimes confused with hurricane palm *(Dictyosperma album)* but can be differentiated by the swollen base, smooth (rather than waxy) crownshaft, shorter leaves, and pendulous inflorescence. New leaves may emerge light bronze in color on young specimens which make attractive container plants (but do not adapt well to very low light). Alexandra palm performs better in the landscape when supplementary irrigation is provided during periods of sustained drought. Likewise, fertilization should be received a minimum of twice per year to prevent disfiguring nutritional deficiencies. Dry winds may also cause some leaf-tip burn. Unfortunately, this species has the reputation for moving poorly from field nurseries. The heart is susceptible to fatal shattering if the crown of the palm is subjected to undue stresses during lifting and transport to the landscape site. Consequently, field grown specimens should be handled very carefully during transplanting. Splinting or otherwise supporting the crown during transportation may be advisable. The former cultivar 'Mt. Lewis' is now treated as a distinct species, *A. purpurea*.

Scientific Name: *Archontophoenix cunninghamiana* (ahr-kont-o-FEE-nix kun-ning-ham-ee-AHN-a)

Common Name(s): piccabeen palm, bangalow palm, picabben palm

Classification: Arecoideae - Areceae
Height: 30' (9 m)
Growth Rate: Moderate

Origin: Australia
USDA Hardiness Zone: 10A-11; damaged at 26° F (-3.3° C); may be killed at 24° F (-4.4° C)

Geoff Stein

Geoff Stein

Fruit detail

Horticultural Characteristics

Salt Tolerance: Low
Drought Tolerance: Moderate
Soil Requirements: Widely adaptable
Light Requirements: Moderate; high
Nutritional Requirements: Moderate
Uses: Specimen tree
Propagation: Seed, germinating in six weeks to three months; best sown fresh; adjacent germination
Human Hazards: None
Pest Problems: None reported
Disease Problems: Fungal leaf spots

Morphology (Identifying Characteristics)

Habit: Solitary; canopy of 8-12 leaves
Trunk or Stem: Slightly swollen at base; ridged leaf scars
Leaf: Pinnately compound, reduplicate; over 100 leaflets
Foliage Color: Green on both sides; brown wooly scales on underside near midrib
Leaf Size: 8-10' (2.4-3 m) long; leaflets to 3' (.9 m) long, about 2" (5 cm) wide
Petiole: Short, 6-12" (15-30.5 cm) long, unarmed
Crownshaft: Smooth, rusty brown to dull purple
Inflorescence: Numerous 3-4' (.9-1.2 m) long pendulous branches
Gender: Separate male and female flowers on the same inflorescence
Flower Color: Pale lavender to purple
Fruit Size: 1/2" (1.3 cm)
Fruit Color: Pink to red

Comments: The piccabeen palm is slightly more cold hardy than its relative, *A. alexandrae*, and usually does not grow as tall. It can be differentiated from the latter by its lack of grayish wax on the leaf underside, less swollen trunk base, frequently colored crownshaft, lilac-colored flowers, and much less strongly-ribbed leaflets. The leaves of the piccabeen palm tend to be more lax than the King Alexander, giving it a slightly less formal appearance. Its cultural requirements and landscape use are similar.

Scientific Name: *Areca catechu* (a-REEK-a KAT-e-choo)

Common Name(s): betel nut palm

Classification: Arecoideae - Areceae
Height: 30' (9.1 m)
Growth Rate: Moderate

Origin: India through Southeast Asia, Malaysia and Pacific (exact origin is uncertain)
USDA Hardiness Zone: 10B-11; damaged at 34° F (1° C); killed at 26° F (-3.3° C)

Geoff Stein

A form with stout trunk and short, blunt leaves

Horticultural Characteristics

Salt Tolerance: Low
Drought Tolerance: Low
Soil Requirements: Acid
Light Requirements: Moderate; high
Nutritional Requirements: Moderate
Uses: Specimen tree, interiorscape
Propagation: Seed, germinating in two to three months; adjacent germination
Human Hazards: Irritant
Pest Problems: None reported
Disease Problems: Ganoderma
Cultivars: Regional cultivars in Asia

Morphology (Identifying Characteristics)

Habit: Solitary; canopy of about a dozen leaves
Trunk or Stem: Slender, smooth, green (eventually gray) with prominent, wide, white ring scars
Leaf: Pinnately compound, reduplicate, arching; with several dozen broad, obliquely toothed leaflets, the terminal two forming a fishtail shape
Foliage Color: Bright green
Leaf Size: 6-8' (1.8-2.4 m) long; leaflets 1-2' (30-60 cm) long, 3-6" (7.5-15 cm) wide
Petiole: Short, unarmed
Crownshaft: Bright green
Inflorescence: About 3' (.9 m) long, borne below the crownshaft, much branched, the branches straight and thin
Gender: Separate male and female flowers on the same inflorescence
Flower Color: Yellowish-white, fragrant
Fruit Size: 2" (5 cm) long
Fruit Color: Orange or red
Fruit: Seeds contain narcotic compounds

Comments: The betel nut palm, immortalized by Bloody Mary in the Rogers and Hammerstein musical "South Pacific," has been spread throughout tropical Asia and the Pacific where it is cultivated for the food storage tissue (endosperm) inside the seed. When chewed with leaves of a pepper vine (*Piper* sp.) and ground lime, a narcotic stimulant is released. Prolonged use stains the gums and teeth red. If large amounts of the nut are ingested, this may cause vomiting, diarrhea, heart and respiratory disturbances, convulsions and coma. Death may occur. The nut is used to make dye in tropical Asia and Malaysia. Arecain is used to treat worms by veterinarians. The palm itself makes a lovely specimen with its boldly ringed trunk and smooth green crownshaft, but is very cold sensitive. Young specimens are quite tolerant of shaded conditions.
Related Species: *A. triandra* (East and Southeast Asia) is a clustering species with thinner trunks but otherwise an appearance similar to the betel nut palm. It prefers a shaded location.

Scientific Name: *Areca vestiaria* (a-REEK-a ves-tee-AHR-ee-a)

Common Name(s): orange crownshaft palm, pinang merah, pinang yaki

Classification: Arecoideae - Areceae
Height: 20' (6.1 m)
Growth Rate: Moderate to fast

Origin: Molucca Islands
USDA Hardiness Zone: 10A-11; no damage at 32° F (0° C)

Geoff Stein

Geoff Stein

Juvenile specimen

Geoff Stein

Fruit detail

Horticultural Characteristics

Salt Tolerance: Moderate
Drought Tolerance: Moderate
Soil Requirements: Moist, but well-drained preferred
Light Requirements: Moderate
Nutritional Requirements: Moderate
Uses: Specimen
Propagation: Seed or careful removal of basal shoots, germinating in a few months; adjacent germination
Human Hazards: None
Pest Problems: None reported
Disease Problems: None reported

Morphology (Identifying Characteristics)

Habit: Clustering or occasionally solitary with a small spreading head
Trunk or Stem: Slender, 3-4" (7.5-10 cm) diameter, green, with prominent light rings, stilt roots sometimes present
Leaf: Pinnately compound with about 20 broad leaflets
Foliage Color: Green, midrib orange
Leaf Size: 3-4' (.9-1.2 m) long; leaflets 1.5' (45 cm) long at midpoint of leaf
Petiole: Short, orange-yellow
Crownshaft: Short and stout, bright orange
Inflorescence: Produced beneath crownshaft in an orange sheath, short, much-branched
Gender: Male and female flowers separate but in the same inflorescence
Flower Color: Yellow-white
Fruit Size: Ovoid, less than 1" (2.5 cm) long
Fruit Color: Orange-yellow

Comments: *Areca vestiaria* is a beautiful clustering species with slender brown trunks, stilt roots, and a stunning orange-red crownshaft. Some forms also produce a colorful new leaf, which often correlates with deeper color on the crownshaft. It is perhaps the most cool-tolerant species in the genus.

Scientific Name: *Arenga hookeriana* (a-RENG-a hook-er-ee-AHN-a)

Common Name(s): Hooker's arenga

Classification: Coryphoideae - Caryoteae
Height: 3-6' (1.2-1.8 m)
Growth Rate: Moderate

Origin: Southern Thailand and northern Malaysia
USDA Hardiness Zone: 10B-11 (10A with protection); no damage at 27° F (-2.8° C)

Horticultural Characteristics

Salt Tolerance: Low
Drought Tolerance: Low
Soil Requirements: Well-drained, slightly acid to slightly alkaline
Light Requirements: Moderate to low
Nutritional Requirements: Moderate
Uses: Shrub, specimen, containers, tall groundcover
Propagation: Seed, germinating in one to six months; remote germination
Human Hazards: Irritant fruit
Pest Problems: None reported
Disease Problems: None reported
Cultivars: None described

Comments: It is still a subject of debate in the palm world whether this species is distinct from the more widely distributed *A. caudata*. The latter is characterized by consistently pinnately compound leaves, whereas *A. hookeriana* is typified by the diamond-shaped entire leaf. However, when seed lots of *A. hookeriana* are grown out—even when collected from a single plant—only a percentage of the offspring produce the more desirable entire leaves; the remaining individuals bear pinnate leaves exactly like *A. caudata*! Whatever the ultimate fate of the nomenclature, few shade-loving palms are as eye-catching as *A. hookeriana*.

Morphology (Identifying Characteristics)

Habit: Clustering, spreading to 6' (1.8 m)
Trunk or Stem: Slender, 1/2-1" (1.3-2.5 cm) in diameter with sparse black fiber
Leaf: Entire to pinnately compound; if entire, then diamond shaped and deeply lobed; if pinnate, then with five leaflets, the terminal one broad and lobed, the remaining four lance-shaped
Foliage Color: Deep green above, densely silver below
Leaf Size: 1-2' (30-60 cm) long, 8-10" (20.3-25.4 cm) wide
Petiole: Short
Crownshaft: None
Inflorescence: 2' (.6 m) long, usually unbranched, produced from the leaf axils
Gender: Male and female flowers on the same inflorescence
Flower Color: Yellow or orange
Fruit Size: 1/4" (.64 cm)
Fruit Color: Red
Fruit: Irritant; contains calcium oxalate crystals

Scientific Name: *Arenga tremula* (a-RENG-a TREM-yoo-la)

Common Name(s): dwarf sugar palm, duma yaka

Classification: Coryphoideae - Caryoteae
Height: 6-12' (1.8-3.6 m)
Growth Rate: Moderate

Origin: Philippines
USDA Hardiness Zone: 10B-11; damaged but recovered at 26° F (-3.3° C)

Horticultural Characteristics

Salt Tolerance: Low
Drought Tolerance: Moderate
Soil Requirements: Widely adaptable
Light Requirements: Moderate; high
Nutritional Requirements: Moderate
Uses: Shrub, screen, specimen plant
Propagation: Seed, often germinating unevenly; division; remote germination
Human Hazards: Irritant
Pest Problems: None reported
Disease Problems: Graphiola false smut

Morphology (Identifying Characteristics)

Habit: Clustering; each stem with 8-10 leaves; each stem dies after fruiting
Trunk or Stem: Slender, clean, distinctly ringed
Leaf: Pinnately compound, induplicate, arching; usually with over 100 mostly 2-ranked leaflets inconspicuously toothed at points along margins
Foliage Color: Dark green above, pale green below
Leaf Size: 7-13' (2.1-4 m) long; leaflets 2-3' (.6-.9 m) long, 1.25" (3.2 cm) wide
Petiole: 2-3' (.6-.9 m) long, unarmed
Crownshaft: None
Inflorescence: 4' (1.2 m) long, held high above the foliage
Gender: Separate male and female flowers on the same inflorescence
Flower Color: Green
Fruit Size: 1/2" (1.3 cm)
Fruit Color: Red
Fruit: Irritant; contains calcium oxalate crystals

Comments: *Arenga tremula* and the related but much hardier *A. engleri* are much more useful as landscape plants than the economically important *A. pinnata.* Though the individual stems die after fruiting, new stems continue to arise from the base. Both are clustering and low-growing, and can be utilized as screening plants. The fruits of all *Arenga* species contain high concentrations of irritating calcium oxalate crystals. *A. engleri* (Taiwan) is probably the hardiest species in the genus (to USDA Hardiness Zone 9A). It grows slightly smaller than *A. tremula*, with fiber-covered stems and leaflets that are silvery on the underside. The short flower stalks are hidden among the leaves and the orange flowers are fragrant. See *Betrock's Cold Hardy Palms* for detailed information.

Scientific Name: *Asterogyne martiana* (ass-te-RAH-ji-nee mahr-tee-AHN-a)

Common Name(s): pata de gallo, cortadera, capoca, pico

Classification: Arecoideae - Geonomeae
Height: 3-5' (.9-1.5 m)
Growth Rate: Moderate to fast

Origin: Central America and northern South America
USDA Hardiness Zone: 10B-11

Geoff Stein

Geoff Stein

Emerging new leaf

Horticultural Characteristics

Salt Tolerance: Low
Drought Tolerance: Low
Soil Requirements: Widely adaptable but must be well-drained
Light Requirements: Low
Nutritional Requirements: Moderate
Uses: Understory, interior
Propagation: Seed, germinating in a few months with heat; adjacent germination
Human Hazards: None
Pest Problems: None reported
Disease Problems: None reported

Comments: One of about five species of American rain forest understory palms, and the most widespread, *A. martiana* is an elegant shade subject with its rosette of shortly bifid leaves. The emerging leaf on well-colored forms can be spectacular. Its low light requirements make it an under-appreciated interior subject.

Morphology (Identifying Characteristics)

Habit: Solitary with 12-15 leaves in a rosette
Trunk or Stem: Short, about 2" (5 cm) diameter and 6' (1.8 m) tall with age
Leaf: Simple, with a deeply bifid apex and deeply impressed veins
Foliage Color: Deep green, but often reddish or copper-colored when new
Leaf Size: 2-3' (.6-.9 m) long, 4-7" (10-17.8 cm) wide
Petiole: Short, 4-8" (10-20 cm) long, unarmed
Crownshaft: None
Inflorescence: Upright, spike-like, arching from between the leaves
Gender: Male and female flowers separate but in the same inflorescence
Flower Color: Orange-brown and fragrant on dull, red stalks
Fruit Size: Olive-shaped, 1/2" (1.3 cm) long
Fruit Color: Purple-black

Scientific Name: *Bactris gasipaes* (BAK-tris GAS-i-peez)

Common Name(s): peach palm, pejibaye, chonta, pejivalle, pupunha

Classification: Arecoideae - Cocoeae
Height: 25' (7.6 m)
Growth Rate: Moderate

Origin: Central and South America (exact origin unknown)
USDA Hardiness Zone: 10B-11; severely damaged or killed at 26° F (-3.3° C)

Horticultural Characteristics

Salt Tolerance: Low
Drought Tolerance: Moderate
Soil Requirements: Acid best
Light Requirements: Moderate; high
Nutritional Requirements: Moderate
Uses: Specimen tree, edible fruit
Propagation: Seed, germinating in two or more months; adjacent germination, division
Human Hazards: Spiny
Pest Problems: None reported
Disease Problems: None reported
Cultivars: Numerous local varieties in Central and South America

Morphology (Identifying Characteristics)

Habit: Clustering, rarely solitary, with 5-6 stems each bearing 8-12 leaves
Trunk or Stem: Light brown; spines between the wide, circling ring scars
Leaf: Pinnately compound, reduplicate; with about 4 dozen pointed, drooping leaflets arranged in groups of 2-5, the terminal leaflets largest
Foliage Color: Green
Leaf Size: 8-12' (2.4-3.7 m) long; leaflets 2' (.6 m) long, 1.25" (3.2 cm) wide
Petiole: 5' (1.5 m) long, spiny, especially at base; some spines on rachis
Crownshaft: None
Inflorescence: 1-5' (.3-1.5 m) long; borne from among the lower leaves, pendulous, branched once
Gender: Separate male and female flowers on the same inflorescence
Flower Color: Yellowish-white
Fruit Size: 2" (5 cm) diameter
Fruit Color: Orange-yellow
Fruit: Edible

Comments: Palms as spiny as the 200 or more species of *Bactris* are rarely favored for landscaping, and it is doubtful that any member of this large, primarily rain forest, genus will soon be encountered more widely than as an occasional curiosity in botanical or collectors' gardens. The single species treated here is important because of its highly valued fruit, an important food source throughout Central and South America where it is cultivated widely. In fact, the exact nativity of peach palm is unknown, and the species is seen only in cultivation. The large fruits must first be boiled in salt water to be rendered edible. So prepared, they have a mealy texture, rich in oil, with a flavor pleasant (or at least inoffensive) to most palates. The cultivated forms produce mostly seedless fruit. The palm heart (inner growing point) of this species has also become an important commercial crop as a substitute for the slow-growing *Euterpe edulis.*

Scientific Name: *Bismarckia nobilis* (bis-MARK-ee-a NO-bi-lis)

Common Name(s): Bismarck palm

Classification: Coryphoideae - Borasseae
Height: 30-60' (9-18 m)
Growth Rate: Slow (towards moderate after trunk development)

Origin: Madagascar
USDA Hardiness Zone: 10A-11; damaged but recovered at 26° F (-3.3° C)

Detail of flowers

Detail of fruit

Horticultural Characteristics

Salt Tolerance: Moderate
Drought Tolerance: High
Soil Requirements: Widely adaptable
Light Requirements: High
Nutritional Requirements: Moderate
Uses: Specimen tree
Propagation: Seeds, often germinating in less than two months; remote germination
Human Hazards: None
Pest Problems: None reported
Disease Problems: None reported

Morphology (Identifying Characteristics)

Habit: Solitary, massive; canopy of 20-30 leaves
Trunk or Stem: Leaf bases adhere when young, later gray and fissured; often swollen at base
Leaf: Costapalmate, induplicate, lopsided hastula; stiff and upright; divided to about 1/3 into approximately 20 segments
Foliage Color: Olive-green to blue-green; slight red edge; waxy white when young
Leaf Size: To 10' (3 m) in diameter
Petiole: Waxy, stout, 4-8' (1.2-2.4 m) long; winged at base and sparsely toothed at edge
Crownshaft: None
Inflorescence: 4' (1.2 m) long; branched; ultimate branches thick and catkin-like
Gender: Separate male and female plants
Flower Color: Brown
Fruit Size: 1.5" (4 cm)
Fruit Color: Brown

Comments: *Bismarckia* is one of the most beautiful and desirable fan palms for use in subtropical landscapes. Its bold and formal appearance dominates the area it inhabits. *Bismarckia* is particularly well adapted to Florida conditions, and with only moderate fertilization the palm remains free of nutritional deficiencies. The Bismark palm is massive in aspect; even relatively young specimens may spread to 20' (6.1 m) or more. Consequently, this beautiful palm is out of scale for small residential yards, and may make a small house appear even smaller. *Bismarckia* transplants with some difficulty, and it is one of the few palms that are regularly root-pruned in field nurseries. The loss of several older leaves is not infrequent shortly after installation. If moving an older established specimen, it may be advisable to remove all the leaves. Young palms (before trunk development) are especially intolerant of being moved due to the burial and underground development of the seedling stem and should only be transplanted out of containers. Bismarcks have been used as far north as Sarasota along Florida's west coast; freeze damage occurs but the palm generally recovers in a single season of growth.

Scientific Name: *Borassus flabellifer* (bo-RAS-sus fla-BEL-li-fir)

Common Name(s): palmyra palm, lontar palm, wine palm, talauriksha palm, toddy palm, tala palm, doub palm

Classification: Coryphoideae - Borasseae
Height: 50-70' (15-20 m)
Growth Rate: Slow

Origin: India, but widely distributed throughout tropical Asia
USDA Hardiness Zone: 10A-11; no problem at 26° F (-3.3° C)

Horticultural Characteristics

Salt Tolerance: Moderate
Drought Tolerance: High
Soil Requirements: Widely adaptable
Light Requirements: High
Nutritional Requirements: Low
Uses: Specimen tree, edible fruit
Propagation: Seed, germinating slowly over six to twelve months; deep remote germination
Human Hazards: Spiny
Pest Problems: None reported
Disease Problems: Moderate susceptibility to lethal yellowing, phytophthora bud rot
Cultivars: Though regional varieties exist, few if any have been formally recognized. Interestingly, some authorities consider the other four to six species of *Borassus* to be variants of the palmyra palm.

Morphology (Identifying Characteristics)

Habit: Solitary, massive; canopy of two to three dozen or more leaves
Trunk or Stem: Gray, smooth or rough, ringed, covered with split leaf bases when young, swollen at base and sometimes also above middle
Leaf: Costapalmate, induplicate; stiff and somewhat folded, divided into 60-80 segments that split at their tips
Foliage Color: Gray-green to blue-green
Leaf Size: 6-10' (1.8-3 m) wide; segments 3-5' (.9-1.5 m) long, 4" (10 cm) wide
Petiole: 3-5' (.9-1.5 m) long, stout; armed with broad, black teeth at margin
Crownshaft: None
Inflorescence: 4-6' (1.2-1.8 m) long with short branches; branches of male flowers particularly thick; borne from among the leaves
Gender: Separate male and female plants
Flower Color: Cream
Fruit Size: 6-8" (15-20 cm) diameter
Fruit Color: Brown
Fruit: Edible

Comments: This magnificent fan palm has been cultivated by humans for millenia, and rivals the coconut in importance to some local economies in Asia. Some biblical scholars have even suggested that the "apple" of which Adam and Eve partook in Eden was probably the fruit of the palmyra palm. Virtually every part of the palmyra palm has found a use, from the large, sturdy leaves as thatch, to the sweet-tasting fruit, eaten raw or cooked. The large inflorescences are tapped for their copious juice which is then condensed into palm sugar or fermented into alcoholic toddy. In the wild, palmyras can form large populations, and occur in hot, monsoon regions. They are equally at home in forested and open habitats. The distribution of this species has no doubt been heavily influenced by mankind. Germinating seedlings descend for many feet below ground before any growth emerges above the surface. The palmyra thrives in any moist, warm, tropical climate, though its ultimate size and spread limits its landscape utility.

Scientific Name: *Brahea armata* (bra-HAI-ah ahr-MAHT-a)

Common Name(s): blue hesper palm, short blue hesper, grey goddess, blue fan palm, Mexican blue fan palm

Classification: Coryphoideae - Corypheae
Height: 30-40' (9-12 m)
Growth Rate: Slow

Origin: Baja, California
USDA Hardiness Zone: 8A-11; little to no damage at 14° F (-10° C); thought to be hardy to 10° F (-12.2° C)

Horticultural Characteristics

Salt Tolerance: Low
Drought Tolerance: High
Soil Requirements: Alkaline, well-drained
Light Requirements: High
Nutritional Requirements: Low
Uses: Specimen tree
Propagation: Seed, germinating in two to three months; remote germination
Human Hazards: Spiny
Pest Problems: Palmetto weevils
Disease Problems: Phytophthora root and bud rots

Morphology (Identifying Characteristics)

Habit: Solitary, robust; canopy of 50-60 leaves
Trunk or Stem: Thick, swollen at base, covered with a shag of dead leaves, eventually gray and ringed
Leaf: Costapalmate, induplicate, very stiff, folded; divided about halfway into 30-40 tapered segments that split at their tips
Foliage Color: Blue-green, very waxy
Leaf Size: 6-8' (1.8-2.4 m) wide; segments 3-4' (.9-1.2 m) long, 2" (5 cm) wide
Petiole: 5' (1.5 m) long, armed with downward pointing teeth; waxy below
Crownshaft: None
Inflorescence: To 15' (4.6 m) long, borne among and extending far beyond the leaves; shortly branched, the ultimate branchlets hairy
Gender: Bisexual flowers
Flower Color: Yellow
Fruit Size: 1" (2.5 cm) long
Fruit Color: Yellow with brown stripes

Comments: Blue hesper palm prospers in southern California, where, despite its slow growth rate, it is prized for its dramatic canopy of ice-blue leaves and long inflorescences. In moist, subtropical and tropical climates such as Florida, the palm grows poorly and is short-lived. Despite this caveat, an old, attractive specimen can be found at Fairchild Tropical Botanic Garden in Miami, Florida. Magnificent specimens of blue hesper palm and other *Brahea* species can be seen at Huntington Botanical Garden in Los Angeles, California. It is also grown with some success in Arizona and southern Texas. Good drainage is essential, and acid soils are not to its liking. The name *B. elegans* (Francheshi palm), which most botanists accept as a synonym for *B. armata*, seems to be applied to forms that top out at 10-15' (3-4.6 m) in height.

Scientific Name: *Brahea edulis* (bra-HAI-a ED-yoo-lis)

Common Name(s): Guadalupe palm

Classification: Coryphoideae - Corypheae
Height: 30' (9 m)
Growth Rate: Slow

Origin: Guadalupe Island (off west coast of Mexico)
USDA Hardiness Zone: 9A-11; no damage at 24° F (-4.4° C); thought to be hardy to 20° F (-6.7° C)

Horticultural Characteristics

Salt Tolerance: Low
Drought Tolerance: Moderate
Soil Requirements: Alkaline
Light Requirements: High
Nutritional Requirements: Low
Uses: Specimen tree, edible fruit
Propagation: Seed, germinating in two to four months; remote germination
Human Hazards: Spiny (variable)
Pest Problems: Palmetto weevils
Disease Problems: Phytophthora root and bud rots

Morphology (Identifying Characteristics)

Habit: Solitary, robust; canopy of several dozen leaves
Trunk or Stem: Brown, ringed
Leaf: Costapalmate, induplicate, stiffly folded; divided about halfway into 70-80 segments that split deeply at their tips
Foliage Color: Green on both sides
Leaf Size: 3-6' (.9-1.8 m) wide; segments 3-4' (.9-1.2 m) long, 1" (2.5 cm) wide
Petiole: 4-5' (1.2-1.5 m) long, with or without teeth on margin
Crownshaft: None
Inflorescence: 4-5' (1.2-1.5 m) long, borne from among the leaves
Gender: Bisexual flowers
Flower Color: Yellow
Fruit Size: 1" (2.5 cm)
Fruit Color: Black
Fruit: Edible

Comments: Guadalupe palm does not make quite as striking a specimen as the blue hesper palm, but does have the distinction of producing an edible fruit. Guadalupe palm does not retain a skirt of dead leaves for as long as most other tall-growing *Brahea* species. It is endangered by goats on its native island, who voraciously consume the seedlings. While it doesn't thrive where atmospheric humidity remains high, it prefers a regular supply of water during the summer months.

Scientific Name: *Butia capitata* (BYOO-tee-a kap-i-TAHT-a)

Common Name(s): pindo palm, jelly palm, wine palm

Classification: Arecoideae - Cocoeae
Height: 15' (4.6 m)
Growth Rate: Slow

Origin: Central-southern Brazil and contiguous Argentina and Uruguay
USDA Hardiness Zone: 8A-10B, 7B with protection; no damage at 14° F (-10° C), thought to be hardy to 10° F (-12.2° C)

Horticultural Characteristics

Salt Tolerance: Low
Drought Tolerance: High
Soil Requirements: Widely adaptable
Light Requirements: Moderate; high
Nutritional Requirements: Moderate
Uses: Small tree, edible fruit
Propagation: Seeds germinating in six months or more; cracking the hard endocarp (shell) speeds germination; adjacent germination
Human Hazards: Fiber spines on petiole
Pest Problems: Scales
Disease Problems: Ganoderma, stigmina leaf spot, graphiola false smut, phytophthora bud rot
Cultivars: 'Bonetti' or 'Bonnetii': this form of *B. capitata* is considered to be the hardiest strain of the species. It has reportedly withstood 9° F (-12.8° C) without damage. It is sometimes listed as a distinct species. It is typically shorter than other forms, with smaller leaves and fruit.

Morphology (Identifying Characteristics)

Habit: Solitary; canopy of 40-50 leaves
Trunk or Stem: Thick, covered with overlapping, stubby and woody leaf bases for many years
Leaf: Pinnately compound, reduplicate, stiffly arching, with numerous leaflets
Foliage Color: Blue-green
Leaf Size: 4-6' (1.2-1.8 m) long; leaflets about 2.5' (76 cm) long, 1" (2.5 cm) wide
Petiole: 4-6' (1.2-1.8 m) long, with slender, fibrous spines on margins
Crownshaft: None
Inflorescence: 3-4' (.9-1.2 m) long; once-branched
Gender: Separate male and female flowers on the same inflorescence
Flower Color: Creamy yellow to reddish
Fruit Size: 1" (2.5 cm)
Fruit Color: Yellow to orange
Fruit: Edible

Comments: Pindo palm is the hardiest feather-leafed palm currently in cultivation. It is used throughout the northern half of Florida as a specimen plant, functioning well in median and even avenue plantings, despite its relatively small stature. Its performance is best above USDA Hardiness Zone 10B, and it is hardy into the Carolinas. The arching, blue-green leaves are crowded with many upward pointing leaflets that form a pronounced V-shape. The species is considerably variable in nature, the forms differing in ultimate height, trunk thickness, leaf color and amount of arching, and fruit color and taste. The best quality pindo fruits are very sweet with a flavor some find reminiscent of a pineapple/banana mixture. They make a tasty jelly. *Butia* hybridizes readily with its close relative the queen palm (*Syagrus romanzoffiana*) and such hybrids (*xButiagrus nabonnandii*, known as mule palm), intermediate in morphology and hardiness, are occasionally offered by nurseries. Hybrids are also known with Chilean wine palm (*Jubaea chilensis*). Some botanists feel that the proper name for *Butia capitata* palms in cultivation in the U.S. is *B. odorata*.
Related Species: *B. yatay* is similar in appearance and hardiness but with more widely spreading leaves. *B. eriospatha* has shorter, bright green leaves and leaf bases covered with brown hair.

Continued on next page

Butia capitata 'Bonnetii' is considered to be the hardiest cultivar

Leaf bases of *Butia capitata* 'Bonnetii'

Detail of trunk with persistent leaf bases

Scientific Name: *Carpenteria acuminata* (kahr-pen-TAHR-ee-a a-kyoo-mi-NAHT-a)

Common Name(s): carpentaria palm, carpy

Classification: Arecoideae - Areceae
Height: 40' (12 m)
Growth Rate: Fast

Origin: Australia
USDA Hardiness Zone: 10B-11; no damage at 30° F (-1° C), thought to be hardy to 28° F (-2.2° C)

Detail of fruit and flowers

Horticultural Characteristics

Salt Tolerance: Low
Drought Tolerance: Low
Soil Requirements: Widely adaptable
Light Requirements: High
Nutritional Requirements: Moderate
Uses: Specimen tree
Propagation: Seeds, which germinate readily when fresh in one to three months; adjacent germination
Human Hazards: Irritant fruit
Pest Problems: Thrips
Disease Problems: Unidentified trunk rot, possibly related to cold damage

Morphology (Identifying Characteristics)

Habit: Solitary; canopy of 10-12 leaves
Trunk or Stem: Slender, smooth, gray, widely-spaced rings
Leaf: Pinnately compound, reduplicate; up to 100 broad leaflets with 1-2 teeth on lower edge; uppermost and lowermost pair of leaflets widest
Foliage Color: Deep green above, waxy blue-green below
Leaf Size: 5-6' (1.5-1.8 m) long; leaflets about 2' (.6 m) long, 1.5" (3.8 cm) wide
Petiole: Short, about 1' (30 cm) long, unarmed; some brown woolly scales at base
Crownshaft: Green, smooth, long
Inflorescence: Appears below crownshaft, 4' (1.2 m) long, branched, spreading; long season of flowering and fruiting
Gender: Separate male and female flowers on the same inflorescence
Flower Color: Greenish-white
Fruit Size: 1/2" (1.3 cm)
Fruit Color: Red
Fruit: Irritant; contains calcium oxalate crystals

Comments: This rainforest palm from northern Australia elicited great excitement when it was first widely introduced into the Florida nursery trade. Fast growing palms are always welcomed by nursery growers, but some of the problems associated with *Carpenteria* have dampened this enthusiasm. The water demands of this palm are considered by some to be out of step with current trends toward water conservative landscaping. Thrips can disfigure the leaves. The palm is considerably cold tender, especially when young, and severe damage or complete loss usually follows a freeze. Despite these caveats, *Carpenteria* is favored for its elegant form and fast growth rate. It adapts well to turf-oriented landscape irrigation, and large specimens are relatively inexpensive (except in the first year or two after a severe freeze!). It looks best when planted in closely-spaced groups of three or more. *Carpenteria* is reportedly short-lived, with an ultimate lifespan not much beyond 40 years. There is only one species in the genus, which is considered closely related to *Veitchia*.

Scientific Name: *Caryota gigas* (kar-ee-O-ta GY-gas)

Common Name(s): Thai mountain giant, giant fishtail palm, mountain fishtail palm

Classification: Coryphoideae - Caryoteae
Height: 60-100' (18-30 m) or more
Growth Rate: Moderate

Origin: Southern China, northern Laos, and northeast Thailand
USDA Hardiness Zone: 10A-10B, 9B with protection; there are anecdotal reports of this species surviving 20° F (-6.5° C)

Geoff Stein

Detail of trunk

Horticultural Characteristics

Salt Tolerance: Low
Drought Tolerance: Low
Soil Requirements: Slightly acid
Light Requirements: High
Nutritional Requirements: Moderate to high
Uses: Specimen tree, best in groups
Propagation: Seed
Human Hazards: Irritant fruit
Pest Problems: None reported
Disease Problems: None reported

Morphology (Identifying Characteristics)

Habit: Solitary, with a sparse canopy of a dozen leaves; dies after flowering and fruiting
Trunk or Stem: Columnar, tan, slightly bulging in the middle, sometimes with short stilt roots at base
Leaf: Bipinnately compound, the tips and secondary leaf stems drooping; leaflets rounded rather than triangular
Foliage Color: Green
Leaf Size: 20' (6 m) long, 10' (3 m) wide
Petiole: 3-6' (.9-1.8 m)
Crownshaft: None
Inflorescence: To 20' (6.1 m) long, much branched and pendulous
Gender: Male and female flowers on the same inflorescence
Flower Color: White
Fruit Size: 3/4" (3.8 cm)
Fruit Color: Red
Fruit: Irritant; contains calcium oxalate crystals

Comments: As its name suggests, *C. gigas* is the most massive of the dozen or so fishtail palm species. In its Asian habitat, *C. gigas* is found at middle elevation on tropical mountains. As a result, it performs very well in cooler tropical climates, such as southern coastal California and elevated parts of Hawaii. It is probably not the best fishtail palm for perennially hot tropical climates. The leaves are awe-inspiringly massive and the overall affect of the canopy is that of a monstrous tree fern. The leaves are few in number however, and are aggregated at the tip of the trunk, thus a grove planting of several specimens of varying height is usually more aesthetically pleasing.

Scientific Name: *Caryota mitis* (kar-ee-O-ta MYT-iss)

Common Name(s): clustering fishtail palm, Burmese fishtail palm, tufted fishtail palm

Classification: Coryphoideae - Caryoteae
Height: 18' (5.5 m)
Growth Rate: Moderate

Origin: Southeast Asia
USDA Hardiness Zone: 10A-11; damaged or killed at 26° F (-3.3° C)

Geoff Stein

Developing and ripe fruit

Horticultural Characteristics

Salt Tolerance: Low
Drought Tolerance: Moderate
Soil Requirements: Widely adaptable
Light Requirements: Moderate; high
Nutritional Requirements: Moderate
Uses: Specimen tree
Propagation: Seeds germinating in three to four months; remote germination
Human Hazards: Irritant
Pest Problems: None reported
Disease Problems: Stigmina and other fungal leaf spots, moderate susceptibility to lethal yellowing

Morphology (Identifying Characteristics)

Habit: Clustering; stems die after fruiting; each stem with 8-10 leaves
Trunk or Stem: Persistent long, pointed leaf bases and black fiber; eventually gray-green with widely spaced dark ring scars
Leaf: Bipinnately compound, induplicate; leaflets composed of about 12 secondary asymmetric, triangular leaflets
Foliage Color: Green
Leaf Size: 4-9' (1.2-2.7 m) long; leaflets 4-7" (10-17.8 cm) long
Petiole: 2-4' (.6-1.2 m) long, unarmed
Crownshaft: None
Inflorescence: 1-2' (30-60 cm) long, composed of numerous pendulous branches
Gender: Separate male and female flowers on the same inflorescence
Flower Color: White
Fruit Size: 1/2" (1.3 cm)
Fruit Color: Dark red at maturity
Fruit: Irritant; contains calcium oxalate crystals

Comments: The individual stems of clustering fishtail palm cease vegetative growth after a period of years and begin to flower from the top down. After the fruit has ripened, the stem dies. Fortunately, in this species new clustering stems are continuously coming along to replace those that have fulfilled their short lease on life. However, some observers claim that the cluster never lives for very long after the main stem dies. The unusual form of the leaves makes this species an eye-catching specimen plant. Young plants do very well in containers as patio plants and can be acclimated to interior conditions as well. Throughout their broad native range, the fishtail palms are utilized as sources of palm sugar and starch. The fruit contains calcium oxalate crystals that are extremely irritating to the skin.

Scientific Name: *Caryota no* (kar-ee-O-ta NO)

Common Name(s): giant fishtail palm

Classification: Coryphoideae - Caryoteae
Height: 60-70' (18.3-21.3 m)
Growth Rate: Fast

Origin: Borneo
USDA Hardiness Zone: 10B-11; damaged below 32° F (0° C)

Horticultural Characteristics

Salt Tolerance: Low
Drought Tolerance: Moderate
Soil Requirements: Widely adaptable
Light Requirements: High
Nutritional Requirements: Moderate
Uses: Specimen tree
Propagation: Seed, germinating over a long period; remote germination
Human Hazards: Irritant fruit
Pest Problems: None reported
Disease Problems: Susceptable to lethal yellowing

Morphology (Identifying Characteristics)

Habit: Solitary with a head of 10-20 leaves in upper part of trunk
Trunk or Stem: Heavy, often bulging in upper part, more than 2' (60 cm) diameter, gray, partly hidden by leaf bases; older trunks attractively ringed
Leaf: Bipinnately compound with "fishtail" leaflets, induplicate
Foliage Color: Dark green
Leaf Size: 10-15' (3-4.6 m) long, 8-10' (2.4-3 m) wide
Petiole: 2-3' (60-91 cm) long
Crownshaft: None
Inflorescence: 6-8' (1.8-2.4 m) long, pendant
Gender: Separate male and female flowers on the same infloresence
Flower Color: Creamy-white
Fruit Size: Globose, about 1" (2.5 cm) diameter
Fruit Color: Purple-black
Fruit: Irritant; contains calcium oxalate crystals

Comments: *Caryota no* is another enormous fishtail palm that makes a striking specimen in hot, tropical climates. As with all of this genus, the tree reaches its final size, then begins to produce flowers and fruit in each leaf axil in turn from the top down, dying when most have matured.

Scientific Name: *Caryota rumphiana* (kar-ee-O-ta rump-fee-AHN-a)

Common Name(s): giant fishtail palm

Classification: Coryphoideae - Caryoteae
Height: 60' (18.3 m)
Growth Rate: Fast

Origin: Southeast Asia to Australia
USDA Hardiness Zone: 10B-11

Geoff Stein

Horticultural Characteristics

Salt Tolerance: Low
Drought Tolerance: Moderate
Soil Requirements: Widely adaptable
Light Requirements: Moderate; high
Nutritional Requirements: Moderate
Uses: Specimen tree
Propagation: Seeds, germinating in two to three months; remote germination
Human Hazards: Irritant fruit
Pest Problems: None reported
Disease Problems: Susceptible to lethal yellowing

Morphology (Identifying Characteristics)

Habit: Solitary; palm dies after fruiting; canopy of 10-20 leaves
Trunk or Stem: Grayish; widely spaced rings; thickest in the middle
Leaf: Bipinnately compound, induplicate; leaflets somewhat pendulous
Foliage Color: Green
Leaf Size: 10-20' (3-6.1 m) long, leaflets up to 15" (38 cm) long
Petiole: 2-5' (.6-1.5 m) long
Crownshaft: None
Inflorescence: 2-4' (.6-1.2 m) long; long, pendent branches
Gender: Separate male and female flowers on the same inflorescence
Flower Color: White
Fruit Size: 1-1.5" (2.5-3.8 cm)
Fruit Color: Purple-black
Fruit: Irritant; contains calcium oxalate crystals

Comments: The canopy of huge, erect, fishtail-like leaves and robust trunk of this species make it a valuable, albeit temporary, specimen plant in subtropical gardens. As with all fishtail palms, the fruit should not be handled without protection from the irritating calcium oxylate crystals that they contain.

Scientific Name: *Caryota urens* (kar-ee-O-ta YOO-renz)

Common Name(s): toddy fishtail palm, jaggery palm, solitary fishtail palm, wine palm, sago palm, kitul tree

Classification: Coryphoideae - Caryoteae
Height: 40' (12.2 m)
Growth Rate: Moderate

Origin: India to Malay peninsula
USDA Hardiness Zone: 10A-11; severely damaged or killed at 26° F (-3.3° C)

Timothy K. Broschat

Horticultural Characteristics

Salt Tolerance: Low
Drought Tolerance: Moderate
Soil Requirements: Widely adaptable
Light Requirements: High
Nutritional Requirements: Moderate
Uses: Specimen tree
Propagation: Seed, germinating in three to four months; remote germination
Human Hazards: Irritant fruit
Pest Problems: None reported
Disease Problems: Moderately susceptible to lethal yellowing

Morphology (Identifying Characteristics)

Habit: Solitary; dies after flowering and fruiting; canopy of 10-20 leaves
Trunk or Stem: Gray, widely-spaced rings, tapered towards apex
Leaf: Bipinnately compound, induplicate; arching; narrow, wedge-shaped, pendulous leaflets
Foliage Color: Green
Leaf Size: 10-12' (3-3.7 m) long; leaflets about 1' (.3 m) long
Petiole: 1-2' (.3-.6 m) long, unarmed, stout
Crownshaft: None
Inflorescence: 10-14' (3-4.3 m) long, pendulous, with numerous branches
Gender: Separate male and female flowers on the same inflorescence
Flower Color: Greenish-white
Fruit Size: 0.5" (1.3 cm) diameter
Fruit Color: Red
Fruit: Irritant; contains calcium oxalate crystals

Comments: This solitary-trunked fishtail palm makes a handsome specimen plant in warm tropical areas with its crown of 10-20 ascending then arching leaves. The very large drooping inflorescences add a further ornamental dimension to the palm which increases as the red fruits appear. The flowering and fruiting process may last as long as seven years, beginning when the palm is 15-20 years old. The tree begins to die as the last fruit cluster forms in the lowest leaf axil. In its native range, the inflorescences are tapped for their sugary sap which is condensed by boiling or may be fermented into an alcoholic beverage ("toddy"). The inner pith of the stems are also a source of starch ("sagu"). Toddy palm looks its best with regular irrigation and fertilization. Young plants make attractive interiorscape subjects for bright indoor exposures. The fruits contain high levels of irritating calcium oxylate crystals and should not be handled for prolonged periods with bare hands.

Scientific Name: *Caryota zebrina* (kar-ee-O-ta ze-BREE-na)

Common Name(s): gecko palm, striped palm, snakeskin palm, palem belang palem tokek, zebra fishtail palm

Classification: Coryphoideae - Caryoteae
Height: 25-60' (7.6-18.3 m)
Growth Rate: Moderate

Origin: New Guinea
USDA Hardiness Zone: 10B-11

Geoff Stein

Geoff Stein

Attractively-striped petiole

Horticultural Characteristics

Salt Tolerance: Low
Drought Tolerance: Low
Soil Requirements: Rich, moist, acid
Light Requirements: Moderate to high
Nutritional Requirements: Moderate to high
Uses: Specimen tree
Propagation: Seed, germinating in one to three months; remote germination
Human Hazards: Irritant fruit
Pest Problems: None reported
Disease Problems: None reported

Morphology (Identifying Characteristics)

Habit: Solitary; flowering and fruiting once then dying
Trunk or Stem: 19-52' (6-16 m) tall, 8-16" (20-40 cm) in diameter, covered with brown fiber
Leaf: Bipinnately compound, primary leaflets about 40, each divided into 14-22 wedge-shaped secondary leaflets
Foliage Color: Dark green
Leaf Size: 16-23' (5-7 m) long; primary leaflets 31.5-59" (80-150 cm) long; secondary leaflets 8-10" (20-25 cm) long, up to 3" (7.6 cm) wide
Petiole: 3.3-6.5' (1-2 m), tiger-striped with alternating bands of light and dark hairs as is the sheathing base
Crownshaft: None
Inflorescence: 1-2.5 m long, branched three times, pendulous
Gender: Male and female flowers on the same inflorescence
Flower Color: Greenish-white
Fruit Size: 1.5 x 2.5 cm
Fruit Color: Red
Fruit: Irritant; contains calcium oxalate crystals

Comments: In the span of four years, two remarkable fishtail palms with striking and similar appearance were described, *C. zebrina* from New Guinea in 2000, and *C. ophiopellis* from the South Pacific Vanuatu islands. Both have beautiful mottling or striping on the young leaf petioles and sheaths that have been likened to snakeskin (the literal translation of "ophiopellis"). *C. zebrina* is the taller growing of the two, slightly hardier, and the most adaptable—its low elevation cousin from Vanuatu is strictly an understory palm that cannot survive in full sun. *C. zebrina* adapts to full sun with age; in hot climates, young plants will benefit from partial shade. Recent DNA studies indicate that this unusual fishtail palm may actually have to be classified as a species of *Arenga*.

Scientific Name: *Chamaedorea cataractarum* (kam-mee-DOOR-ee-a kat-a-RAK-ta-rum)

Common Name(s): cat palm, cascade palm, guayita de los arroyos, cataract palm

Classification: Arecoideae - Chamaedoreae
Height: 5' (1.5 m)
Growth Rate: Moderate

Origin: Southern Mexico
USDA Hardiness Zone: 10A-11; no problem at 26° F (-3.3° C)

Horticultural Characteristics

Salt Tolerance: Low
Drought Tolerance: Low
Soil Requirements: Widely adaptable
Light Requirements: Moderate; low
Nutritional Requirements: Moderate
Uses: Shrub, foliage plant, massed in beds
Propagation: Seed, germinating irregularly over one to six months; adjacent germination
Human Hazards: Irritant fruits
Pest Problems: Mealybugs, mites
Disease Problems: None reported

Morphology (Identifying Characteristics)

Habit: Trunkless; clustering just above the base
Trunk or Stem: Stems very short, bearing two to six leaves
Leaf: Pinnately compound, reduplicate; with numerous narrow leaflets
Foliage Color: Dark green
Leaf Size: 3-4' (.9-1.2 m) long; leaflets about 1' (30 cm) long, 3/4" (1.9 cm) wide
Petiole: Slender, unarmed, about 1' (30 cm) long
Crownshaft: None
Inflorescence: 1.5-2' (.46-.6 m) long, yellowish-green, branched
Gender: Separate male and female plants
Flower Color: Yellow
Fruit Size: 1/4" (.64 cm) diameter
Fruit Color: Black
Fruit: Irritant; contains calcium oxalate crystals

Comments: This small *Chamaedorea* species is virtually trunkless. Each stem splits just above soil level, and a beautiful, well-rounded clump is eventually formed. Cat palm is of easy culture, and is useful as a low shrubby accent in the shaded garden. It also makes an attractive potted specimen. Cat palm is somewhat more tolerant of higher light levels than many other *Chamaedorea* species, but will still bleach in sunny locations unless water and fertilizer are regularly provided.

Scientific Name: *Chamaedorea costaricana* (kam-mee-DOOR-ee-a kos-ta-REEK-a-na)

Common Name(s): Costa Rican bamboo palm, pacayita, Pacaya, tenera

Classification: Arecoideae - Chamaedoreae
Height: 10-12' (3-3.7 m)
Growth Rate: Moderate

Origin: Central America
USDA Hardiness Zone: 10B-11; hardy to 28° F (-2.2° C)

Donald R. Hodel

Horticultural Characteristics

Salt Tolerance: Low
Drought Tolerance: Moderate
Soil Requirements: Widely adaptable
Light Requirements: Low; moderate
Nutritional Requirements: Moderate
Uses: Specimen plant, shrub, screen
Propagation: Seed, germinating irregularly over one to six months, division; remote germination
Human Hazards: Fruit mildly irritating
Pest Problems: Mites, mealybugs, banana moth, scales
Disease Problems: None reported

Morphology (Identifying Characteristics)

Habit: Densely clustering, eventually forming clumps over 6' (1.8 m) wide; each stem with 12-24 leaves
Trunk or Stem: Slender, smooth, green, with widely spaced ring scars
Leaf: Pinnately compound, reduplicate, drooping, with numerous (40 or more), narrow, thin-textured leaflets
Foliage Color: Pale green
Leaf Size: 2-4' (.6-1.2 m) long
Petiole: 1-2' (.3-.6 m) long, unarmed
Crownshaft: None
Inflorescence: Pendulous, 2-3' (.6-.9 m) long, yellowish-green in flower; female turning red in fruit
Gender: Separate male and female plants
Flower Color: Yellow
Fruit Size: 1/4" (.64 cm) diameter
Fruit Color: Black
Fruit: Mildly irritating; contains calcium oxalate crystals

Comments: Costa Rican bamboo palm is one of the strongest growers in this group of *Chamaedorea.* The species produces many stems in dense clusters which may eventually achieve a basal spread of 6' (1.8 m) or more. It most closely resembles *C. seifrizii* but is larger and more vigorous than that species.

Scientific Name: *Chamaedorea elegans* (kam-mee-DOOR-ee-a EL-e-ganz)

Common Name(s): parlor palm, Neanthe bella, chate

Classification: Arecoideae - Chamaedoreae
Height: 3' (.9 m) typically, but capable of reaching 6' (1.8 m) or more
Growth Rate: Slow

Origin: Mexico, Guatemala, Belize
USDA Hardiness Zone: 10A-11; no problem at 27° F (-2.8° C)

Donald R. Hodel

Infructescences

Horticultural Characteristics

Salt Tolerance: Low
Drought Tolerance: Moderate
Soil Requirements: Widely adaptable
Light Requirements: Low; moderate
Nutritional Requirements: Moderate
Uses: Foliage plant, specimen plant
Propagation: Seed, germinating irregularly over a year; air layering; adjacent germination
Human Hazards: Irritant
Pest Problems: Mites, mealybugs, scales
Disease Problems: Gliocladium blight, phytophthora bud rot

Morphology (Identifying Characteristics)

Habit: Solitary; canopy of 5-15 leaves
Trunk or Stem: Slender, green, with closely spaced ring scars; aerial roots produced at stem nodes; leaves clustered near top
Leaf: Pinnately compound, reduplicate, deep green; leaflets lance-shaped, 20-40 regularly arranged along rachis
Foliage Color: Green
Leaf Size: 1.5-3' (.45-.9 m) long; leaflets 6-9" (15.2-22.9 cm) long, about 1" (2.5 cm) wide
Petiole: 5-15" (12.7-38 cm) long, unarmed
Crownshaft: None
Inflorescence: .5-3' (.15-.9 m) long, twice branched, greenish in flower, female turns orange-red in fruit, erect
Gender: Separate male and female plants
Flower Color: Yellow
Fruit Size: About 1/4" (.64 cm) diameter
Fruit Color: Black
Fruit: Irritant; contains calcium oxalate crystals

Comments: Parlor palm, one of the most popular indoor palms in the world and a frequent component of dish gardens, is an extremely variable species in the wild. In the outdoor landscape, it can be used as a small accent in low light, but is more conspicuous if several are planted close together. Young plants massed together can even function as a ground-cover of sorts. As a houseplant, *C. elegans* will inhabit a dark corner for many months with little ill effect, but mites can be troublesome at low relative humidity. Parlor palm varies in the eventual height that individuals will reach, as well as in the size of the leaves.

Scientific Name: *Chamaedorea metallica* (kam-mee-DOOR-ee-a me-TAL-lik-a)

Common Name(s): miniature fishtail palm, metallica palm, metallic palm

Classification: Arecoideae - Chamaedoreae
Height: 4' (1.2 m)
Growth Rate: Slow

Origin: Mexico
USDA Hardiness Zone: 10A-11; no problem at 26° F (-3.3° C)

Fairchild Tropical Botanic Garden

Geoff Stein

Horticultural Characteristics

Salt Tolerance: Low
Drought Tolerance: Moderate
Soil Requirements: Widely adaptable
Light Requirements: Low; moderate
Nutritional Requirements: Moderate
Uses: Specimen plant; foliage plant
Propagation: Seed, germinating in several months; adjacent germination
Human Hazards: Fruit a mild irritant
Pest Problems: Mealybugs, scales
Disease Problems: None reported

Morphology (Identifying Characteristics)

Habit: Solitary; canopy of 10-15 leaves
Trunk or Stem: Slender, dark green; ring scars closely spaced; aerial roots near base; leaves clustered near top
Leaf: Simple, two-lobed, reduplicate; slightly toothed on upper margins; puckered on surface; occasionally pinnately compound
Foliage Color: Metallic blue-green
Leaf Size: 10-12" (25-30 cm) long, 5-8" (12.7-20.3 cm) wide
Petiole: Short, slender, 4-6" (10-15 cm) long
Crownshaft: None
Inflorescence: Erect; the male branched, 1-1.5' (30-45.7 cm) long; the female usually an unbranched spike (occasionally with a few branches)
Gender: Separate male and female plants
Flower Color: Orange
Fruit Size: About 1/2" (1.3 cm) diameter
Fruit Color: Black
Fruit: Mildly irritating; contains calcium oxalate crystals

Comments: This fishtail-leafed *Chamaedorea* is unique in the genus for the beautiful, shiny blue-green cast of its broad and (usually) only two-lobed leaves. It is most striking when several plants are placed close together, whether in the landscape or in containers. The leaves look their best if the plant is protected from drying winds and strong sunlight. This species prospers in soils with increased amounts of organic material. On sandy soils, regular application of mulch is beneficial. *C. metallica* makes an excellent indoor plant as well, and will occupy a dark corner for months in good condition.
Similar Species: *C. ernesti-augusti* is an allied species similar in appearance to *C. metallica* but lacking the distinctive metallic sheen and color. It produces aerial roots at nodes along the entire stem like *C. elegans*, and can reach over 6' (1.8 m) in height.

Scientific Name: *Chamaedorea microspadix* (kam-ee-DOOR-ee-a myk-ro-SPAY-dix)

Common Name(s): hardy bamboo palm, palmilla, bamboo palm

Classification: Arecoideae - Chamaedoreae
Height: 8' (2.4 m)
Growth Rate: Moderate

Origin: Mexico
USDA Hardiness Zone: 9A-11 (8B with protection); variable damage below 19° F (-7.2° C)

Female plant in fruit

Horticultural Characteristics

Salt Tolerance: Low
Drought Tolerance: Moderate
Soil Requirements: Widely adaptable
Light Requirements: Low; moderate
Nutritional Requirements: Moderate
Uses: Shrub, specimen plant, screen
Propagation: Seed, germinating over several months; adjacent germination
Human Hazards: Fruit mildly irritating
Pest Problems: Mealybugs
Disease Problems: None reported

Comments: Hardy bamboo palm, like *C. radicalis*, extends the outdoor utility of the genus *Chamaedorea* to areas where freezing temperatures are experienced in winter. With some protection, plants have reportedly withstood temperatures below 20° F (-6.7° C) with little or no damage. Certainly the hardiest reed-stem *Chamaedorea* currently enjoying wide cultivation, *C. microspadix* superficially resembles the tender bamboo palms such as *C. seifrizii*, but can be distinguished by the distance often observed between stems in the cluster and the fewer leaflets. Hardy bamboo palm makes a fine specimen plant in part shade, and can also be used as a coarse screening plant. It is equally at home in the interior, and is one of the more mite-resistant species of *Chamaedorea*.

Morphology (Identifying Characteristics)

Habit: Clustering, stems sometimes widely separated, each bearing four to eight leaves
Trunk or Stem: Slender, green, with prominent, moderately wide-spaced ring scars; leaves present for more than half their length
Leaf: Pinnately compound, reduplicate, with only 16-20 broad, thin, regularly arranged leaflets
Foliage Color: Dull green
Leaf Size: 15-24" (38-61 cm) long; leaflets 6-10" (15-25 cm) long, 1-2" (2.5-5 cm) wide
Petiole: Short, slender, unarmed
Crownshaft: None
Inflorescence: 1-2' (30-60 cm) long, branched once, drooping, yellowish-green; borne below the leaves
Gender: Separate male and female plants
Flower Color: Cream
Fruit Size: About 1/4" (.64 cm) diameter
Fruit Color: Orange-red
Fruit: Mildly irritating; contains calcium oxalate crystals

Scientific Name: *Chamaedorea radicalis* (kam-mee-DOOR-ee-a rad-i-KAL-is)

Common Name(s): radicalis palm

Classification: Arecoideae - Chamaedoreae
Height: 5' (1.5 m), but capable of reaching 10' (3 m)
Growth Rate: Slow

Origin: Mexico
USDA Hardiness Zone: 9A-11; no problem at 22° F (-5.6° C), thought to be hardy to 20° F (-6.5° C)

Horticultural Characteristics

Salt Tolerance: Low
Drought Tolerance: Moderate
Soil Requirements: Widely adaptable
Light Requirements: Low; moderate
Nutritional Requirements: Moderate
Uses: Shrub, foliage plant
Propagation: Seed, germinating over several months; adjacent germination
Human Hazards: Fruit mildly irritating
Pest Problems: None reported
Disease Problems: None reported

Comments: This often stemless and hardy *Chamaedorea* is becoming more widely available. It prospers in warm, shady sites in the landscape. Somewhat more open in growth than cat palm, it can be used similarly as an understory shrub in combination with other tropicals. It reportedly performs well in the interior as well. It begins to flower when quite young.

Morphology (Identifying Characteristics)

Habit: Often trunkless, clustering from the base, each stem with 6-8 leaves
Trunk or Stem: Short, slender
Leaf: Pinnately compound, reduplicate, with several dozen narrow leaflets
Foliage Color: Dark green
Leaf Size: About 3' (.9 m) long; leaflets about 1' (30 cm) long, 1" (2.5 cm) wide
Petiole: Short, unarmed
Crownshaft: None
Inflorescence: About 4' (1.2 m) long, held above the leaves, branched once, greenish in flower; female turns orange in fruit
Gender: Separate male and female plants
Flower Color: Yellow-orange
Fruit Size: Slightly less than 1/2" (1.3 cm) diameter
Fruit Color: Orange
Fruit: Mildly irritating; contains calcium oxalate crystals

Scientific Name: *Chamaedorea seifrizii* (kam-mee-DOOR-ee-a see-FRITZ-ee-eye)

Common Name(s): bamboo palm, reed palm, chiat, xate

Classification: Arecoideae - Chamaedoreae
Height: 7' (2.1 m) but can achieve 12' (3.7 m)
Growth Rate: Moderate

Origin: Mexico and northern Central America
USDA Hardiness Zone: 10A-11; damaged but recovered at 26° F (-3.3° C)

Horticultural Characteristics

Salt Tolerance: Low
Drought Tolerance: Moderate
Soil Requirements: Widely adaptable
Light Requirements: Low; moderate
Nutritional Requirements: Moderate
Uses: Shrub, screen, specimen plant, foliage plant
Propagation: Seed, germinating over six or more months; adjacent germination
Human Hazards: Fruit mildly irritating
Pest Problems: Mites, mealy bugs, scales
Disease Problems: Gliocladium blight, phytophthora bud rot

Morphology (Identifying Characteristics)

Habit: Clustering densely, each stem bearing six to nine leaves
Trunk or Stem: Upright, slender, dark green with widely spaced and conspicuous ring scars
Leaf: Pinnately compound, reduplicate; 2-3 dozen narrow leaflets crowded on the stem
Foliage Color: Dull, medium green
Leaf Size: About 2' (61 cm) long; leaflets 8" (20.3 cm) long, 1/2-3/4" (1.3-1.9 cm) wide
Petiole: Short, unarmed
Crownshaft: None
Inflorescence: Short, 1/2"-1' (15-30 cm) long, branched once, greenish in flower, females turning orange in fruit, borne below the leaves
Gender: Separate male and female plants
Flower Color: Yellow
Fruit Size: 1/4" (.64 cm) diameter
Fruit Color: Black
Fruit: Mildly irritating; contains calcium oxalate crystals

Comments: One of the most popular *Chamaedorea* species, *C. seifrizii* eventually forms fairly dense clumps of very erect stems with an overall aspect of bamboo. The canopy of leaves is open, and concentrated in the upper half of the stem. Reed palm is relatively sun-tolerant, but is most at home in shady locations, especially in hot climates. Most nurseries grow this palm in full sun for the first year or two of production to simulate cluster development before moving them under shade. It is also tolerant of less fertile soils than many other *Chamaedorea* species.

Scientific Name: *Chamaedorea tepejilote* (kam-mee-DOOR-ee-a te-pay-hee-LO-tee)

Common Name(s): Pacaya, palmito dulce, tepejilote

Classification: Arecoideae - Chamaedoreae
Height: 10' (3 m)
Growth Rate: Fast

Origin: Mexico to Colombia
USDA Hardiness Zone: 10B-11; no problem at 34° F (1.1° C); thought to be hardy to at least 30° F (-1.1° C)

Donald R. Hodel

Horticultural Characteristics

Salt Tolerance: Low
Drought Tolerance: Moderate
Soil Requirements: Widely adaptable
Light Requirements: Low; moderate
Nutritional Requirements: Moderate
Uses: Specimen plant, shrub, foliage plant
Propagation: Seed, germinating in several months; air-layering; adjacent germination
Human Hazards: Irritant fruit
Pest Problems: Mites, scales, mealybugs
Disease Problems: Gliocladium blight
Cultivars: A variable species with many regional cultivars in Central America selected on the basis of the quality of the edible male inflorescences (known as pacaya or pacayaita) which are highly prized, especially in Guatemala.

Morphology (Identifying Characteristics)

Habit: Solitary (sometimes clustering); bears five to seven leaves
Trunk or Stem: Slender, green, conspicuously ringed, producing aerial roots
Leaf: Pinnately compound, reduplicate, with 2-3 dozen ribbed leaflets that fall from the stem with age
Foliage Color: Deep green
Leaf Size: To 5' (1.5 m) long; leaflets 18-24" (46-60 cm) long, 1.5-2" (3.8-5 cm) wide
Petiole: Short, about 18" (46 cm) long, unarmed
Crownshaft: Short, green
Inflorescence: To 2' (.6 m) long, borne below the crown, shortly once-branched, greenish; females are longer, thicker than males
Gender: Separate male and female plants
Flower Color: Yellow
Fruit Size: 1/2" (1.3 cm) diameter
Fruit Color: Black
Fruit: Irritant; contains calcium oxalate crystals

Comments: The male inflorescences of this solitary *Chamaedorea* species are a prized market commodity in Guatemala and other parts of Central America. They are pickled, or sliced fresh and used in soups, omelettes and other dishes. Pacaya is much faster growing than many of the more popular *Chamaedorea* species, and is becoming more widely available for this reason. Solitary forms are often planted as multiple specimens, and in this fashion can be mistaken for one of the bamboo or reed palms. Like most members of the genus, it favors a shaded spot in the tropical garden, and is useful as a specimen or accent in close quarters where larger palms might be outsized.

Scientific Name: *Chamaerops humilis* (ka-MEE-rahps HYOO-mi-lis)

Common Name(s): European fan palm, Mediterranean fan palm

Classification: Coryphoideae - Corypheae
Height: 10' (3 m)
Growth Rate: Slow

Origin: Mediterranean region
USDA Hardiness Zone: 8A-11; no problem at 16-17° F (-8.9 to -8.3° C); thought to be hardy to 0° F (-17.8° C)

Detail of stem

Horticultural Characteristics

Salt Tolerance: Moderate (possibly high for natively coastal forms)
Drought Tolerance: High (once well-established)
Soil Requirements: Widely adaptable, well-drained
Light Requirements: Moderate; high
Nutritional Requirements: Moderate
Uses: Specimen plant, shrub, container plant
Propagation: Seeds, germinating in two to three months; possibly division; remote germination
Human Hazards: Spiny
Pest Problems: Scales, palm aphid, ambrosia beetle
Disease Problems: Potassium deficiency (Florida), ganoderma, fungal leaf spots
Cultivars: Many forms occur throughout the range of this species, some of which have been named in the past. The most stable variant is so-called variety *cerifera*, the name given to forms with very waxy, silvery leaves. These forms are reportedly slower growing than the typical European fan palms, but may be slightly hardier. The formal varietal name *C. humilis* var. *elatior* has been applied to solitary-stemmed, non-suckering individuals. A particularly tightly suckering, low-growing, green-leafed form is marketed as the cultivar 'Green Mound'.

Morphology (Identifying Characteristics)

Habit: Usually clustering, but solitary forms occur; canopy of 15-30 leaves
Trunk or Stem: About 1' (30 cm) diameter; dead leaves persist below crown; covered for many years with dense, brown fibers
Leaf: Palmate, very deeply divided into several dozen narrow segments which split at their tips
Foliage Color: Green, blue-green or silvery green; glossy or dull
Leaf Size: About 3' (.9 m) in diameter
Petiole: 3-5' (.9-1.5 m) long; armed with fierce orange teeth that point toward leaf
Crownshaft: None
Inflorescence: Short, about 6" (15 cm) long, with thick branches, hidden among the leaves
Gender: Usually separate male and female plants
Flower Color: Yellow
Fruit Size: About 1/2" (1.3 cm) diameter
Fruit Color: Yellow, orange or brown

Chamaerops humilis 'Green Mound'

Flower stems

Developing fruit

Comments: This hardy fan palm occurs throughout the Mediterranean region, from coastal zones to over 3000' (914.4 m) in elevation, and in various types of vegetation. In mountain habitats, it has even been known to receive snow cover. Throughout this broad range, it is typically found on poor, rocky soils, and thus is very adaptable to a wide range of soil types in the landscape as long as they are well-drained. It is highly prized in warm temperate areas where few palms are reliably winter hardy, and a large clump makes a striking specimen plant. The skirt of dead leaves below the crown is usually trimmed off to accent the mat of dark fibers that clothe the trunk for many years. The variation in leaf color and habit is extraordinary. In a nursery row of European fan palms, it is sometimes difficult to find any two that look exactly alike. Its slow rate of growth allows this palm to be grown in a large container for many years. Growth of *C. humilis* is best in full sun, but it also retains an excellent appearance in light shade. Pollen from mature male trees may cause allergies.

Scientific Name: *Chambeyronia macrocarpa* (kam-bay-RO-nee-a mak-ro-KAHRP-a)

Common Name(s): red-leaf palm, red feather palm, flame palm, flame thrower palm, houailou red leaf palm, blushing palm

Classification: Arecoideae - Areceae
Height: 60' (18.3 m)
Growth Rate: Slow

Origin: New Caledonia
USDA Hardiness Zone: 10B-11; variable damage at 28° F (-2.2° C)

Geoff Stein

Geoff Stein

Developing fruit

Geoff Stein

New leaves are bright red

Horticultural Characteristics

Salt Tolerance: Low
Drought Tolerance: Low
Soil Requirements: Moist, high organic preferred
Light Requirements: Shade when young, higher as plant matures
Nutritional Requirements: Responds to rich soil
Uses: Understory palm for many years
Propagation: Seed, germinating in a few weeks when fresh; adjacent germination
Human Hazards: None
Pest Problems: None reported
Disease Problems: None reported
Cultivars: Morphological variants are reported from different localities in New Caledonia, including ones with striped, yellow, and white-haired crownshafts.

Morphology (Identifying Characteristics)

Habit: Solitary with a crown of 10 arching leaves
Trunk or Stem: Slender, strongly-ringed with leaf scars, enlarged at the base
Leaf: Pinnately compound with 60-80 spaced, arching leaflets, reduplicate, unarmed
Foliage Color: Dark green, new leaf deep red beneath, fading to green
Leaf Size: 4-8' (1.2-2.4 m) long, leaflets to 18" (46 cm) long
Petiole: Short
Crownshaft: Well-defined
Inflorescence: Below crownshaft, branched on a short stalk
Gender: Male and female flowers separate but in the same inflorescence
Flower Color: Cream or pink
Fruit Size: Ovoid, 2.5" x 1.5" (6.4 x 3.7 cm)
Fruit Color: Deep red

Comments: A very desirable palm for understory use on moist, rich soil where the bright, new, red leaves show off to advantage. The leaf development is slow and each may be in color for several months.

Scientific Name: *Coccothrinax argentata* (kok-ko-THRY-nax ahr-jen-TAHT-a)

Common Name(s): silver palm, Florida silver palm, silver thatch palm, yuraguana de costa

Classification: Coryphoideae - Corypheae
Height: 15' (4.6 m), but frequently smaller
Growth Rate: Slow

Origin: Florida and the Bahamas
USDA Hardiness Zone: 10A-11; thought to be hardy to 26° F (-3.3° C)

Developing fruit

Horticultural Characteristics

Salt Tolerance: High
Drought Tolerance: High
Soil Requirements: Widely adaptable
Light Requirements: Moderate; high
Nutritional Requirements: Low
Uses: Small specimen tree; seaside locations
Propagation: Seed, germinating in three to six months with heat; remote germination
Human Hazards: None
Pest Problems: None reported
Disease Problems: Phytophthora bud rot if over-watered, graphiola false smut
Comments: Florida's native silver palm can sometimes be found growing with its roots wedged within cracks on limestone outcrops, its trunk blackened by pineland fires. As this suggests, it is an extremely tough and durable palm, with an intensely silver underside to the leaves that seems to glint in the sun.
Related Species: *C. argentea*, native to Hispaniola, is larger in all respects than *C. argentata*, with more rigid leaves that are less silvery on the underside.

Morphology (Identifying Characteristics)

Habit: Solitary; canopy of 12-16 leaves
Trunk or Stem: Slender, smooth, light gray, indistinctly ringed, matted with fiber in upper regions
Leaf: Palmate, induplicate, divided to about 3/4 into 40+ segments which are split at their tip and droop
Foliage Color: Green above, densely silver below
Leaf Size: About 3' (.9 m) in diameter; segments 1" (2.5 cm) wide
Petiole: About 2.5' (.76 m) long, unarmed
Crownshaft: None
Inflorescence: 2' (.6 m) long, with short branches
Gender: Bisexual flowers
Flower Color: White
Fruit Size: 1/2" (1.3 cm) diameter
Fruit Color: Black

Scientific Name: *Coccothrinax barbadensis* (kok-ko-THRY-nax bahr-ba-DEN-sis)

Common Name(s): silver palm, Lesser Antilles silver thatch, latanier, balai

Classification: Coryphoideae - Corypheae
Height: 25' (7.6 m)
Growth Rate: Slow

Origin: West Indies
USDA Hardiness Zone: 10A-11; thought to be hardy to 27° F (-2.8° C)

Horticultural Characteristics

Salt Tolerance: Moderate
Drought Tolerance: High
Soil Requirements: Widely adaptable
Light Requirements: Moderate; high
Nutritional Requirements: Low
Uses: Small specimen tree; seaside landscapes
Propagation: Seed, germinating in three months or more; best at high temperature; remote germination
Human Hazards: None
Pest Problems: None reported
Disease Problems: None reported

Morphology (Identifying Characteristics)

Habit: Solitary; canopy of 12-15 leaves
Trunk or Stem: Slender, light gray-brown, slightly ringed, upper portion matted with brown leaf base fibers
Leaf: Palmate, induplicate, nearly circular, divided 1/2 to 2/3 into broad, 2-lobed segments
Foliage Color: Green above, silvery below
Leaf Size: About 3' (.9 m) in diameter; segments 2" (5 cm) wide
Petiole: About 3' (.9 m) long, unarmed
Crownshaft: None
Inflorescence: 1-2' (.3-.6 m) long, branched
Gender: Flowers bisexual
Flower Color: White
Fruit Size: 3/8" (95 mm) diameter
Fruit Color: Shiny brown to black

Comments: This slow-growing silver palm attains larger size and spread than the Florida native *C. argentata*. Like most *Coccothrinax* species, it is very tolerant of dry, alkaline soils and inland coastal exposures.

Scientific Name: *Coccothrinax crinita* (kok-ko-THRY-nax kri-NEET-a)

Common Name(s): old man palm, guano barbudo, guano petate, thatch palm, mat palm, old man thatch palm

Classification: Coryphoideae - Corypheae
Height: 15' (4.6 m)
Growth Rate: Slow

Origin: Cuba
USDA Hardiness Zone: 10A-11; thought to be hardy to 28° F (-2.2° C)

Juvenile specimen

Horticultural Characteristics

Salt Tolerance: Moderate
Drought Tolerance: Moderate
Soil Requirements: Widely adaptable
Light Requirements: Moderate; high
Nutritional Requirements: Low
Uses: Small specimen tree, container plant
Propagation: Seed, germinating in six months; remote germination
Human Hazards: None
Pest Problems: Nematodes
Disease Problems: Phytophthora bud rot if over-watered

Morphology (Identifying Characteristics)

Habit: Solitary; canopy of 15-25 leaves
Trunk or Stem: Slender, densely covered with long, straw-colored hair-like fiber that makes the trunk look thicker
Leaf: Palmate, induplicate, almost circular, rigid, divided more than 3/4 into 30 or more segments that are split at their tips
Foliage Color: Dark green above, grayish below
Leaf Size: To 5' (1.5 m) in diameter; segments about 2" (5 cm) wide
Petiole: 4' (1.2 m) long, unarmed
Crownshaft: None
Inflorescence: 5' (1.5 m) long, branched
Gender: Bisexual flowers
Flower Color: Yellow
Fruit Size: 1" (2.5 cm) long
Fruit Color: Purple

Comments: This delightful fan palm is remarkable for the long shag of hair that clothes the stem, even when the plant is young. It is very slow-growing, however, and large specimens fetch a handsome price. Old man palm is no more demanding than other members of the same genus, and adapts well to alkaline soils and inland coastal exposures.

Scientific Name: *Coccothrinax miraguama* (kok-ko-THRY-nax meer-a GWAHM-a)

Common Name(s): miraguama palm

Classification: Coryphoideae - Corypheae
Height: 20' (6.1 m)
Growth Rate: Moderate

Origin: Cuba
USDA Hardiness Zone: 10B-11; no problem at 32° F (0° C)

Horticultural Characteristics

Salt Tolerance: Moderate
Drought Tolerance: High
Soil Requirements: Widely adaptable
Light Requirements: Moderate; high
Nutritional Requirements: Low
Uses: Small tree
Propagation: Seed, germinating in two to three months
Human Hazards: None
Pest Problems: None reported
Disease Problems: Potassium deficiency (Florida)
Cultivars: Several regional varieties have been described by botanists

Morphology (Identifying Characteristics)

Habit: Solitary; canopy of 20-30 leaves
Trunk or Stem: Variable; smooth and gray with indistinct ring scars or covered with matted fiber and protruding leaf bases
Leaf: Palmate, induplicate, circular, stiff; divided halfway or more into 40-60 pointed segments that abruptly taper inward near the tip
Foliage Color: Dark green above, silvery below
Leaf Size: 2-5' (.6-1.5 m) wide; segments 2' (.6 m) long, 2" (5 cm) wide
Petiole: 3-4' (.9-1.2 m) long, thin, unarmed
Crownshaft: None
Inflorescence: 3' (.9 m) long, branched, borne from among the leaves
Gender: Bisexual flowers
Flower Color: Yellowish-white
Fruit Size: 1/2" (1.3 cm) diameter
Fruit Color: Red ripening to black

Comments: Miraguama palm is one of the most attractive species in the genus, with a faster than average growth rate. The leaves form neat circles giving the canopy a more formal appearance than most *Coccothrinax* species. Miraguama palm makes a fine showing in group plantings. Individuals can vary as to the degree of matting on the trunk as well as in trunk thickness and height.

Scientific Name: *Cocos nucifera* (KO-kos noo-SIF-e-ra)

Common Name(s): coconut palm, dwarf golden malay, tall Jamaican

Classification: Arecoideae - Cocoeae
Height: 50-80' (15.2-24.4 m)
Growth Rate: Moderate

Origin: Probably the Pacific Islands, but now distributed worldwide in the tropics
USDA Hardiness Zone: 10B-11; severely damaged or killed at 26° F (-3.3° C); often damaged below 30° F (-1.1° C)

Byron Keith

Byron Keith

Byron Keith

C. nucifera 'Dwarf Golden Malayan' fruit

Horticultural Characteristics

Salt Tolerance: High
Drought Tolerance: High
Soil Requirements: Widely adaptable
Light Requirements: High
Nutritional Requirements: Moderate
Uses: Shade tree; specimen tree; edible fruit; commercial source of oil & fiber
Propagation: Seed, germinating in four to six months; adjacent germination
Human Hazards: None
Pest Problems: Palm aphid, coconut mite, red ring nematode (outside U.S.)
Disease Problems: Susceptible to lethal yellowing (varies with cultivar); potassium deficiency, phytophthora bud rot, ganoderma
Cultivars: 'Atlantic Tall' ('Jamaican Tall'), 'Panama Tall': very susceptible to lethal yellowing. 'Malayan Dwarf': green and golden forms, slender trunk, begins flowering when young, greens more susceptible to lethal yellowing than goldens. 'Maypan': hybrid of 'Panama Tall' and golden 'Malayan Dwarf,' resistant to lethal yellowing. 'Fiji Dwarf': variable resistance to lethal yellowing, very ornamental variety. Many others.

Morphology (Identifying Characteristics)

Habit: Solitary, very rarely producing a sucker or two, bearing 20-30 leaves
Trunk or Stem: Sometimes curved, base often swollen, grayish-brown, with large, crescent-shaped leaf scars; fiber matting above
Leaf: Pinnately compound, reduplicate, slightly twisted, eventually drooping, with 150-200 leaflets
Foliage Color: Dark to light green or yellowish-green
Leaf Size: 15 (4.5 m) or more feet long; leaflets 3' (.9 m) long, 1.5" (3.8 cm) wide
Petiole: 3-4' (.9-1.2 m) long, unarmed
Crownshaft: None
Inflorescence: 3-5' (.9-1.5 m) long, thick, few-branched or spike-like; surrounded at base by a persistant, conspicuous bract
Gender: Separate male and female flowers on the same inflorescence
Flower Color: White
Fruit Size: 1' (30 cm) long
Fruit Color: Green, yellow, orange; eventually brown

Continued on next page

Cocos nucifera 'Fiji Dwarf'

Comments: Coconut palms are the universal symbol of the tropics worldwide, and arguably the world's most economically important palm. Copra (the dried "meat" of the seed), from which oil is extracted, is a significant cash crop thoughout the tropics. Coir, the fiber from the fruit husk, is widely used in manufacturing. The fruits yield several food products at different stages of development, and the leaves are used for thatch or are woven into baskets, mats, and clothing. Even the trunks have been utilized for construction. The trees are valued for their ability to adapt to exposed coastal locations, prospering best in areas with high rainfall, high water tables (though long-term flooding is not tolerated) and warm temperatures. In frost-free but cool climates, the palms grow more slowly and may not flower. Lethal yellowing is the most serious problem of coconuts. The disease is presently incurable, and is spread by a tropical leaf hopper. A program of antibiotic injections will temporarily suspend the decline of infected palms while resistant replacements are being established nearby. Dwarf varieties are so-named not because they necessarily stay shorter than the tall varieties, but because they begin to fruit at a smaller size. Tall varieties are conspicuously swollen at their stem base and have vaguely 3-sided fruits, while the true dwarfs are not particularly swollen at the base and bear round fruits. Unfortunately, some growers merely collect seed nuts from presumed dwarf varieties in the local landscape, rather than buy certified seed. These locally sourced nuts may not come true-to-type and may be as susceptible to lethal yellowing as the talls.

Scientific Name: *Copernicia baileyana* (ko-pur-NIS-ee-a bay-lee-YAHN-a)

Common Name(s): Bailey copernicia, yarey, yarey hembra, yareyon, Bailey's palm, Bailey fan palm

Classification: Coryphoideae - Corypheae
Height: 40' (12.2 m)
Growth Rate: Slow

Origin: Cuba
USDA Hardiness Zone: 10B-11; hardy to 30° F (-1.1° C)

Juvenile specimen

Horticultural Characteristics

Salt Tolerance: Low
Drought Tolerance: High
Soil Requirements: Widely adaptable
Light Requirements: High
Nutritional Requirements: Low
Uses: Specimen tree
Propagation: Seeds, germinating in one to three months; remote germination
Human Hazards: Spiny
Pest Problems: None reported
Disease Problems: None reported

Morphology (Identifying Characteristics)

Habit: Solitary, bearing 50 or more leaves
Trunk or Stem: Smooth, gray, massive to 5' (1.5 m) wide, leaf scars inconspicuous; broad leaf bases persisting on upper portions
Leaf: Costapalmate, induplicate, divided about 1/3 into over a hundred stiff segments that split at their tips
Foliage Color: Green
Leaf Size: 5' (1.5 m) diameter, segments 2" (5 cm) wide
Petiole: 4-5' (1.2-1.5 m) long, broad, armed with coarse teeth
Crownshaft: None
Inflorescence: 5-7' (1.5-2.1 m) long, much-branched, produced from among and extending past the leaves
Gender: Bisexual flowers
Flower Color: Cream
Fruit Size: 3/4" (1.9 cm) diameter
Fruit Color: Dark brown

Comments: This Cuban relative of the carnauba wax palm is highly regarded for the imposing girth of its trunk, topped by a dense crown of beautiful, rigid leaves. It requires ample room, is slow to establish, but is arguably one of the most magnificent fan palms in the world. The *Copernicia* palms as a group, consist of about two dozen species, the majority of which are native to Cuba.

Scientific Name: *Copernicia hospita* (ko-pur-NIS-ee-a HAHS-pi-ta)

Common Name(s): hospita palm, guano cano, yarey

Classification: Coryphoideae - Corypheae
Height: 30' (9 m) but can reach 50' (15 m)
Growth Rate: Slow

Origin: Cuba
USDA Hardiness Zone: 10B-11

Horticultural Characteristics

Salt Tolerance: Moderate
Drought Tolerance: High
Soil Requirements: Widely adaptable
Light Requirements: High
Nutritional Requirements: Low
Uses: Specimen tree
Propagation: Seed, germinating in one to three months; remote germination
Human Hazards: Spiny
Pest Problems: None reported
Disease Problems: None reported

Morphology (Identifying Characteristics)

Habit: Solitary; canopy of 20-30 leaves
Trunk or Stem: Gray, indistinctly ringed; dead leaves form a skirt below the crown
Leaf: Costapalmate, induplicate, wedge-shaped with wide costa and long hastula; divided about 1/3 into 18-30 segments; margins toothed
Foliage Color: Blue-green, waxy
Leaf Size: 5-7' (1.5-2.1 m) long, 2' (.6 m) wide; segments 2" (5 cm) wide
Petiole: 3-4' (.9-1.2 m) long, armed with teeth
Crownshaft: None
Inflorescence: About 6' (1.8 m) long, slender, branched, extending out from the leaves
Gender: Bisexual flowers
Flower Color: Brown
Fruit Size: About 3/8" (9 mm) diameter
Fruit Color: Green

Comments: Hospita palm is one of the striking Cuban *Copernicia* species. The leaves form an erect crown on mature trees of impressive dimensions and appearance. The segments of the leaf are rigid. The leaves are further marked distinctively by the long, broad leaf stem extension (costa) that penetrates several feet into the leaf blade and an often equally long hastula on the upper surface which juts out from the blade. The leaves are also spiny margined, and small teeth are also found on some of the ribs within the blade. This Cuban species is well-adapted to seasonally dry, warm tropical areas, though its slow rate of growth keeps it uncommon. "Young" specimens (without much trunk development) are supremely distinctive looking.
Similar Species: *C. rigida* (jata palm), also from Cuba, is very similar to the hospita palm, but bears only green leaves.

Scientific Name: *Copernicia macroglossa* (ko-pur-NIS-ee-a mak-ro-GLAHS-a)

Common Name(s): Cuban petticoat palm, jata de guanabacoa, petticoat palm, jata de guanbacoa

Classification: Coryphoideae - Corypheae
Height: 15' (4.5 m)
Growth Rate: Slow

Origin: Cuba
USDA Hardiness Zone: 10B-11; damaged but recovered at 26° F (-3.3° C)

Horticultural Characteristics

Salt Tolerance: Moderate
Drought Tolerance: High
Soil Requirements: Widely adaptable
Light Requirements: High
Nutritional Requirements: Low
Uses: Specimen tree
Propagation: Seed, germinating in one to three months; remote germination
Human Hazards: Spiny
Pest Problems: None reported
Disease Problems: None reported

Morphology (Identifying Characteristics)

Habit: Solitary; canopy of 12-15 leaves
Trunk or Stem: Gray, slender, but clothed to base for many years with a skirt of dead leaves (unless these are trimmed)
Leaf: Costapalmate, induplicate, broadly wedge-shaped, with teeth scattered along margin; divided about 1/3 into sixty segments
Foliage Color: Light green, waxy
Leaf Size: 5-7' (1.5-2.1 m) wide
Petiole: Absent to very short, 1' (30 cm) or less
Crownshaft: None
Inflorescence: About 6' long, slender, branched, extending beyond the leaves
Gender: Bisexual flowers
Flower Color: Brown
Fruit Size: 3/4" (3.8 cm) diameter
Fruit Color: Green

Comments: The trunk of Cuban petticoat palm, when fully "shagged" with dead leaves, appears deceptively massive; below the thatch of its petticoat, the actual trunk is no more than 8" (20.3 cm) thick. The leaves of this species lack a well-developed leaf stem (petiole), but are broader and with a less conspicuous leaf stem extension into the blade. The hastula is quite long. Typically, the canopy of Cuban petticoat palm consists of about a dozen erect green leaves. The leaves droop as they age and will persist for many years unless removed.

Scientific Name: *Copernicia prunifera* (ko-pur-NIS-ee-a proo-NIF-e-ra)

Common Name(s): carnauba wax palm, carnauba

Classification: Coryphoideae - Corypheae
Height: 30' (9.1 m)
Growth Rate: Slow to moderate

Origin: Brazil
USDA Hardiness Zone: 10B-11; damaged below 28° F (-2.2° C)

Horticultural Characteristics

Salt Tolerance: Moderate
Drought Tolerance: Moderate
Soil Requirements: Widely adaptable
Light Requirements: High
Nutritional Requirements: Low
Uses: Specimen tree; leaf wax is a commercial product in Brazil
Propagation: Seed, germinating in one to three months; remote germination
Human Hazards: Spiny
Pest Problems: None reported
Disease Problems: None reported

Morphology (Identifying Characteristics)

Habit: Solitary; canopy of about two dozen leaves
Trunk or Stem: Gray, smooth, leaf scars only partially circle trunk; leaf bases oddly persist on lower trunk
Leaf: Palmate, induplicate; divided more than halfway into 30-60 narrow segments that barely split at their tips
Foliage Color: Blue-green, very waxy
Leaf Size: 3.5' (1 m) wide, segments 1/2" (1.3 cm) wide
Petiole: 2.5-3' (.76-.9 m) long; armed throughout length with large, curved black teeth
Crownshaft: None
Inflorescence: 5-7' (1.5-2.1 m) long, slender, branched
Gender: Bisexual flowers
Flower Color: Brown
Fruit Size: 1" (2.5 cm) long
Fruit Color: Brown

Comments: One of three *Copernicia* species that occur in South America, the carnauba wax palm is valued in Brazil for the copious quantity of heat resistant wax found on its leaves. Leaves are harvested, dried, and the wax beaten from them for processing into various waxes and polishes. In its native habitat, the carnauba wax palm is subject to flooding, and thus may have landscape tolerance for less well-drained sites than Cuban *Copernicia* species. The carnauba wax palm is also slightly faster growing than its West Indian cousins. The leaf bases of carnauba wax palms curiously persist on the lower 1/3 of the trunk while falling cleanly from the upper portions. While not as drought tolerant or dramatic in appearance as the sessile-leafed *Copernicia* species (those lacking leaf stems), carnauba wax palm makes an attractive specimen tree in tropical gardens.
Similar Species: *C. alba*, the carnaday palm, occurs in Paraguay, northern Argentina, Bolivia, and contiguous southwestern Brazil. It often forms enormous populations. Resembling the carnauba wax palm in most respects, it is also a secondary commercial source of industrial grade wax.

Scientific Name: *Corypha umbraculifera* (ko-RYF-a um-brak-yoo-LIF-e-ra)

Common Name(s): talipot palm

Classification: Coryphoideae - Corypheae
Height: 60-90' (18.3-27.4 m)
Growth Rate: Moderate (slow when young until above-ground trunk forms)

Origin: Exact origin unknown, possibly India and Sri Lanka
USDA Hardiness Zone: 10B-11; severely damaged or killed at 26° F (-3.3° C)

Horticultural Characteristics

Salt Tolerance: Low
Drought Tolerance: High
Soil Requirements: Widely adaptable
Light Requirements: High
Nutritional Requirements: Moderate
Uses: Specimen tree
Propagation: Seed, germinating in two to three months (best if fresh); remote germination
Human Hazards: Spiny
Pest Problems: None reported
Disease Problems: None reported

Morphology (Identifying Characteristics)

Habit: Solitary; flowers, fruits, then dies; canopy of about three dozen leaves
Trunk or Stem: Gray, robust, leaf bases persist when young; ringed with spiraled, swollen leaf scars
Leaf: Costapalmate, induplicate, round, divided to about 1/2 into 80-100 tapering segments that are split at their tips
Foliage Color: Light to deep green
Leaf Size: 12-18' (3.7-5.5 m) in diameter; segments 6.5' (2 m) long, 2.5" (6.4 cm) wide
Petiole: 6-12' (1.8-3.7 m) long, thick, gray to yellow, black teeth on margins, base split
Crownshaft: None
Inflorescence: Appearing terminal and held well above the leaves, 30-40' (9.1-12.2 m) tall and as wide, much branched and bearing millions of flowers
Gender: Bisexual flowers
Flower Color: Yellowish-white
Fruit Size: 2" (5 cm) diameter
Fruit Color: Green-brown

Comments: Talipot palm is one of about eight *Corypha* species, two of which are cultivated in tropical landscapes for their spectacular flowering habits. After devoting 30-80 years to robust trunk and leaf development, all *Corypha* species produce a spectacular terminal inflorescence that erupts like a fountain high above the crown of leaves. As the fruits form over the course of a year, the leaves yellow and droop into brown obsolescence. By the time the palm's dramatic display of fecundity is over, the plant is dead. Even as young plants, talipot palms require a great deal of room for their massive canopies of large leaves (the largest among fan palms). The huge foliage of all *Corypha* species is valued in their native habitats for thatch, and palm sugar is made from sap collected from the trunk or inflorescence. Talipot palm often is slow to establish; growth quickens after trunk development. Though drought tolerant, it responds to irrigation during dry periods. *C. utan*, the gebang palm, broadly distributed throughout tropical Asia, is smaller than the talipot, less hardy and slightly susceptible to lethal yellowing.

Scientific Name: *Cryosophila stauracantha* (KRY-o-sahf-i-la stow-ra-KANTH-a)

Common Name(s): rootspine palm, give and take, silver rootspine palm, escoba

Classification: Coryphoideae - Corypheae
Height: 30' (9.1 m)
Growth Rate: Moderate

Origin: Central America, Nicaragua to Panama
USDA Hardiness Zone: 10A-11; damaged at 26° F (-3.3° C)

Geoff Stein

Geoff Stein

Inflorescence with conspicuous bracts

Horticultural Characteristics

Salt Tolerance: Low
Drought Tolerance: Low
Soil Requirements: Found on alkaline soils, but has a fairly wide tolerance
Light Requirements: Moderate
Nutritional Requirements: Moderate
Uses: Specimen
Propagation: Seed, reported to germinate erratically; remote germination
Human Hazards: Spines on trunk sharp enough to pierce skin
Pest Problems: None reported
Disease Problems: None reported

Morphology (Identifying Characteristics)

Habit: Solitary with a crown of 10-15 upright leaves
Trunk or Stem: Slender, usually less than 6" (15 cm) diameter, covered for much of height with branching, spiny aerial roots
Leaf: Palmately compound, induplicate, almost circular in outline, divided for half length or more into 30-50 leaflets, hastula short
Foliage Color: Dark green above, grayish below
Leaf Size: To 6' (1.8 m) across
Petiole: Up to 6' (1.8 m) long, hairy and split at base
Crownshaft: None
Inflorescence: Hanging from between leaves, 2' (60 cm) long with velvety, papery sheaths when first produced
Gender: Flowers perfect (with both male and female parts)
Flower Color: Creamy-white
Fruit Size: Ovoid, about 1" (2.5 cm) long
Fruit Color: White

Comments: *Cryosophila* is a small group of American palms characterized by the presence of rootspines. *C. stauracantha* is a plant of lowland rain forests but with a reasonably wide tolerance of conditions under cultivation. The circular leaves with their eye-catching silvery-white underside create a graceful accent for a sheltered spot in partial shade.

Scientific Name: *Cyrtostachys renda* (sir-toe-STAY-kiss REN-da)

Common Name(s): red sealing wax palm, lipstick palm, maharajah palm, sealing wax palm, pinang rajah

Classification: Arecoideae - Areceae
Height: 15' (4.5 m)
Growth Rate: Slow

Origin: Malay Peninsula and Borneo
USDA Hardiness Zone: 11 (may be damaged at temperatures above freezing)

Geoff Stein

Geoff Stein

Detail of red crownshaft

Horticultural Characteristics

Salt Tolerance: Low
Drought Tolerance: Moderate
Soil Requirements: Widely adaptable
Light Requirements: Moderate; high
Nutritional Requirements: Moderate
Uses: Specimen plant, foliage plant
Propagation: Seed, germinating in two to three months with high heat, division; adjacent germination
Human Hazards: None
Pest Problems: None reported
Disease Problems: None reported

Morphology (Identifying Characteristics)

Habit: Clustering; each stem with 10 or fewer leaves
Trunk or Stem: Slender, smooth, green or brownish; conspicuously ringed
Leaf: Pinnately compound, reduplicate; leaflets evenly spaced, narrow, and forming a "V"
Foliage Color: Green and red
Leaf Size: 3-4' (.9-1.2 m) long; leaflets 8-12" (20.3-30 cm) long, 1/2-2/3" (1.3-1.7 cm) wide
Petiole: Red, about 1' (2.5 cm) long
Crownshaft: Smooth, green to bright red, 2-3' (.6-.9 m) long
Inflorescence: Red, short, slender, branched, borne below the crownshaft
Gender: Separate male and female flowers on the same inflorescence
Flower Color: Green
Fruit Size: 3/8" (9 mm) diameter
Fruit Color: Black

Comments: Though few locations in the United States can provide a safe outdoor haven for the red sealing wax palm, its deserved reputation as one of the world's most beautiful palms justifies its treatment here. A denizen of moist, even swampy, rain forests, *C. renda* will not tolerate drought or drying winds, and pales at the slightest touch of winter chill. Nonetheless, the abiding beauty of its red crownshafts and leaf stems render it an item that few palm enthusiasts can resist. Except in the warm tropics, red sealing wax palm is best maintained as a container plant that can be easily protected when temperatures drop below 40° F (4.4° C). Seedlings generally take a long time to express the characteristic red coloration and are also variable in crownshaft color; faster results and guaranteed color can be obtained by carefully dividing established clumps.

Scientific Name: *Dictyosperma album* (dik-tee-o-SPURM-a AL-bum)

Common Name(s): hurricane palm, princess palm

Classification: Arecoideae - Areceae
Height: 30' (9.1 m)
Growth Rate: Moderate

Origin: Mascarene Islands
USDA Hardiness Zone: 10B-11; severely damaged or killed at 26° F (-3.3° C)

Inflorescence

Horticultural Characteristics

Salt Tolerance: Moderate
Drought Tolerance: Moderate
Soil Requirements: Widely adaptable
Light Requirements: High
Nutritional Requirements: Moderate
Uses: Specimen tree
Propagation: Seed, germinating in two to four months; adjacent germination
Human Hazards: None
Pest Problems: None reported
Disease Problems: Moderately susceptible to lethal yellowing
Cultivars: Var. *rubrum*: reddish leaves on young plants; reddish-brown wax on crownshaft; var. *furfuraceum*: wooly, white hairs on crownshaft; var. *aureum*: shorter trunk, orange-yellow leaves on young plants

Morphology (Identifying Characteristics)

Habit: Solitary; canopy of 10-20 leaves
Trunk or Stem: Relatively slender, gray, ridged leaf scars and numerous vertical fissures, swollen at base
Leaf: Pinnately compound, reduplicate; twisted 90° near tip; marginal reins frequent; leaflets numerous, sharply pointed and ribbed
Foliage Color: Green, brown scales on underside of leaflets
Leaf Size: 8-12' (2.4-3.7 m) long; leaflets to 3' (.9 m) long, 2-3" (5-7.5 cm) wide
Petiole: .5-1' (15-30 cm) long; unarmed
Crownshaft: Wide; light green covered with gray to brownish waxy scales
Inflorescence: 1.5' (46 cm) long; horn-like in bud
Gender: Male and female flowers on the same inflorescence
Flower Color: Creamy-yellow to reddish (depending on variety)
Fruit Size: 1/2" (1.3 cm)
Fruit Color: Purple-black

Comments: This beautiful palm, somewhat similar in appearance to *Archontophoenix* (see comments on that species for distinguishing characteristics), earns one of its common names by an alleged resistance to hurricane-force winds. Drying winds can burn the foliage, however, and a protective exposure is advisable in areas with low humidity. During periods of prolonged drought, supplementary irrigation is advantageous. Considered close to extinction in its native habitat, the princess palm is widely cultivated as an elegant vertical accent in tropical and subtropical landscapes.

Scientific Name: *Dypsis cabadae* (DIP-sis ka-BAH-dee)

Common Name(s): cabada palm

Classification: Arecoideae - Areceae
Height: 30' (9.1 m)
Growth Rate: Moderate

Origin: Comoros Islands (near Madagascar)
USDA Hardiness Zone: 10B-11; no damage at 30° F (-1.1° C)

Boldly ringed green trunks

Horticultural Characteristics

Salt Tolerance: Low
Drought Tolerance: High
Soil Requirements: Widely adaptable
Light Requirements: Moderate; high
Nutritional Requirements: Moderate
Uses: Multi-trunked specimen tree, large shrub
Propagation: Seed, germinating in one to two months; adjacent germination
Human Hazards: None
Pest Problems: None reported
Disease Problems: Slightly susceptible to lethal yellowing, stigmina leaf spot, potassium deficiency, ganoderma

Morphology (Identifying Characteristics)

Habit: Clustering, each stem with 6-10 leaves
Trunk or Stem: Smooth, bright green, prominently ringed with grayish leaf scars
Leaf: Pinnately compound, reduplicate; numerous leaflets in one plane; arching near the tip
Foliage Color: Medium green
Leaf Size: 8-10' (2.4-3 m); leaflets approximately 2' (.6 m) long, 2" (5 cm) wide
Petiole: Short, 1-2' (.3-.6 m) long, unarmed
Crownshaft: Greenish-gray
Inflorescence: To 5' (1.8 m) long, branched, appearing below the crownshaft
Gender: Separate male and female flowers on the same inflorescence
Flower Color: Yellow
Fruit Size: 1/2" (1.3 cm)
Fruit Color: Red

Comments: Formerly known as *Chrysalidocarpus cabadae*, this elegant clustering palm grows larger and slightly more slowly than its relative, the areca (*D. lutescens*). The cabada palm makes a striking architectural accent in the landscape, with its smooth, boldly-ringed green trunks. The cabada palm may be slow to cluster; several specimens can be planted close together to create a fuller effect. Young plants frequently have reddish-brown petioles and leaf sheaths; this fades with age. The cabada palm is very effective in courtyard settings or other close spaces where its eye-catching trunk can be shown to advantage. The cabada palm was described from a plant in a Cuban garden and was only recently encountered in the wild.

Scientific Name: *Dypsis decaryi* (DIP-sis de-KAHR-e-eye)

Common Name(s): triangle palm

Classification: Arecoideae - Areceae
Height: 25' (7.6 m)
Growth Rate: Moderate

Origin: Madagascar
USDA Hardiness Zone: 10B-11; severely damaged or killed below 28° F (-2.2° C)

Horticultural Characteristics

Salt Tolerance: Low
Drought Tolerance: Moderate
Soil Requirements: Widely adaptable, well-drained
Light Requirements: Moderate; high
Nutritional Requirements: Moderate
Uses: Specimen tree
Propagation: Seed, germinating in one to two months; adjacent germination
Human Hazards: None
Pest Problems: None reported
Disease Problems: Potassium deficiency (Florida); bacterial bud rot if overwatered, slight susceptibility to lethal yellowing
Comments: Formerly known as *Neodypsis decaryi*, the triangle palm is one of the most unique of all landscape palms in appearance, due to the very precise three-planed arrangement of the leaves. Though a true crownshaft is not formed, the tightly overlapping and bulging leaf bases form a stocky triangle above the short trunk. The leaf bases are covered with brownish-red hairs that easily rub off. Long "reins" frequently hang down from the blue-green leaves. The stiff, planar canopy of triangle palm results in a very bold and formal appearance that dominates the area of the landscape it inhabits. Consequently, its placement should be carefully considered. Though drought tolerant in humid subtropical and tropical zones once established, a triangle palm requires periodic irrigation as it settles into place. In dry summer regions such as California, irrigation is essential. The planting site should be well-drained, and regular fertilization is a must on poor, infertile soils. The leaves are damaged at temperatures below freezing, and older specimens may require two years or more to renew a full canopy after a severe freeze.

Morphology (Identifying Characteristics)

Habit: Solitary; robust canopy of about 20 leaves
Trunk or Stem: Short, dark brown, with narrow, gray leaf scars; leaves radiate out in three planes
Leaf: Pinnately compound, reduplicate; stiff, curved downward near tip; 100-200 pointed leaflets forming a narrow "V"; marginal reins frequent
Foliage Color: Blue-green; patches of red scales on underside of leaflets
Leaf Size: 8-10' (2.4-3 m) long; leaflets 1-2' (.3-.6 m) long, 1.5" (3.8 cm) wide
Petiole: About 1' (2.5 cm) long, unarmed; bases covered with red scurf
Crownshaft: Not really formed; overlapping and bulging leaf bases form distinctive triangular configuration
Inflorescence: 4-5' (1.2-1.5 m) long, emerging from among the leaves, branched
Gender: Separate male and female flowers on the same inflorescence
Flower Color: Yellow
Fruit Size: 1" (2.5 cm)
Fruit Color: Yellow-green

Scientific Name: *Dypsis leptocheilos* (DIP-sis lep-toe-KY-los)

Common Name(s): teddy bear palm, redneck palm

Classification: Arecoideae - Areceae
Height: 30' (9.1 m)
Growth Rate: Moderate

Origin: Madagascar
USDA Hardiness Zone: 10B-11; severely damaged or killed below 28° F (-2.2° C)

Horticultural Characteristics

Salt Tolerance: Low
Drought Tolerance: Moderate
Soil Requirements: Widely adaptable
Light Requirements: High
Nutritional Requirements: Moderate
Uses: Specimen tree
Propagation: Seed, germinating in several months; adjacent germination
Human Hazards: None
Pest Problems: Thrips
Disease Problems: None reported

Morphology (Identifying Characteristics)

Habit: Solitary; canopy of 30-50 leaves
Trunk or Stem: Brown, attractively ringed with wide, whitish ring scars
Leaf: Pinnately compound, reduplicate, erect
Foliage Color: Bright green
Leaf Size: 6-12' (1.8-3.7 m) long; leaflets 1-1.5' (30-46 cm) long, 1.5" (3.8 cm) wide
Petiole: Short, 1/2"-1' (15-30 cm) long, green
Crownshaft: Covered with fur-like rust-red scales
Inflorescence: Short, borne from below the crownshaft
Gender: Separate male and female flowers on the same inflorescence
Flower Color: White
Fruit Size: About 1" (2.5 cm)
Fruit Color: Yellowish-orange

Comments: Originally identified as the species *D. lastelliana*, this relative of the triangle palm has been grown successfully in southern California and Hawaii. In South Florida, it performs best in a sheltered location. It suffers where exposed to drying winds. The crownshaft of leaf bases is attractively covered with rust-red hairs. As the palms age, if older bases are pulled away, a waxy underlay of white to bluish-white marks the younger ring scars. The canopy of redneck palm is bright green and spreading; the leaflets stand at right angles from the rachis. The closely related *D. lastelliana* has a larger trunk, more erect leaves, and is a more demanding garden subject than *D. leptocheilos*.

Scientific Name: *Dypsis lutescens* (DIP-sis loo-TES-senz)

Common Name(s): areca palm, butterfly palm, golden cane palm, yellow bamboo palm

Classification: Arecoideae - Areceae
Height: 20' (6.1 m)
Growth Rate: Moderate

Origin: Madagascar
USDA Hardiness Zone: 10A-11; damaged at 26° F (-3.3° C)

Horticultural Characteristics

Salt Tolerance: Moderate
Drought Tolerance: High
Soil Requirements: Widely adaptable
Light Requirements: Moderate; high
Nutritional Requirements: High
Uses: Shrub, hedge, specimen plant
Propagation: Seed, germinating in two months or less when fresh; division; adjacent germination
Human Hazards: None
Pest Problems: Caterpillars, mealybugs, banana moth (Florida)
Disease Problems: Potassium deficiency (Florida), gliocladium blight, phytophthora bud rot, ganoderma, graphiola false smut
Comments: Formerly known as *Chrysalidocarpus lutescens*, the areca palm is so widely planted throughout subtropical and tropical climates, it is often treated with contempt by palm enthusiasts. Despite its ubiquity in cultivation, the species is extremely rare in its native Madagascar and is actually considered threatened with extinction in the wild. Though most often thickly planted as a screen or boundary hedge, areca palm can make an attractive specimen plant in time when a measure of clear trunk is achieved, and the cluster is opened up by judicious thinning out of some stems. Unfortunately, containerized specimens are usually produced by potting numerous seedlings together which, when planted in the landscape, form dense and frequently stunted clusters. On soils with low fertility, the foliage is usually marred with nutritional deficiencies, but, with regular fertilization, the leaflets will hold a medium green coloration that contrasts nicely with the naturally yellow-tinged leafstems. Arecas are also widely produced for the foliage plant market, but suffer in dim light and low humidity.

Morphology (Identifying Characteristics)

Habit: Clustering, new stems arising above the soil line, each with six to eight leaves
Trunk or Stem: Slender, green to yellowish-green, with conspicuous and closely spaced ring scars
Leaf: Pinnately compound, reduplicate, with 80-100+ leaflets held in a "V"; petiole and rachis yellow or orange tinged
Foliage Color: Green to yellowish green
Leaf Size: To 8' (2.4 m) long; leaflets 1.5-2' (.46-.6 m) long, 1.5" (3.8 cm) wide
Petiole: 2' (.6 m) long, unarmed, yellowish-green
Crownshaft: Grayish-green
Inflorescence: 3' (.9 m) long, borne below the leaves, few-branched, drooping
Gender: Separate male and female flowers on the same inflorescence
Flower Color: yellow
Fruit Size: 1" (2.5 cm) long
Fruit Color: Yellow to purple

Scientific Name: *Dypsis madagascariensis* (DIP-sis mad-a-gas-kar-ee-EN-sis)

Common Name(s): lucubensis palm

Classification: Arecoideae - Areceae
Height: 30' (9.1 m)
Growth Rate: Moderate

Origin: Madagascar
USDA Hardiness Zone: 10B-11

Geoff Stein

Horticultural Characteristics

Salt Tolerance: Low
Drought Tolerance: Moderate
Soil Requirements: Widely adaptable
Light Requirements: Moderate; high
Nutritional Requirements: Moderate
Uses: Specimen tree
Propagation: Seed, germinating in two to five months; adjacent germination
Human Hazards: None
Pest Problems: None reported
Disease Problems: Potassium deficiency (Florida)

Morphology (Identifying Characteristics)

Habit: Solitary or clustering; canopy of 9-12 leaves arranged in three vertical rows
Trunk or Stem: Green for many years, eventually gray, prominently ringed with raised leaf scars
Leaf: Pinnately compound, reduplicate; with over 200 lax leaflets in variously ranked groups of 3-4 giving the leaf a plume-like appearance
Foliage Color: Deep green
Leaf Size: 10' (3 m) long; leaflets 1.5-2' (.46-.6 m) long, 1" (2.5 cm) wide
Petiole: 6" (15 cm) long or less, unarmed
Crownshaft: Short, bright green, waxy white near top
Inflorescence: 2-4' (.6-1.2 m) long, densely branched
Gender: Separate male and female flowers on the same inflorescence
Flower Color: Yellow
Fruit Size: 1/2" (1.3 cm) long

Comments: Solitary forms of this species were formerly known as *Chrysalidocarpus lucubensis*. The crown, though sparse in leaf number, has an attractive tiered arrangement augmented by the full, plume-like character of the leaves.

Scientific Name: *Elaeis guineenisis* (e-LEE-is gin-ee-EN-sis)

Common Name(s): African oil palm, oil palm, macaw fat

Classification: Arecoideae - Cocoeae
Height: 35' (10.7 m) but capable of reaching over 50' (15.2 m)
Growth Rate: Moderate

Origin: Africa
USDA Hardiness Zone: 10B-11; severely damaged or killed at 26° F (-3.3° C)

Geoff Stein

Male flowers

Detail of fruit

Horticultural Characteristics

Salt Tolerance: Moderate
Drought Tolerance: Moderate
Soil Requirements: Widely adaptable
Light Requirements: High
Nutritional Requirements: Moderate
Uses: Specimen tree
Propagation: Seed, germinating in two to five months; tissue culture; adjacent germination
Human Hazards: Spiny
Pest Problems: None reported
Disease Problems: None reported
Cultivars: Various commercial varieties selected for oil characteristics

Morphology (Identifying Characteristics)

Habit: Solitary; canopy of 40-50 leaves
Trunk or Stem: Heavy, often bulging at the middle; rings wide but do not circle the trunk; triangular leaf bases adhere for some time
Leaf: Pinnately compound, reduplicate, plume-like; leaflets numerous, narrow and long, radiating in clusters; lower leaflets short and with midrib spines
Foliage Color: Green
Leaf Size: 12-16' (3.7-4.9 m) long; leaflets 2-4' (.6-1.2 m) long, about 2" (5 cm) wide
Petiole: 2-5' (.6-1.5 m) long, broad, armed (persistent midribs of lower leaflets)
Crownshaft: None
Inflorescence: Short, dense, head-like; emerging from among the lower leaf axils; 4-12" (10-30 cm) long, with short, finger-like branches
Gender: Male and female flowers usually on different inflorescences
Flower Color: Cream
Fruit Size: 2" (5 cm) diameter
Fruit Color: Usually black and red, but some varieties have different colors

Comments: The African oil palm is, after the coconut, the most important commercially exploited palm species. Commercial oils are extracted from both the fruit ("palm oil") and the seed ("palm kernel oil"). The oils are widely used for industrial as well as culinary purposes. Large plantations of this species are found throughout the tropics. While well adapted to warm humid climates worldwide, the robust size of the African oil palm limits its usefulness as a landscape palm. It is probably most appropriate for avenue and park plantings where its stately crown can be used to good advantage. Trees begin to bear fruit in about five years, which is held in very dense clusters of up to several hundred. The largest leaves (which appear every 2-3 weeks on established, well-growing trees) last for over three years. African oil palms adapt to poorly drained soils and will tolerate flooding for short periods. **Related Species:** *E. oleifera*: this Central and South American oil palm is smaller than the African (to about 15' [4.57 m]). The thick trunk creeps along the ground, rooting on its underside, for a number of years before turning upward.

Scientific Name: *Euterpe edulis* (yoo-TURP-ee ED-yoo-lis)

Common Name(s): palmito palm, yayih, juncara palm, assai palm, juçara palm

Classification: Arecoideae - Areceae
Height: 30-40' (9.14-12.2 m)
Growth Rate: Slow

Origin: Atlantic coast of Brazil south to NE Argentina and SE Paraguay
USDA Hardiness Zone: 10B-11; though southernmost populations may be hardier

Horticultural Characteristics

Salt Tolerance: Low
Drought Tolerance: Low
Soil Requirements: Acid
Light Requirements: Moderate; high (when mature)
Nutritional Requirements: Moderate
Uses: Specimen tree, palm heart
Propagation: Seed, germinating in one month; adjacent germination
Human Hazards: None
Pest Problems: None reported
Disease Problems: None reported

Morphology (Identifying Characteristics)

Habit: Solitary (rarely clustering); canopy of 8-15 leaves
Trunk or Stem: Slender, 4-6" (10-15 cm) diameter; green and brownish-gray, conspicuously ringed with wide, brownish leaf scars; often with visible roots at base
Leaf: Pinnately compound, reduplicate, arching, with numerous narrow, drooping leaflets
Foliage Color: Green
Leaf Size: 8-12' (2.4-3.7 cm) long; leaflets 3' (.9 m) long, 1/2-1" (1.3-2.5 cm) wide
Petiole: 1' (.3 m) or less long; unarmed
Crownshaft: Long, slender, green (sometimes orange to reddish)
Inflorescence: 3' (.9 m) long, slender, much-branched, borne below the crownshaft
Gender: Separate male and female flowers on the same inflorescence
Flower Color: White
Fruit Size: 1" (2.5 cm) long
Fruit Color: Purple

Comments: *Euterpe edulis*, the palmito, was at one time the commercial source of palm hearts (the innermost unexpanded leaves within the crownshaft), the harvest of which kills the palm. Wild stands of the species were exploited for this product until the disappearance of the Atlantic Coastal rain forest no longer made it economically feasible. It is an attractive landscape palm where well-adapted, particularly those forms with crownshaft color, best situated in groups of three or more. Like many wet rain forest palms, *E. edulis* benefits from shade during its early years of growth, and a generous supply of moisture throughout its life. Regular fertilization is beneficial on poor, sandy soils, and alkalinity is not well tolerated. Protection from drying winds is also essential.
Related Species: *E. oleracea*, known as assai palm, is a clustering species from the Amazon basin. A thick, purple-colored drink (assai) is prepared from the ripe fruits that remains popular throughout Amazonian Brazil. Though fast-growing and very graceful in appearance, the assai palm is quite tender, and requires protection where freezing temperatures are periodically experienced.

Scientific Name: *Gaussia maya* (GOWS-see-a MAH-ya)

Common Name(s): maya palm, cambo, palma cimaronna, palmasito

Classification: Ceroxyloideae
Typical Height: 30' (9.1 m)
Growth Rate: Moderate

Origin: Guatemala and Belize
USDA Hardiness Zone: 10B-11; severely damaged or killed at 26° F (-3.3° C)

Horticultural Characteristics

Salt Tolerance: Low
Drought Tolerance: Moderate
Soil Requirements: Widely adaptable
Light Requirements: Moderate; high
Nutritional Requirements: Moderate
Uses: Specimen tree
Propagation: Seed, germinating in two months
Human Hazards: Irritant fruit
Pest Problems: None reported
Disease Problems: None reported

Morphology (Identifying Characteristics)

Habit: Solitary; canopy of five to seven leaves
Trunk or Stem: Light brown (green just below crown) with widely-spaced and ridged leaf scars; root stubs at base
Leaf: Pinnately compound, reduplicate, ascending, with over 100 many-ranked leaflets that fall from the leaf stem as they age
Foliage Color: Green
Leaf Size: 9' (2.7 m) long; leaflets 2' (.6 m) long, 2" (5 cm) wide
Petiole: 4' (1.2 m) long, unarmed; base deeply notched on side opposite the blade
Crownshaft: Not well formed
Inflorescence: 3' (.9 m) long, with about a dozen short branches; borne low on the trunk; horn-like in bud
Gender: Separate male and female flowers on the same inflorescence
Flower Color: Greenish-white
Fruit Size: 3/4" (1.9 cm) diameter
Fruit Color: Red
Fruit: Irritant; contains calcium oxalate crystals

Comments: Formerly known as *Opsiandra maya*, the maya palm requires warmth and a steady supply of moisture for best growth, but is quite tolerant of a wide range of soil types. It makes an attractive specimen despite its relatively sparse crown of ascending leaves. It will tolerate full sun, but looks best if situated in part shade. The leaflets are arranged in many planes, giving the leaves a plume-like appearance which helps offset their small number. The first inflorescences of the maya palm remain in bud for several years as the trunk continues to grow, producing additional inflorescences above them. At some point, old and young buds begin to open sequentially from oldest to youngest, with the result that maya palms usually carry flowers and fruits at the same time and at all stages of development. Maya palm does have a reputation for blowing over in high winds. Three other species of *Gaussia* are known, from Puerto Rico, Mexico and Cuba.

Scientific Name: *Heterospathe elata* (het-eh-roh-SPAYTH-ee ee-LAHT-a)

Common Name(s): sagisi palm

Classification: Arecoideae - Cocoeae
Height: 40' (12.2 m)
Growth Rate: Slow

Origin: Philippines
USDA Hardiness Zone: 10B-11; severely damaged or killed at 26° F (-3.3° C)

Geoff Stein

Horticultural Characteristics

Salt Tolerance: Low
Drought Tolerance: Moderate
Soil Requirements: Widely adaptable
Light Requirements: Moderate; high
Nutritional Requirements: Moderate
Uses: Specimen tree, foliage plant
Propagation: Seed, germinating in two months; adjacent germination
Human Hazards: None
Pest Problems: None reported
Disease Problems: None reported

Morphology (Identifying Characteristics)

Habit: Solitary; canopy of 10-16 leaves
Trunk or Stem: Smooth, with broad yellowish-brown ring scars, eventually gray and fissured, swollen at base
Leaf: Pinnately compound, reduplicate, with 130 tapered leaflets; stiffly arched and twisted sharply at the middle
Foliage Color: Green, but young leaves emerge pinkish-brown
Leaf Size: 5-10' (1.5-3 m) long; leaflets 2-3' (.6-.9 m) long, 1-1.5" (2.5-3.8 cm) wide
Petiole: 2' (.6 m) long, unarmed; base quite fibrous
Crownshaft: None
Inflorescence: 4' (1.2 m) long, borne among the leaves, branched to several orders
Gender: Separate male and female flowers on the same inflorescence
Flower Color: White
Fruit Size: 1/4-1/2" (.64-1.27 cm) diameter
Fruit Color: White

Comments: The Sagisi palm is one of several dozen rain forest palms of the southern Pacific region. It is finding wider use as a specimen tree in warm, relatively frost-free areas. It is valued for its attractive display of emergent leaf color, and shows promise as an interiorscape plant as well. Sagisi palm prospers with better than cursory maintenance; regular fertilization is essential on soils of low fertility. In the landscape it should not be situated where cold air is likely to settle during winter. The leaves are very sharply twisted such that the leaflets near the tip of the leaf are held in a vertical plane.

Scientific Name: *Howea forsteriana* (HOW-ee-a for-ster-ee-AHN-a)

Common Name(s): kentia palm, sentry palm, thatch palm, forster sentry palm, thatch leaf palm

Classification: Arecoideae - Areceae
Height: 30' (9.1 m) but can reach 60' (18.2 m)
Growth Rate: Slow

Origin: Lord Howe Islands
USDA Hardiness Zone: 9B-11; recoverable damage at 25° F (-3.9° C)

Horticultural Characteristics

Salt Tolerance: Low
Drought Tolerance: Moderate
Soil Requirements: Widely adaptable
Light Requirements: low; moderate; high only in temperate subtropical climates
Nutritional Requirements: Moderate
Uses: Specimen tree, foliage plant
Propagation: Seed, germinating in two months to one year; adjacent germination
Human Hazards: None
Pest Problems: Red scale
Disease Problems: Phytophthora bud rot, stigmina and other fungal leaf spots

Morphology (Identifying Characteristics)

Habit: Solitary; canopy of about three dozen leaves
Trunk or Stem: Swollen at base, gray, ring scars wavy and slightly raised
Leaf: Pinnately compound, reduplicate, arching; with numerous, evenly spaced, drooping leaflets
Foliage Color: Dark green above, lighter green below
Leaf Size: 12' (3.7 m) long; leaflets about 2.5' (.76 m) long, 2" (5 cm) wide
Petiole: 4-5' (1.2-1.5 m) long, unarmed, sheathing base becoming fibrous
Crownshaft: None
Inflorescence: 3.5' (1 m) long, consisting of 3-7 spikes fused at the base
Gender: Male and female flowers on the same inflorescence
Flower Color: White
Fruit Size: 1.5" (3.8 cm) long
Fruit Color: Red

Comments: Kentia palm is the world's most popular indoor palm, capable of retaining a good to excellent appearance for long durations under interiorscape conditions. However, as a landscape ornamental, the kentia is best reserved for cooler subtropical climates, as the species suffers with incessant heat and frequent drying winds. Light frosts are tolerated, but freezing temperatures will damage or even kill the palms. In cool, coastal climates such as in California, parts of Hawaii, and similar regions, kentias adapt well to full sun after attaining a reasonable size. If their culture is attempted in warmer or dryer areas, partial shade is recommended throughout their life. Despite its slow growth and the high cost of seed, kentia palm remains the reigning queen of interior palms due to its dark green, full and graceful crown of large leaves. As foliage plants they are frequently planted two to three per container, a practice which some feel disrupts the natural beauty of the palm.
Similar Species: *H. belmoreana* is a shorter, slightly less robust cousin of the kentia. Not as adaptable indoors as the kentia, the Belmore sentry palm has lighter green leaves and a simple-spiked inflorescence.

Detail of stem

Fruit

Geoff Stein

Flower spikes

Geoff Stein

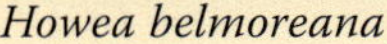
Howea belmoreana

Geoff Stein

Developing fruit of *Howea belmoreana*

Scientific Name: *Hyophorbe lagenicaulis* (hy-o-FOR-bee lag-e-ni-KAW-lis)

Common Name(s): bottle palm

Classification: Ceroxyloideae - Hyophorbeae
Height: 12' (3.7 m)
Growth Rate: Slow

Origin: Round Island (Mascarenes)
USDA Hardiness Zone: 10B-11; variably damaged below 30° F (-1.1° C)

Horticultural Characteristics

Salt Tolerance: Moderate
Drought Tolerance: Moderate
Soil Requirements: Widely adaptable
Light Requirements: Moderate; high
Nutritional Requirements: Moderate
Uses: Small specimen tree
Propagation: Seed, germinating in three to six months; adjacent germination
Human Hazards: Irritant fruit
Pest Problems: None reported
Disease Problems: Potassium deficiency (Florida)

Morphology (Identifying Characteristics)

Habit: Solitary; crown of four to eight leaves
Trunk or Stem: Gray, smooth, closely ringed and usually vertically fissured, enormously swollen at base
Leaf: Pinnately compound, reduplicate, arching, with 140 leaflets held in an upward "V"; leaflets with several ribs
Foliage Color: Green to grayish-green
Leaf Size: 5-6' (1.5-1.8 m) long; leaflets about 2' (.6 m) long, 2" (5 cm) wide
Petiole: 8-10" (20.3-25.4 cm) long, unarmed, arching
Crownshaft: Smooth, green, waxy, broadest at base
Inflorescence: About 30" (.76 m) long, several borne in a circle just below crownshaft, densely branched; hornlike and erect in bud
Gender: Separate male and female flowers on the same inflorescence
Flower Color: Cream
Fruit Size: 1" (2.5 cm) long
Fruit Color: Black

Comments: Bottle palm is cultivated throughout the world for its wonderfully novel shape and beautifully-sculpted crownshaft. It is thus ironic that on Round Island in the Mascarene chain (the only known habitat for this popular palm), only 15 or so individuals remain. Despite the bizarrely swollen trunk, which most people assume to be a water storage adaptation, bottle palm requires irrigation during dry periods to look its best, especially if planted in full sun. Bottle palm thrives on heat and is very salt tolerant, but is severely damaged, if not killed outright, by freezing temperatures. Regular fertilization is essential to keep bottle palm's sparse canopy in good condition. In Florida it is particularly susceptible to potassium deficiency.

Scientific Name: *Hyophorbe verschaffeltii* (hy-o-FOR-bee ver-sha-FELT-tee-eye)

Common Name(s): spindle palm

Classification: Ceroxyloideae - Hyophorbeae
Height: 20' (6.1 m)
Growth Rate: Slow

Origin: Rodrigues Island (Mascarenes)
USDA Hardiness Zone: 10B-11; severely damaged or killed at 28° F (-3.3° C)

Inflorescences in bud

Flowers

Horticultural Characteristics

Salt Tolerance: Moderate
Drought Tolerance: Moderate
Soil Requirements: Widely adaptable
Light Requirements: High
Nutritional Requirements: High
Uses: Small specimen tree
Propagation: Seed, germinating in three to six months; adjacent germination
Human Hazards: Irritant fruit
Pest Problems: None reported
Disease Problems: Potassium and magnesium deficiency (Florida), slight susceptibility to lethal yellowing

Morphology (Identifying Characteristics)

Habit: Solitary; crown of 5-10 leaves
Trunk or Stem: Stout, gray, closely ringed, swollen at middle or just below crownshaft (but not excessively)
Leaf: Pinnately compound, reduplicate, arching; 100-150 leaflets held in several planes lack secondary ribs and droop slightly above the middle
Foliage Color: Bright green above, grayish-green below
Leaf Size: 5-8' (1.5-2.4 m) long; leaflets about 2.5' (.76 m) long, 2" (5 cm) wide
Petiole: To 1' (30 cm) long, unarmed
Crownshaft: Smooth, bright green, waxy, swollen at base
Inflorescence: 2.5' (.76 m) long, several borne in circle just below crownshaft, densely branched, hornlike and erect in bud
Gender: Separate male and female flowers on same inflorescence
Flower Color: Cream
Fruit Size: 3/4" (1.9 cm) long
Fruit Color: Orange to red
Fruit: Irritant; contains calcium oxalate crystals

Comments: Spindle palm grows slightly taller and is slightly hardier than the bottle palm. It can be easily separated from the latter by the less swollen trunk (which is never, on mature specimens, widest at the bottom), and the several-ranked leaflets that give the leaves a less formal appearance than those of bottle palm. Though still quite striking in appearance, spindle palm does not cast quite as novel an aspect as *H. lagenicaulis*, and thus combines more easily in the landscape with other palms. The leaves, especially on young plants, are noticeably triangular in arrangement on the stem. As with its sister species, spindle palm requires regular care to look its best, including supplementary irrigation during dry periods. It should be situated in full sun.

Scientific Name: *Hyphaene thebaica* (hy-FEE-nee thee-BAY-i-ka)

Common Name(s): gingerbread palm, doum palm, African doum palm

Classification: Coryphoideae - Borasseae
Height: 30-60' (9.1-8.3 m)
Growth Rate: Slow

Origin: Northern Africa
USDA Hardiness Zone: 10A-11

Fruit

Horticultural Characteristics

Salt Tolerance: Moderate
Drought Tolerance: High
Soil Requirements: Widely adaptable
Light Requirements: High
Nutritional Requirements: Low
Uses: Specimen tree
Propagation: Seed, germinating in six months or more; requires deep container; remote germination
Human Hazards: Spiny
Pest Problems: None reported
Disease Problems: None reported

Morphology (Identifying Characteristics)

Habit: Solitary or multi-trunked, branching; 20-30 leaves
Trunk or Stem: Black, deeply fissured, with brown leaf scars and tufts of fiber; covered with white to gray leaf bases when young
Leaf: Costapalmate, induplicate, round; arched and folded inward at tip of costa; divided 1/2 to 2/3 into several dozen pointed stiff segments
Foliage Color: Deep green to silvery-green
Leaf Size: Averaging 4' (1.2 m) in diameter
Petiole: 3-4' (.9-1.2 m) long; edged with sharp, hooked black teeth that turn gray with age
Crownshaft: None
Inflorescence: Averaging 4' (1.2 m) long; with short, thick branches
Gender: Separate male and female plants
Flower Color: Purplish-brown or yellow
Fruit Size: About 3" (7.5 cm) long
Fruit Color: Brown
Fruit: Edible, though barely palatable

Comments: The gingerbread or doum palms comprise a group of about 10 species not yet well circumscribed from each other. They are a rarity within the palm family insofar as trunks of many of the species regularly branch well above the base. They are denizens of very arid regions by-and-large, but grow where sub-surface water can be mined by their deeply penetrating root systems. Their slow rate of growth and difficult handling has kept them from becoming well represented in nurseries and landscapes, but they are extremely tough palms, with some species that may even be hardy slightly north of USDA Hardiness Zone 10. Thriving cultivated specimens of several species can be found in south Florida, southern California, and other subtropical and tropical regions. The sizable fruits are edible, though barely palatable, and have been utilized as subsistence or survival food. They are often pear- or top-shaped. A few of the other species and their place of origin are: *H. compressa* (East Africa), *H. coriacea* (Southeast Africa) and *H. dichotoma* (India).

Scientific Name: *Johannesteijsmannia altifrons* (yo-hahn-nes-tish-MAHN-nee-a AL-ti frahnz)

Common Name(s): joey palm, diamond joey, joey

Classification: Coryphoideae - Corypheae
Height: 4-6' (1.2-1.8 m)
Growth Rate: Slow

Origin: Thailand and the Malay Peninsula
USDA Hardiness Zone: 11 (10B with protection)

Geoff Stein

Horticultural Characteristics

Salt Tolerance: Low
Drought Tolerance: Low
Soil Requirements: Rich, moist but well-drained, acid
Light Requirements: Low
Nutritional Requirements: Moderate, but consistently supplied
Uses: Understory palm, interior
Propagation: Seed germinates in 45 days if not allowed to dry out; otherwise erratic and slow; remote germination
Human Hazards: Sharp teeth on lower portions of petiole and lower leaf margins
Pest Problems: None reported
Disease Problems: None reported

Morphology (Identifying Characteristics)

Habit: Solitary, producing a cluster of several dozen leaves
Trunk or Stem: None above ground
Leaf: Large, entire, costapalmate, induplicate but appearing reduplicate, diamond-shaped
Foliage Color: Glossy green
Leaf Size: 10' (3 m) or more long
Petiole: To 6' (1.8 m) long, armed with short teeth which continue on the lower part of the blade
Crownshaft: None
Inflorescence: Branched, formed between leaves
Gender: Flowers bisexual (perfect)
Flower Color: Creamy-white with strong smell
Fruit Size: Globose, about 1.5" (3.8 cm) diameter, surface corky-warted
Fruit Color: Brown

Comments: The genus *Johannesteijsmannia* consists of four species of tropical Asian understory palms closely related to *Licuala. J. altifrons*, now endangered in its habitat, is a magnificent palm for shade. The huge, diamond-shaped glossy green leaves are unmatched by any other palm on earth except its sister species, the rare *J. magnifica* (the leaves of which are beautifully waxy white below). Joey palm needs a rich soil, year-round warmth, regular irrigation and protection from drying winds.

Scientific Name: *Jubaea chilensis* (joo-BEE-a chi-LEN-sis)

Common Name(s): Chilean wine palm, coquito palm, palma chilena

Classification: Arecoideae - Cocoeae
Height: 50-80' (15.2-24.4 m)
Growth Rate: Slow

Origin: Chile
USDA Hardiness Zone: 8B-10A; May be lightly damaged below 15° F (-9.4° C); thought to be hardy to 4° F (-15.6° C)

Horticultural Characteristics

Salt Tolerance: Low
Drought Tolerance: High (once established)
Soil Requirements: Widely adaptable
Light Requirements: High
Nutritional Requirements: Moderate
Uses: Specimen tree; sap collected for sugar and alcohol (palm is killed)
Propagation: Seed, germinating erratically in six months to over a year; adjacent germination
Human Hazards: None
Pest Problems: None reported
Disease Problems: None reported

Morphology (Identifying Characteristics)

Habit: Solitary, robust, massive crown of several dozen leaves
Trunk or Stem: Thick, 4-6' (1.2-1.8 m) diameter, dark gray, conspicuously marked with raised, diamond shaped leaf scars
Leaf: Pinnately compound, reduplicate, stiff, spreading; with several hundred narrow, pointed leaflets that split at their tips
Foliage Color: Dull green above, gray below
Leaf Size: 6-12' (1.8-3.6 m) long; leaflets 2' (.6 m) long, 1" (2.5 cm) wide
Petiole: Short, with hairy fibers at margins
Crownshaft: None
Inflorescence: About 4' (1.2 m) long, densely branched, borne among the lower leaves
Gender: Separate male and female flowers on the same inflorescence
Flower Color: Purple
Fruit Size: 1.25" (3.2 cm) diameter
Fruit Color: Orange-yellow

Comments: This rare and amazing species quite possibly has the thickest trunk of any palm so far known. Chilean wine palm occurs in a few coastal valleys in Chile that remain devoid of extremes of both heat and cold. Native populations were exploited for the sugary sap for many years. This practice severely reduced their numbers since the trunk is cut down at harvest. The species is now protected by law. Sap reportedly can be collected from felled trunks for up to two years. Chilean wine palm grows poorly in hot, humid tropical and subtropical climates. It is best suited for coastal California, the Mediterranean coast, and similar climatic zones in Australia and South Africa.

Scientific Name: *Kentiopsis oliviformis* (kent-ee-AHP-sis o-liv-i-FOR-mis)

Common Name(s): none known

Classification: Arecoideae - Areceae
Height: 30' (9.1 m), to 100' (30.5 m) in the wild
Growth Rate: Slow

Origin: New Caledonia
USDA Hardiness Zone: 10B-11

Geoff Stein

Horticultural Characteristics

Salt Tolerance: Low
Drought Tolerance: Moderate
Soil Requirements: Well-drained, slightly alkaline to slightly acid
Light Requirements: High
Nutritional Requirements: Moderate, may have specific micronutrient needs
Uses: Specimen
Propagation: Seed, germinating in one to three months when fresh, otherwise can be erratic; adjacent germination
Human Hazards: None
Pest Problems: None reported
Disease Problems: None reported

Morphology (Identifying Characteristics)

Habit: Solitary with an arching head of 10-12 leaves
Trunk or Stem: Medium, strongly-ringed, heavier or swollen at the base
Leaf: Pinnately compound with more than 100 slender, tapering leaflets, reduplicate
Foliage Color: Dark green
Leaf Size: 6-8' (1.8-2.4 m) long, leaflets 18-24" (46-60 cm) long
Petiole: Short
Crownshaft: Purplish to brownish green, 3-4' (.9-1.2 m) long
Inflorescence: Short, upright, stiff branches borne below the crownshaft
Gender: Male and female flowers separate but in the same inflorescence
Flower Color: Whitish-green
Fruit Size: Olive-shaped, about 1" (2.5 cm) long
Fruit Color: Red

Comments: Reputed by some to be a difficult palm to grow; other growers find it trouble-free. It is the tallest native palm in New Caledonia, and is best adapted to seasonally dry tropical climates. It makes a handsome specimen plant and also looks excellent in a small group planting.

Scientific Name: *Kerriodoxa elegans* (ker-ree-o-DOX-a EL-e-ganz)

Common Name(s): white elephant palm

Classification: Coryphoideae - Corypheae
Height: 15' (4.6 m)
Growth Rate: Slow to moderate

Origin: Southern Thailand
USDA Hardiness Zone: 10A-11 (possibly 9B with protection), only slight damage at 26° F (-3.3° C)

Horticultural Characteristics

Salt Tolerance: Low
Drought Tolerance: Moderate
Soil Requirements: Well-drained
Light Requirements: Moderate to high
Nutritional Requirements: Moderate
Uses: Specimen or large container
Propagation: Seed, germinating in a few months with heat; remote germination
Human Hazards: Petiole edges hard and sharp
Pest Problems: None reported
Disease Problems: None reported

Comments: White elephant palm is an eye-catching specimen plant for partial shade. Though not exceedingly tall, the very broad leaves form a sizable spreading crown. The contrast between the dark petioles and the glossy green blades is spectacular. It has reportedly over-wintered in USDA Hardiness Zone 9B, but exposure to cold, drying winds is detrimental.

Morphology (Identifying Characteristics)

Habit: Solitary with 8-12 leaves held stiffly extended
Trunk or Stem: Medium-slender, about 8" (20.3 cm) diameter, closely-ringed
Leaf: Palmate, induplicate, almost circular, split about 1/3 or 1/2 of their radius into pleated, slightly pendulous segments
Foliage Color: Dark green above, chalky-white below
Leaf Size: About 6' (1.8 m) wide
Petiole: 2-3' (.6-.9 m) long, unarmed but sharp-edged, brown-black in color
Crownshaft: None
Inflorescence: Borne from among the leaves, hairy; male flower stems 1' (30 cm) long and much-branched; female to 3' (.9 m)
Gender: Male and female flowers on separate plants
Flower Color: Creamy-yellow
Fruit Size: Globose, about 2" (5 cm) diameter with a corky, veined surface
Fruit Color: Orange-yellow

Scientific Name: *Latania loddigesii* (la-TAN-ee-a lo-di-GAI-zee-eye)

Common Name(s): blue latan palm

Classification: Coryphoideae - Borasseae
Height: 30' (9.1 m)
Growth Rate: Slow

Origin: Mauritius Island (Mascarenes)
USDA Hardiness Zone: 10B-11; thought to be hardy to 29° F (-1.6° C)

Horticultural Characteristics

Salt Tolerance: Moderate
Drought Tolerance: High
Soil Requirements: Widely adaptable
Light Requirements: High
Nutritional Requirements: Moderate
Uses: Specimen tree
Propagation: Seed (which must be fresh), germinating in one to two months; remote germination
Human Hazards: None
Pest Problems: Palmetto weevils
Disease Problems: Slight susceptibility to lethal yellowing
Comments: The latan palms are lovely tropical fan palms, as striking when young, due to their specific coloration, as they are as mature specimens. Much of the color fades as these palms age, thus older individuals of the different species can be difficult to distinguish from each other without attention to some rather inconspicuous features. Blue latans are highlighted with mottled blue, most of the color concentrated in the leaf stems and veins. It is also the "scurfiest" of the species, with a dense deposit of woolly wax on the leaf undersides. Small seedlings can be an intense purple-red, and easily confused with red latan. As they age, they become less red than the red latan. The seed of the blue latan has a distinctive, convoluted surface ornamentation at its broader end, and sure identity is best confirmed by observation of seeds. All latan palms are adapted to a seasonally dry tropical climate, and prosper with hot, wet summers and warm but drier winters. In the wild, they often occur close to the shore (but on cliffs and in canyons where they would not receive direct salt spray). Older specimens are at some risk in areas known to harbor lethal yellowing disease.

Morphology (Identifying Characteristics)

Habit: Solitary; canopy of one to two dozen leaves
Trunk or Stem: Grayish-brown, swollen at base, slightly bulged near wavy narrow ring scars
Leaf: Costapalmate, stiffly folded, divided to 1/2 into about 30 stiff, unsplit segments with finely-toothed margins; hastula pointed and flat
Foliage Color: Blue-green; waxy, almost woolly below; red veins when young
Leaf Size: 6-8' (1.8-2.4 m) wide, segments several feet long, 3" (7.6 cm) wide
Petiole: 4-6' (1.2-1.8 m) long, bluish (red when young), toothed (when young); base split
Crownshaft: None
Inflorescence: 3-6' (.9-1.8 m) long, from among the leaves; males with clusters of short, clubby branches; females with single short branches
Gender: Separate male and female plants
Flower Color: Brownish-yellow
Fruit Size: 2-3" (5-7.5 cm) long, 1" (2.5 cm) wide
Fruit Color: Brownish-green

Scientific Name: *Latania lontaroides* (la-TAN-ee-a lon-ta-ROY-deez)

Common Name(s): red latan palm

Classification: Coryphoideae - Borasseae
Height: 30' (9.1 m)
Growth Rate: Slow

Origin: Reunion Island (Mascarenes)
USDA Hardiness Zone: 10A-11; thought to be hardy to 26° F (-3.3° C)

Red leaf bases of juvenile plant

Horticultural Characteristics

Salt Tolerance: Moderate
Drought Tolerance: High
Soil Requirements: Widely adaptable
Light Requirements: High
Nutritional Requirements: Moderate
Uses: Specimen tree
Propagation: Seed (which must be fresh), germinating in one to two months; remote germination
Human Hazards: None
Pest Problems: Palmetto weevils
Disease Problems: Slight to moderate susceptibility to lethal yellowing

Morphology (Identifying Characteristics)

Habit: Solitary; canopy of 12-24 leaves
Trunk or Stem: Grayish-brown, swollen at base, bulged near the wide ring scars
Leaf: Costapalmate, stiffly folded, divided to 1/2 into about 30 unsplit segments with finely-toothed margins; hastula broad, blunt and raised
Foliage Color: Gray-green and slightly waxy (red and shiny green when young); red margins and veins
Leaf Size: 6-8' (1.8-2.4 m) wide, segments several feet long, 3" (7.6 cm) wide
Petiole: 4-6' (1.2-1.8 m) long, reddish, slightly toothed when young; base sheath split; scurfy
Crownshaft: None
Inflorescence: 3-6' (.9-1.8 m) long, from among the leaves; males with clusters of short, clubby branches; females with single short branches
Gender: Separate male and female plants
Flower Color: Brownish-yellow
Fruit Size: 2-3" (5-7.6 cm) long, 1" (2.5 cm) wide
Fruit Color: Brownish-green

Comments: The red latan eventually loses most of the red foliar highlights that make it such a distinctive young specimen. It can be distinguished from the blue latan by its pointed and upraised hastula on the upper leaf surface, less waxy scurf on the leaf underside and wide leaf scars on a gray trunk. The seed lacks the attractive sculpturing found on that of the blue latan palm. It is also slightly hardier. Any toothing that occurs on the leaf segment margins or petiole usually disappears as the palm ages. Culture is the same as for the blue latan. **Related Species:** The yellow latan (*L. verschaffeltii*), from Rodiquez Island, has yellow to yellow-orange petioles and leaf veins. The hastula is small, blunt and flat. The trunk only rarely bulges around the leaf scars. The dark seeds are three-lobed and have a conspicuous ridge running down the middle. Hybrids are known between it and the red latan.

Scientific Name: *Licuala grandis* (li-KWAH-la GRAN-dis)

Common Name(s): licuala palm, Vanuatu fan palm, palas paying, ruffled fan palm

Classification: Coryphoideae - Corypheae
Height: 8' (2.4 m)
Growth Rate: Slow

Origin: New Hebrides Islands
USDA Hardiness Zone: 10B-11; severely damaged or killed below 28° F (-2.2° C)

Geoff Stein

Horticultural Characteristics

Salt Tolerance: Low
Drought Tolerance: Low
Soil Requirements: Widely adaptable
Light Requirements: Moderate
Nutritional Requirements: High
Uses: Small tree
Propagation: Seed, germinating in three to six months with heat; remote germination
Human Hazards: Spiny
Pest Problems: None reported
Disease Problems: None reported

Morphology (Identifying Characteristics)

Habit: Solitary; canopy of 10-20 leaves
Trunk or Stem: Slender, gray-brown; ridged, non-circling leaf scars; covered with fiber and projecting leaf bases for many years
Leaf: Palmate, induplicate, almost circular; usually undivided; densely pleated along ribs
Foliage Color: Green, shiny
Leaf Size: About 3' (.9 m) wide
Petiole: About 3' (.9 m) long, armed with hooked teeth in the lower 2/3
Crownshaft: None
Inflorescence: 6' (1.8 m) long, loosely branched, produced from among the leaves
Gender: Bisexual flowers
Flower Color: White
Fruit Size: 1/2" (1.3 cm) diameter
Fruit Color: Red

Comments: *Licuala grandis*, with its seemingly perfectly circular leaves (in fact, they are not) is one of the most attractive palms available for tropical landscapes. The corrugated and (usually) unsegmented leaves are a bright, shiny green and immediately catch the eye with their elegant and symmetrical shape. *Licuala grandis* is a wet rainforest understory plant, and requires part shade for best appearance, in a situation protected from drying winds. It should receive irrigation during prolonged dry periods. A well-drained but organic soil is ideal; on sandy soils, maintenance of an organic mulch is strongly recommended. This slow-growing species can also be maintained for many years in a large container or tub on a shaded patio.
Similar Species: The genus *Licuala* consists of 100 or more single-stemmed or clustering species that are not well understood taxonomically. The following solitary species are occasionally cultivated: *L. lauterbachii* (New Guinea) is a tender species that grows to 12' (3.7 m) and bears nearly circular leaves split into about 30 segments. *L. paludosa* (Malaysia and southeast Asia) resembles a single-stemmed, spiny licuala (*L. spinosa*).

Scientific Name: *Licuala ramsayi* (li-KWAH-la RAM-say-eye)

Common Name(s): Australian fan palm

Classification: Coryphoideae - Corypheae
Height: 40-45' (12.2-13.7 m)
Growth Rate: Slow

Origin: Australia (Queensland)
USDA Hardiness Zone: 10B-11; slight damage at 26° F (-3.3° C)

Geoff Stein

Horticultural Characteristics

Salt Tolerance: Moderate, found in coastal swamps
Drought Tolerance: Low
Soil Requirements: Moist
Light Requirements: Moderate; low when small
Nutritional Requirements: Moderate
Uses: Specimen
Propagation: Seed, germinating erratically and slowly even with heat; remote germination
Human Hazards: Sharp teeth on leaf stem
Pest Problems: None reported
Disease Problems: None reported

Morphology (Identifying Characteristics)

Habit: Solitary with about 12 leaves in an open crown
Trunk or Stem: Slender, about 8" (20.3 cm) diameter
Leaf: Palmate, circular in outline, deeply divided into many, uneven, wedge-shaped segments with toothed tips
Foliage Color: Dark green
Leaf Size: 5-6' (1.5-1.8 m) across
Petiole: 5-6' (1.5-1.8 m) long, armed with spines along the margins
Crownshaft: None
Inflorescence: Borne between leaves, hanging
Gender: Flowers perfect (bisexual)
Flower Color: White
Fruit Size: Globose, 1/2" (1.3 cm) diameter
Fruit Color: Orange-red

Comments: The pinwheel-like leaf of this species is its standout feature. It is the largest of the *Licualas* in cultivation, and spectacular singly or in groups. Young plants do well in the interior.

Scientific Name: *Licuala spinosa* (li-KWAH-la spi-NO-sa)

Common Name(s): spiny licuala, mangrove fan palm

Classification: Coryphoideae - Corypheae
Height: 12' (3.7 m)
Growth Rate: Slow

Origin: Malaysia, Philippines, Indonesia
USDA Hardiness Zone: 10A-11; 9B with protection; damaged but recovered from 26° F (-3.3° C)

Horticultural Characteristics

Salt Tolerance: Low
Drought Tolerance: Moderate
Soil Requirements: Widely adaptable
Light Requirements: Moderate
Nutritional Requirements: Moderate
Uses: Shrub
Propagation: Seed, germinating in three to six months with heat; remote germination
Human Hazards: Spiny
Pest Problems: None reported
Disease Problems: None reported

Morphology (Identifying Characteristics)

Habit: Clumping; each stem with about 10 leaves
Trunk or Stem: Slender, covered with fiber and leaf bases
Leaf: Palmate, circular, divided deeply into 20 or so wedge-shaped segments that are toothed at their truncated tips
Foliage Color: Green, shiny
Leaf Size: About 3' (.9 m) wide; segments several inches wide
Petiole: 3-5' (.9-1.5 m) long, armed with sharp, hooked teeth
Crownshaft: None
Inflorescence: 4-8' (1.2-2.4 m) long, loosely branched
Gender: Bisexual flowers
Flower Color: White
Fruit Size: 1/2" (1.3 cm) diameter
Fruit Color: Red

Comments: Despite the ferocious armament along the leaf stems and its slow rate of growth, spiny licuala is prized for its attractively-segmented, circular leaves. It is one of the more sun-tolerant species in the genus, but leaves maintain their best appearance with some shade. Its water demands are directly proportional to the amount of sunlight the palm receives. Spiny licuala also appears to be slightly hardier than *L. grandis.*

Similar Species: *L. rumphii* (Eastern Indonesia) is a tightly clumping species slightly smaller than spiny licuala. The leaves form about 3/4 of a circle and are divided to the stem into several broad segments. *L. gracilis* (Java) is a dwarf clumper that rarely exceeds 5' (1.5 m) in height.

Scientific Name: *Livistona australis* (liv-i-STON-a aw-STRAL-is)

Common Name(s): Australian fan palm, Australian cabbage tree palm, Gippsland palm, Australian palm, fan palm

Classification: Coryphoideae - Livistoneae
Height: 40' (12.2 m)
Growth Rate: Slow

Origin: Australia
USDA Hardiness Zone: 9A-11; thought to be hardy to at least 22° F (-5.6° C)

Horticultural Characteristics

Salt Tolerance: Moderate
Drought Tolerance: Moderate
Soil Requirements: Widely adaptable
Light Requirements: Moderate; high
Nutritional Requirements: Moderate
Uses: Specimen tree
Propagation: Seed, germinating in one to two months; remote germination
Human Hazards: Sharp teeth on petiole (chiefly when young)
Pest Problems: None reported
Disease Problems: Potassium deficiency (Florida)

Morphology (Identifying Characteristics)

Habit: Solitary, robust, canopy of 30-50 leaves
Trunk or Stem: Gray or brown, closely ringed with ridged leaf scars, fissured; leaf bases and fiber persist for several years
Leaf: Costapalmate, induplicate, thin-textured, circular; divided to about 2/3 into numerous, deeply split segments that droop at their tips
Foliage Color: Deep, glossy green; sometimes tinged brown
Leaf Size: 6-8' (1.8-2.4 m) diameter; segments 3' (.9 m) long, 1.5" (3.8 cm) wide
Petiole: About 6' (1.8 m) long, narrow, marginally toothed on young specimens
Crownshaft: None
Inflorescence: About 4' (1.2 m) long, shortly branched, borne among the leaves
Gender: Bisexual flowers (sometimes function as males only)
Flower Color: Creamy-yellow
Fruit Size: 3/4" (1.9 cm) long
Fruit Color: Reddish-brown to black

Comments: After Chinese fan palm, Australian fan palm is probably the hardiest *Livistona* species in wide cultivation. It grows considerably taller than Chinese fan palm, however, and can easily be distinguished from that species by its conspicuously ridged trunk. It also does not appear to be susceptible to lethal yellowing. Early Australian settlers harvested the heart for cabbage, fashioned hats and baskets from the leaves and utilized the trunks for light construction. Aborigines made fishing lines and nets from leaf fiber, used the leaves for roofing and pieces of the outer trunk to make spearheads. Australian fan palm is one of the most carefree species in the genus and adapts well to a wide variety of soil types. Young plants are particularly attractive and function well as indoor foliage.

Scientific Name: *Livistona chinensis* (liv-i-STON-a chi-NEN-sis)

Common Name(s): Chinese fan palm

Classification: Coryphoideae - Livistoneae
Height: 25' (7.6 m)
Growth Rate: Slow

Origin: China, southern Japan
USDA Hardiness Zone: 9A-11; thought to be hardy to at least 20° F (-6.7° C)

Horticultural Characteristics

Salt Tolerance: Moderate
Drought Tolerance: Moderate
Soil Requirements: Widely adaptable
Light Requirements: Moderate; high
Nutritional Requirements: Moderate
Uses: Specimen tree
Propagation: Seed, germinating in one to two months; remote germination
Human Hazards: Spiny (variable)
Pest Problems: None reported
Disease Problems: Moderate susceptibility to lethal yellowing, ganoderma
Cultivars: Var. *subglobosa* has been applied to wild forms with spherical (rather than ovoid) fruits.

Morphology (Identifying Characteristics)

Habit: Solitary; canopy of 30-50 leaves
Trunk or Stem: Brown initially, gray with age, closely ringed with incomplete leaf scars, eventually corky below
Leaf: Costapalmate, induplicate, divided to about 2/3 into 60-100 deeply split segments that are pendant in their lower half
Foliage Color: Olive green
Leaf Size: About 6' (1.8 m) diameter; segments 3-4' (.9-1.2 m) long, 2" (5 cm) wide
Petiole: 6' (1.8 m) long, teeth (if present) along margins of lower half
Crownshaft: None
Inflorescence: 6' (1.8 m) long, produced from among the leaves, densely branched
Gender: Bisexual flowers
Flower Color: Cream
Fruit Size: 1/2-1" (1.3-2.5 cm) long
Fruit Color: Grayish-blue

Comments: By far the most widely planted member of the genus, Chinese fan palm makes a slow-growing but handsome specimen, forming a wide-spreading attractive crown even as a young plant. This has even led to their use as a groundcover in landscaping, an outrageous practice since at least half of the palms will require removal as they age. The long leaf segment tips hang gracefully giving the canopy a weeping appearance. They are tolerant of relatively infertile soils, but respond favorably to good nutrition. It is probably the hardiest of the *Livistonas*, and can withstand several degrees below freezing without any damage. Full sun is best for the Chinese fan palm; in anything more than light shade, the leaves have a tendency to "stretch." *L. boninensis*, found on the Ogasawara Islands southeast of Japan, has at times been considered a variety of *L. chinensis*, which it resembles in most respects, but exceeds in height (to 60 or more feet [18.3 m]). It is probably only slightly less hardy.

Continued on next page

Fruiting stems

Detail of leaf showing hastula

Detail of fruit

Scientific Name: *Livistona decipiens* (liv-i-STON-a dee-SIP-ee-enz)

Common Name(s): ribbon fan palm, weeping cabbage palm, fountain palm, ribbon palm

Classification: Coryphoideae - Livistoneae
Height: 30' (9.1 m)
Growth Rate: Slow to moderate

Origin: Australia
USDA Hardiness Zone: 9A-11; thought to be hardy to 23° F (-5° C)

Horticultural Characteristics

Salt Tolerance: Low
Drought Tolerance: Moderate
Soil Requirements: Widely adaptable
Light Requirements: Moderate; high
Nutritional Requirements: Moderate
Uses: Specimen tree
Propagation: Seed, germinating in one to two months; remote germination
Human Hazards: Spiny
Pest Problems: None reported
Disease Problems: None reported

Morphology (Identifying Characteristics)

Habit: Solitary, robust; canopy of 40-60 leaves
Trunk or Stem: Brown, with circling reddish-brown ring scars, slightly swollen at base
Leaf: Costapalmate, induplicate, with long costa; divided deeply into many folded segments that split at their middle and hang down gracefully
Foliage Color: Deep green above, waxy gray below
Leaf Size: 7-9' (2.1-2.7 m) wide; segments 4-5' (1.2-1.5 m) long, 3/4" (3.8 cm) wide
Petiole: 6' (1.8 m) long; armed with small, sharp teeth
Crownshaft: None
Inflorescence: 4' (1.2 m) long, from among the leaves
Gender: Bisexual flowers
Flower Color: Yellow
Fruit Size: 5/8" (1.6 cm) diameter

Comments: Ribbon fan palm most closely resembles Australian fan palm but does not grow as tall as the latter and bears larger leaves. It is most notable for its deeply divided leaves, the long segments of which hang downward like a curtain for several feet. This effect is best exhibited in a sheltered position; in the open the leaves tend to become tattered by the wind.

Scientific Name: ***Livistona mariae*** (liv-i-STON-a MAHR-ee-eye)

Common Name(s): Central Australian fan palm, Central Australian cabbage palm

Classification: Coryphoideae - Livistoneae
Height: 40' (12.2 m)
Growth Rate: Moderate

Origin: Australia
USDA Hardiness Zone: 10A-10B; damaged but recovered at 26° F (-3.3° C)

Geoff Stein

Horticultural Characteristics

Salt Tolerance: Moderate
Drought Tolerance: High
Soil Requirements: Widely adaptable
Light Requirements: High
Nutritional Requirements: Moderate
Uses: Specimen tree
Propagation: Seed, usually germinating within three months; remote germination
Human Hazards: Sharp teeth on petiole
Pest Problems: None reported
Disease Problems: Potassium deficiency

Morphology (Identifying Characteristics)

Habit: Solitary; canopy of several dozen leaves
Trunk or Stem: Covered with burlap-like fiber and protruding leaf bases for years, eventually gray and ringed; swollen at base
Leaf: Costapalmate, induplicate; divided to more than half the diameter; tips drooping
Foliage Color: Dark green; purple-red when young (especially in full sun)
Leaf Size: 6' (1.8 m) or more in diameter
Petiole: Long, to 6' (1.8 m); sharply toothed in the lower half
Crownshaft: None
Inflorescence: Long, erect, branched
Gender: Bisexual flowers
Flower Color: Yellow
Fruit Size: 1" (2.5 cm)
Fruit Color: Black

Geoff Stein

Comments: *Livistona mariae* is known only from the Alice Springs area in central Australia. This is hot, dry territory, but the palm occurs in close proximity to year-round water from springs. This robust fan palm appears very adaptable to South Florida conditions. It is among the largest-leafed *Livistona* species and requires ample room for its sizable canopy. The leaves of young plants turn purplish-red in full sun and also are toothed on their margins.

Scientific Name: *Livistona rotundifolia* (liv-i-STON-a ro-tun-di-FO-lee-a)

Common Name(s): footstool palm, round leaf fan palm, serdang

Classification: Coryphoideae - Livistoneae
Height: 35' (10.7 m)
Growth Rate: Moderate

Origin: Philippines, Indonesia
USDA Hardiness Zone: 10B-11; damaged but recovered at 26° F (-3.3° C)

Geoff Stein

Geoff Stein

Leaf base fibers

Geoff Stein

Leaf scars

Horticultural Characteristics

Salt Tolerance: Low
Drought Tolerance: Moderate
Soil Requirements: Widely adaptable
Light Requirements: Moderate; high
Nutritional Requirements: Moderate
Uses: Specimen tree, foliage plant
Propagation: Seed, germinating in one to two months; remote germination
Human Hazards: Spiny
Pest Problems: None reported
Disease Problems: Slight susceptibility to lethal yellowing, phytophthora bud rot

Morphology (Identifying Characteristics)

Habit: Solitary; canopy of 30-50 leaves
Trunk or Stem: Smooth, pale gray with reddish leaf scars, fissured; covered with fiber and wedge-shaped leaf bases for many years
Leaf: Costapalmate, induplicate; divided to 1/2 or less into 60 or more straight, shortly split segments
Foliage Color: Deep, glossy green
Leaf Size: 5-7' (1.5-2.1 m) wide; segments about 2" (5 cm) wide
Petiole: 6-8' (1.8-2.4 m) long, slender; armed with curved teeth, especially in lower half
Crownshaft: None
Inflorescence: 8' (2.4 m) long, split into three main branches each with many short, secondary branches
Gender: Bisexual flowers
Flower Color: Yellow
Fruit Size: 3/4" (3.8 cm) long
Fruit Color: Brownish-black (red before ripening)

Comments: This beautiful but less hardy *Livistona* makes a lovely container specimen when young, the leaves forming almost perfect circles. Juvenile leaves are also only shallowly divided. Unlike many of the hardier species, the segments of the bright green, glossy leaves do not droop regularly. The trunk, whether covered with a mat of fiber and protruding leaf bases or clean and revealing the red ring scars, is also striking in appearance.
Similar Species: *L. robinsoniana* (Philippines) is similar in aspect but taller growing.

Scientific Name: *Livistona saribus* (liv-i-STON-a sar-REE-bus)

Common Name(s): taraw palm, serdang

Classification: Coryphoideae - Livistoneae
Height: 60' (18.3 m)
Growth Rate: Moderate

Origin: Southeast Asia, Indonesia & Philippines
USDA Hardiness Zone: 9A-11; thought to be hardy to at least 22° F (-5.6° C)

Horticultural Characteristics

Salt Tolerance: Moderate
Drought Tolerance: High
Soil Requirements: Widely adaptable
Light Requirements: Moderate; high
Nutritional Requirements: Moderate
Uses: Specimen tree
Propagation: Seed, germinating within two months; remote germination
Human Hazards: Spiny
Pest Problems: None reported
Disease Problems: None reported

Morphology (Identifying Characteristics)

Habit: Solitary; canopy of several dozen leaves
Trunk or Stem: Robust, pale gray, ringed; wedge-shaped leaf bases adhere when young
Leaf: Costapalmate, induplicate; divided about mid-depth into forked segments that droop at the tips
Foliage Color: Deep green
Leaf Size: 4-5' (1.2-1.5 m) in diameter
Petiole: To 6' (1.8 m) long; armed with long, straight, sharp teeth, especially in lower half
Crownshaft: None
Inflorescence: 5' (1.5 m) or more long, openly branched
Gender: Bisexual flowers
Flower Color: Yellow
Fruit Size: 3/4" (3.8 cm)
Fruit Color: Glossy blue-gray, often with white spots

Detail of leaf stem

Detail of trunk

Comments: This southeast Asian fan palm appears well adapted to Florida conditions. The dense crown requires ample room for development. It responds well to irrigation and fertilization when young and prefers some shade until it has developed a trunk several feet tall. Palm enthusiasts favor the red-petioled forms, but they have repeatedly proven to be less hardy than those with green leaf stems.

Scientific Name: *Lytocaryum weddellianum* (lyt-o-KAHR-ee-um wed-del-ee-AHN-um)

Common Name(s): Weddell palm, feather palm, miniature coconut palm

Classification: Arecoideae - Cocoeae
Height: 6-8' (1.8-2.4 m)
Growth Rate: Slow

Origin: Brazil
USDA Hardiness Zone: 10A-11; damaged below 25° F (-3.9° C)

Geoff Stein

Horticultural Characteristics

Salt Tolerance: Low
Drought Tolerance: Low
Soil Requirements: Rich, moist, acidic and well-drained
Light Requirements: Low to moderate
Nutritional Requirements: Moderate
Uses: Interior palm or for deep shade
Propagation: Seed, germinating over a period of months even with heat; adjacent germination
Human Hazards: None
Pest Problems: None reported
Disease Problems: None reported
Cultivars: A "var. *cinerea*" has been offered in Europe

Morphology (Identifying Characteristics)

Habit: Solitary, crowned with a graceful head of arching leaves
Trunk or Stem: Very slender, unarmed
Leaf: Pinnately compound, reduplicate, about 50 pairs of slender, closely-spaced, tapering leaflets
Foliage Color: Dark green above, gray-green below
Leaf Size: 3-4' (.9-1.2 m) long; leaflets 4-6" (10-15.2 cm) long, 1/4-1/2" (.64-1.3 cm) wide
Petiole: Short, 1' (30 cm) long; hairy when leaf is young
Crownshaft: None
Inflorescence: Arching from between the leaves
Gender: Separate male and female flowers on the same inflorescence
Flower Color: Yellow
Fruit Size: Ovoid, less than 1" (2.5 cm) long
Fruit Color: Brown

Comments: Weddell palm, somewhat reminiscent of pygmy date palm in appearance, is an outstanding small palm for interior use since it is very tolerant of low light. The graceful, arching leaves have a delicate appearance, particularly as a small plant. Its slow rate of growth has kept it out of the American foliage market, but it has been popular in Europe for over a century. In the landscape, it makes a delightful accent below a canopy of trees, but requires regular irrigation and rich soil to look its best.

Scientific Name: *Mauritia flexuosa* (maw-RIT-ee-a flex-yoo-O-sa)

Common Name(s): moriche, buriti, aguaje, morete, miriti, caranday-guazu, canangucho

Classification: Calamoideae - Lepidocaryeae
Height: 80-100' (24.4-30.5 m)
Growth Rate: Slow to moderate

Origin: Tropical northern South America
USDA Hardiness Zone: 10B-11

Horticultural Characteristics

Salt Tolerance: Low
Drought Tolerance: Low
Soil Requirements: Acid, moist to wet
Light Requirements: High
Nutritional Requirements: Moderate
Uses: Specimen plant, waterside
Propagation: Seed, germinating in one and a half months if fresh; seed should never be allowed to dry out
Human Hazards: Small spines along leaf margin not terribly hazardous
Pest Problems: Giant palm weevil (*Rhynchophorus palmarum*)
Disease Problems: None reported

Morphology (Identifying Characteristics)

Habit: Solitary, canopy of 8-20 leaves
Trunk or Stem: Columnar, 1-2' (.3-.6 m) in diameter, light gray to white and smooth with age, gray-green to tan when younger
Leaf: Costapalmate, reduplicate, circular in shape, divided into 200 stiff to drooping segments split almost to the base
Foliage Color: Olive green on upper surface, lighter green to whitish below
Leaf Size: 8' (2.4 m) long, 15' (4.6 m) wide; segments 6-7' (1.8-2.1 m) long
Petiole: Up to 30' (9.1 m) long and 4' (1.2 m) wide at base, light green to almost white at sheathing base
Crownshaft: None
Inflorescence: Borne from among the leaves, 6' (1.8 m) long, twice-branched, secondary branches pendulous for 1-2' (.3-.6 m), covered with conspicuous bracts
Gender: Separate male and female plants
Flower Color: Cream
Fruit Size: 3" (7.6 m)
Fruit Color: Brownish-red or orange
Fruit: Edible

Comments: The buriti palm forms extensive populations in flooded savannahs throughout its broad range, but can also be found in isolated stands wherever permanent moisture is assured. It is one of the most economically important palms of the greater Amazon region. The fruit pulp is consumed fresh, used to flavor ice cream or made into preserves and, once dried, ground into flour. Oil is also extracted from the fruits. The stems are a source of starch and sugary sap. The larvae of giant palm weevils are collected from infested palms and consumed by local tribes. The leaf fiber is used to fashion many utilitarian objects. As an ornamental, it makes a majestic specimen plant, but will not prosper without constant moisture.

Scientific Name: *Nannorrhops ritchiana* (NAN-o-rahps rich-ee-AHN-a)

Common Name(s): mazari palm

Classification: Coryphoideae - Corypheae
Height: 10' (3 m), but with a range of 5-25' (1.5-7.6 m)
Growth Rate: Slow

Origin: Afghanistan, Pakistan to Arabia
USDA Hardiness Zone: 8A-11; hardy to at least 10° F (-12.2° C) There is variation depending on source, with some reports of survival from sub-zero temperatures.

Horticultural Characteristics

Salt Tolerance: Moderate
Drought Tolerance: High
Soil Requirements: Widely adaptable if well-drained
Light Requirements: High
Nutritional Requirements: Low
Uses: Shrub
Propagation: Seed, germinating slowly
Human Hazards: None
Pest Problems: None reported
Disease Problems: Slight susceptibility to lethal yellowing
Cultivars: *Nannorrhops* 'Iran Silver'. This form is found at high elevation in inland mountainous areas of Iran. The leaves are a beautiful intense silver color. It is exceedingly drought tolerant and reportedly more cold hardy than typical mazari palms. There is no consensus on whether this form deserves recognition as a second species in the genus, since silver forms of *N. ritchiana* occur elsewhere throughout the range of the species. Several names have been applied at times (*N. naudiniana*, *N. stocksiana* or *N. arabica*).

Morphology (Identifying Characteristics)

Habit: Clustering, branching; stems die back after flowering; 30-40 leaves
Trunk or Stem: Short, mostly underground, prostrate (erect with age); thick, covered with leaf stem bases and orange fiber
Leaf: Costapalmate, stiff, twisted; divided deeply into about 30 segments that split for half their length
Foliage Color: Blue-green
Leaf Size: 4' (1.2 m) wide; segments 4' (1.2 m) long, 1.5' (46 cm) wide
Petiole: 1-3' (.3-.9 m) long, unarmed or with small marginal teeth
Crownshaft: None
Inflorescence: 4-6' (1.2-1.8 m) long, from the apex of the stem and held high above leaves, much-branched
Gender: Bisexual flowers
Flower Color: White
Fruit Size: 1/2" (1.3 cm) diameter
Fruit Color: Brownish-orange
Fruit: Edible

Continued on next page

Nannorrhops 'Iran Silver'

Flower stems

Stems showing characteristic orange fiber

Comments: This unusual species may be the hardiest of all palms, adapted through its native range to extremes of summer heat and winter cold. The mazari palm is also extremely slow-growing, even in very mild winter areas. As each stem prepares to flower, new leaves emerge progressively smaller. The branched flowerstem is produced from the tip of the stem and towers above the leaf canopy. After fruiting, the stem eventually dies back, but not before branching just below the crown. With its habit of both clustering below ground and branching above, the mazari palm can form a specimen of impressive spread if not height. The powdery blue-green leaves create an eye-catching accent. Throughout its desert range, it is a source of palm cabbage, and fiber for weaving and rope manufacture. The fruits are also eaten.

Scientific Name: *Neoveitchia storckii* (nee-o-veech-ee-a STORK-ee-a)

Common Name(s): unleito

Classification: Arecoideae - Areceae
Height: 40' (12.2 m)
Growth Rate: Moderate

Origin: Fiji
USDA Hardiness Zone: 10B-11

Geoff Stein

Flowers and fruit

Horticultural Characteristics

Salt Tolerance: Low
Drought Tolerance: Low
Soil Requirements: Prefers deep, well-drained soil, slightly acid to slightly alkaline
Light Requirements: High, once early growth is completed
Nutritional Requirements: Moderate
Uses: Specimen
Propagation: Seed, germinating erratically even with heat
Human Hazards: None
Pest Problems: None reported
Disease Problems: None reported

Morphology (Identifying Characteristics)

Habit: Solitary, with a heavy crown of large leaves
Trunk or Stem: Heavy, darkly ringed with wavy leaf scars, gray and smooth in its oldest portions, often swollen at the base
Leaf: Pinnately compound, reduplicate, arching near the tip, with 60-70 pairs of long, broad leaflets; twisted at or near midpoint such that the leaflets above this point are oriented vertically
Foliage Color: Dark green
Leaf Size: 10-15' (3-4.5 m) long; leaflets 18-30" (46-76 cm) long
Petiole: 1-2' (.3-.6 m) long
Crownshaft: Not fully developed (leaf sheath split opposite the petiole), almost black in its lower portions, green above
Inflorescence: Borne below the leaves, 2-3' (.6-.9 m) long, cream-colored
Gender: Separate male and female flowers on the same inflorescence
Flower Color: White
Fruit Size: Ovoid, about 2" (5 cm) long
Fruit Color: Orange

Comments: The large leaves and loose crownshaft belie the fact that this genus of two species is closely related to *Veitchia*. *N. storckii* is endangered in its native Fiji where the trunks are valued for construction. The dark coloration of the tightly sheathing leaf bases contrasts attractively with the deep green of the blades.

Scientific Name: *Normanbya normanbyi* (nor-MAN-bee-a nor-MAN-bee-eye)

Common Name(s): Queensland black palm, black palm

Classification: Arecoideae - Areceae
Height: Up to 60' (18.3 m) in the wild, usually smaller in cultivation
Growth Rate: Moderate

Origin: Northern Australia and New Guinea
USDA Hardiness Zone: 10B-11; damaged below 28° F (-2.2° C)

Geoff Stein

Horticultural Characteristics

Salt Tolerance: Low
Drought Tolerance: Low
Soil Requirements: Acid, organic, moist
Light Requirements: Moderate to high (with age)
Nutritional Requirements: High
Uses: Specimen tree
Propagation: Seed, germinating erratically over six months or longer; adjacent germination
Human Hazards: None
Pest Problems: None reported
Disease Problems: None reported

Morphology (Identifying Characteristics)

Habit: Solitary, canopy of 10-12 leaves
Trunk or Stem: 6" (15 cm) in diameter, light tan above, whitish-gray in older portions with widely-spaced white ring scars
Leaf: Pinnately compound, reduplicate, arching, with numerous split, wedge-shaped and jagged-tipped leaflets arranged in different planes
Foliage Color: Dark green above, silvery-white or blueish below
Leaf Size: 8' (2.4 m) long
Petiole: Short, about 1' (30 cm) long
Crownshaft: 2-3' (60-91 cm) long, cylindrical but swollen at base, white to silvery-green
Inflorescence: Borne below the crownshaft, 2' (60 cm) long, semi-erect, with about a dozen short branches
Gender: Male and female flowers on the same inflorescence
Flower Color: White
Fruit Size: 2" (5 cm)
Fruit Color: Pinkish-red to purple

Comments: Queensland black palm is often compared in appearance to foxtail palm (*Wodyetia bifurcata*), but is considered more attractive or elegant by some palm enthusiasts. It is not as forgiving as its hardier look-alike, however, and requires steady moisture and an acid soil rich in organic matter. When young, *N. normanbyi* prefers partial shade.

Scientific Name: *Phoenix canariensis* (FEE-nix ka-nar-ee-EN-sis)

Common Name(s): Canary Island date, Canary date

Classification: Coryphoideae - Phoeniceae
Height: 40' (12.2 m)
Growth Rate: Slow

Origin: Canary Islands
USDA Hardiness Zone: 9A-11; hardy to at least 21° F (-6.1° C)

Horticultural Characteristics

Salt Tolerance: Moderate
Drought Tolerance: High
Soil Requirements: Widely adaptable; well-drained
Light Requirements: High
Nutritional Requirements: Moderate
Uses: Specimen tree
Propagation: Seed, germinating in two to three months; remote germination
Human Hazards: Spiny; male plants produce copious quantities of potentially allergenic pollen
Pest Problems: Palmetto weevils, palm-leaf skeletonizer
Disease Problems: Lethal yellowing; magnesium deficency; ganoderma; stigmina leaf spot, graphiola false smut, phytophthora bud rot

Morphology (Identifying Characteristics)

Habit: Solitary, massive; canopy of 50-100 leaves
Trunk or Stem: Thick, to 3' (.9 m) in diameter, with distinctive diamond leaf scar pattern; swollen mass of aerial roots often forms at base
Leaf: Pinnately compound, induplicate; stiffly arched, sometimes twisted; several hundred narrow leaflets, the lower ones modified into spines
Foliage Color: Dull deep green
Leaf Size: 10-20' (3-6.1 m) long; leaflets about 1.5' (46 cm) long, 1" (2.5 cm) wide
Petiole: Short, strongly armed with leaflet spines in lower third
Crownshaft: None
Inflorescence: 3-4' (.9-1.2 m) long; orange; densely branched
Gender: Separate male and female plants
Flower Color: Yellow
Fruit Size: 3/4" (3.8 cm)
Fruit Color: Orange
Fruit: Edible but not very palatable

Comments: Canary Island date palm is highly prized for its formal aspect in the landscape which complements Mediterranean style architecture, and for its hardiness which allows its use thoroughout most of Florida and California. The leaf scar pattern on the trunk is very ornamental. The spread of Canary Island dates requires ample room for development even when the palms are young. Extremely tough and durable, this species endures dry conditions and, with the exception of easily correctable magnesium deficiency, poor soils as well. Poorly-drained sites, however, should be avoided. Over-irrigation may increase susceptibility to various fungal diseases. Transplanting large specimens should be handled carefully; stressed plants are easily invaded by palmetto weevils which quickly destroy the irreplaceable "heart." A fair number of the Canary Island date palms sold are actually hybrids of this and other *Phoenix* species. Blue-green leafed specimens sold as Canary Islands are assuredly hybrid individuals.

Continued on next page

Flowers and developing fruit

Aerial root "buss" of Canary Island date palm

Scientific Name: *Phoenix dactylifera* (FEE-nix dak-ti-LIF-e-ra)

Common Name(s): date palm, date, edible date palm

Classification: Coryphoideae - Phoeniceae
Height: 70' (21.3 m)
Growth Rate: Slow

Origin: North Africa, but exact origin unknown
USDA Hardiness Zone: 9A-11; damaged but recovered at 19° F (-7.2°C)

Horticultural Characteristics

Salt Tolerance: High
Drought Tolerance: High
Soil Requirements: Widely adaptable
Light Requirements: High
Nutritional Requirements: Moderate
Uses: Specimen tree
Propagation: Seed, germinating in two to three months, suckers, tissue culture; remote germination
Human Hazards: Spiny; male plants produce copious quantities of potentially allergenic pollen
Pest Problems: Scales
Disease Problems: At least slightly to moderately susceptible to lethal yellowing, stigmina leaf spot, graphiola false smut
Cultivars: Hundreds, if not thousands, of cultivars throughout the Middle East selected largely for fruit characteristics. Common cultivars used in landscaping include 'Medjool', 'Zahedi', and 'Deglet Noor'.
Comments: The edible or "true" date palm is becoming much more widely used in landscaping than previously, especially since large specimens have become available from date groves in California and Arizona that have ceased production. They are adaptable landscape palms, with a broad range of environmental tolerance, but fruit poorly in the humid tropics and subtropics. The canopy of date palm is often sparse in comparison to Canary Island date. Their wide use in areas where lethal yellowing disease is resident should also be carefully considered as no variety is known to be resistant.

Morphology (Identifying Characteristics)

Habit: Slowly clustering (main trunk dominates for many years), 20-40 leaves
Trunk or Stem: Robust, gray and patterned with broad leaf scars after persistent leaf bases fall; offsets (suckers) often at base
Leaf: Pinnately compound, induplicate, erect at first, then drooping; with 200+ stiff, pointed leaflets, the lower ones modified into spines
Foliage Color: Gray-green
Leaf Size: To 20' (6.1 m) long; leaflets 1-2' (30-60 cm) long, 1" (2.5 cm) wide
Petiole: 4' (1.2 m) long, armed with leaflet spines
Crownshaft: None
Inflorescence: 4' (1.2 m) long, densely branched, borne from among the leaves
Gender: Separate male and female plants
Flower Color: White
Fruit Size: 1.2-1.5" (3-3.8 cm) long
Fruit Color: Yellow, orange or red
Fruit: Edible

Scientific Name: *Phoenix loureiri* (FEE-nix loo-RAY-ri)

Common Name(s): Loureir's date palm, dwarf date palm, voiavoi

Classification: Coryphoideae - Phoeniceae
Height: 12-15' (3.7-4.6 m)
Growth Rate: Moderate

Origin: India east to Taiwan and the Philippines
USDA Hardiness Zone: 9B-11; the species has reportedly remained undamaged at 24° F (-4.4° C), and regional variants may be hardy to USDA Hardiness Zone 8B

Geoff Stein

Geoff Stein

Flowers

Geoff Stein

Geoff Stein

P. loureiri var. *humilis* fruit

Horticultural Characteristics

Salt Tolerance: Low to moderate (coastal and island populations)
Drought Tolerance: Moderate
Soil Requirements: Widely adaptable but avoid highly alkaline soils
Light Requirements: Moderate to high
Nutritional Requirements: Moderate
Uses: Specimen plant, screen or border, containers
Propagation: Seed, germinating readily in one to two months
Human Hazards: Leaflet spines
Pest Problems: None reported
Disease Problems: None reported
Cultivars: Var. *loureiri* and var. *humilis* are recognized on the basis of obscure anatomical characters, but variation in the species seems to be more related to habitat. Forms from open, seasonally dry areas tend to be shorter, more clustering and have bluer leaves than forms from the forest understory.

Morphology (Identifying Characteristics)

Habit: Solitary or clustering
Trunk or Stem: 10-12' (3-3.7 m) tall, 1' (30 cm) in diameter, covered with brown fiber and stubby leaf bases for many years
Leaf: Pinnately compound, induplicate, narrow, sharply-pointed, leaflets radiating in different planes from the rachis; lower leaflets modified into spines
Foliage Color: Deep green to blue-green
Leaf Size: 6' (1.8 m) long
Petiole: Short, with leaflet spines
Crownshaft: None
Inflorescence: Borne from among the leaves
Gender: Separate male and female plants
Flower Color: Cream
Fruit Size: 1/2" (1.3 cm) long
Fruit Color: Black
Comments: *Phoenix loureiri* is sometimes confused with pygmy date palm, but is both more robust and much hardier than that species, and has plumose leaves. It has yet to become widely available in the United States, perhaps due to erratic seed supplies, but holds great promise as a small-statured date palm for USDA Hardiness Zones 8 and 9. There is considerable variation within the species both in habit and appearance.

Scientific Name: *Phoenix reclinata* (FEE-nix rek-li-NAHT-a)

Common Name(s): Senegal date, reclinata palm, African wild date palm

Classification: Coryphoideae - Phoeniceae
Height: 25' (7.6 m)
Growth Rate: Moderate

Origin: Africa
USDA Hardiness Zone: 10A-11; damaged below 25° F (-3.9° C)

Horticultural Characteristics

Salt Tolerance: Moderate
Drought Tolerance: High
Soil Requirements: Widely adaptable
Light Requirements: High
Nutritional Requirements: Moderate
Uses: Multi-trunked specimen tree
Propagation: Seed, germinating in two to three months, division; remote germination
Human Hazards: Spiny
Pest Problems: Palm leaf skeletonizer
Disease Problems: Ganoderma, stigmina leaf spot, graphiola false smut

Morphology (Identifying Characteristics)

Habit: Clustering, some stems lean or curve forward, each with 25-50 leaves
Trunk or Stem: Slender, covered with fiber matting and old leaf stems, eventually clean and ringed with leaf scars
Leaf: Pinnately compound, induplicate; with 200-250 leaflets radiating at different angles, the lower ones modified into long spines
Foliage Color: Dark green
Leaf Size: About 15' (4.6 m) long; leaflets 1.5' (46 cm) long, 1.75" (4.4 cm) wide
Petiole: 4' (1.2 m) long, armed with leaflet spines
Crownshaft: None
Inflorescence: 3' (.9 m) long, branched
Gender: Separate male and female plants
Flower Color: Cream
Fruit Size: 1/2" (1.3 cm) long
Fruit Color: Reddish-brown

Comments: Senegal date palm suckers vigorously and a single plant can consist of more than 20 stems if left unpruned. It hybridizes readily with other date species, and a fair amount of the material in the nursery trade is probably of mixed parentage. These hybrids are often hardy to USDA Hardiness Zone 9B or even 9A. It is valued as a specimen plant for accent, but sufficient room is necessary both to allow its natural spread and distance from its dagger-like leaflet spines. Senegal date looks best if trimmed up to reveal the slender, matted trunks. A more open cluster can be achieved by selectively pruning out some of the stems.

Scientific Name: *Phoenix roebelenii* (FEE-nix ro-be-LEN-ee-eye)

Common Name(s): pygmy date palm, dwarf date palm, miniature date palm roebelinii palm, pigmy date palm

Classification: Coryphoideae - Phoeniceae
Height: 10' (3 m)
Growth Rate: Slow

Origin: Southeast Asia
USDA Hardiness Zone: 10A-11; damaged below 25° F (-3.9° C)

Horticultural Characteristics

Salt Tolerance: Low
Drought Tolerance: Moderate
Soil Requirements: Widely adaptable
Light Requirements: Moderate; high
Nutritional Requirements: Moderate
Uses: Small tree, container plant
Propagation: Seed, germinating in two to three months; remote germination
Human Hazards: Spiny
Pest Problems: None reported
Disease Problems: Pestalotiopsis, magnesium, manganese and potassium deficiencies, stigmina leaf spot, graphiola false smut

Comments: Pygmy date palm is one of the most widely used date palms in the United States. Though usually single-trunked in nature, multiples are frequently produced in nurseries. This species' small stature, slow rate of growth, ease of culture, and graceful crown have made it a popular accent plant in tropical landscapes. The crown requires occasional trimming of the older leaves. Pygmy date palm is also one of the most adaptable dates for container culture, though it does not hold up very well in dimly lit interiors.

Morphology (Identifying Characteristics)

Habit: Solitary, with a dense crown of 50 or more leaves
Trunk or Stem: Relatively slender, often thinnest at base, covered with peg-like leaf bases; mass of aerial roots frequently at base
Leaf: Pinnately compound, induplicate, the lowest drooping; leaflets numerous, evenly spaced along rachis, the lower ones spine-like
Foliage Color: Glossy green
Leaf Size: 3-5' (.9-1.5 m) long; leaflets 8-15" (20-38 cm) long, 1/2" (1.3 cm) wide
Petiole: 2-6" (5-15 cm) long, armed with leaflet spines
Crownshaft: None
Inflorescence: 1.5' (46 cm) long, produced among the leaves, branched
Gender: Separate male and female plants
Flower Color: Cream
Fruit Size: 1/2" (1.3 cm) long
Fruit Color: Black

Scientific Name: *Phoenix rupicola* (FEE-nix roop-i-KO-la)

Common Name(s): cliff date, wild date palm, India date palm, Indian wine palm

Classification: Coryphoideae - Phoeniceae
Height: 25' (7.6 m)
Growth Rate: Slow

Origin: India
USDA Hardiness Zone: 10A-11; damaged below 25° F (-3.9° C)

Chuck Hubbuch

Horticultural Characteristics

Salt Tolerance: Moderate
Drought Tolerance: High
Soil Requirements: Widely adaptable
Light Requirements: High
Nutritional Requirements: Moderate
Uses: Specimen tree
Propagation: Seed, germinating in two to three months; remote germination
Human Hazards: Spiny
Pest Problems: None reported
Disease Problems: Stigmina leaf spot

Morphology (Identifying Characteristics)

Habit: Solitary; canopy of 30-50 leaves
Trunk or Stem: Frequently with only a few leaf bases persisting; swollen near the crown with fiber matting
Leaf: Pinnately compound, induplicate, twisted and drooping; with about 200 thin-textured leaflets; lower leaflets modified into spines
Foliage Color: Bright green
Leaf Size: 10' (3 m) long; leaflets 1.5' (46 cm) long, 1" (2.5 cm) wide
Petiole: 3" (7.6 cm) long, armed with leaflet spines
Crownshaft: None
Inflorescence: 3" (7.6 cm) long, branched, borne from among the leaves
Gender: Separate male and female plants
Flower Color: White
Fruit Size: 3/4" (3.8 cm)
Fruit Color: Yellow, ripening to purple-brown

Comments: This small but attractive date palm is seeing wider use in the landscape due to its moderate stature and graceful form. The bright green leaflets all lie in one plane, and are softer-textured than most dates.

Scientific Name: *Phoenix sylvestris* (FEE-nix sil-VES-tris)

Common Name(s): toddy palm, wild date palm, silver date palm, sugar date palm, khajuri, India date

Classification: Coryphoideae - Phoeniceae
Height: 40' (12.2 m)
Growth Rate: Slow

Origin: India
USDA Hardiness Zone: 9A-11; has remained undamaged at 22° F (-5.6° C)

Detail of trunk

Horticultural Characteristics

Salt Tolerance: Moderate
Drought Tolerance: High
Soil Requirements: Widely adaptable
Light Requirements: High
Nutritional Requirements: Moderate
Uses: Specimen tree
Propagation: Seed, germinating in two to three months; remote germination
Human Hazards: Spiny; male plants produce copious quantities of potentially allergenic pollen
Pest Problems: None reported
Disease Problems: Graphiola false smut

Morphology (Identifying Characteristics)

Habit: Solitary; canopy of 100 leaves
Trunk or Stem: Robust, with diamond-shaped leaf scars and frequently a skirt of aerial roots at base and persistant leaf bases above
Leaf: Pinnately compound, induplicate; lower leaflets modified into spines; 200-250 leaflets arranged in groups of two or three, often criss-crossing
Foliage Color: Blue-green
Leaf Size: 9-12' (2.7-3.7 m) long; leaflets .5-1.5' (15-46 cm) long, 1" (2.5 cm) wide
Petiole: 3' (.9 m) long, armed with leaflet spines
Crownshaft: None
Inflorescence: 2-3' (.6-.9 m) long, much branched; borne from among the leaves
Gender: Separate male and female plants
Flower Color: White
Fruit Size: 1" (2.5 cm)
Fruit Color: Orange-yellow, ripening to reddish-purple

Comments: Toddy palm has characteristics in common with the edible date, *P. dactylifera*, and the Canary Island date, *P. canariensis*. It does not sucker and bears shorter leaves than either species. The sap is collected from the cut inflorescences in India and boiled down into sugar (jaggery) or fermented into an alcoholic beverage (toddy). It can be expected that hybrid seed will be formed where it is grown close to other date palm species. Like most of the larger date palms, it makes a durable specimen plant.

Scientific Name: *Pinanga coronata* (pi-NAING-a kor-o-NAHT-a)

Common Name(s): ivory cane palm, ivory crownshaft palm

Classification: Arecoideae - Areceae
Height: 12' (3.7 m)
Growth Rate: Moderate

Origin: Java and Sumatra
USDA Hardiness Zone: 10B-11; severely damaged or killed at 26° F (-3.3° C)

Geoff Stein

Geoff Stein

Infructescence

Horticultural Characteristics

Salt Tolerance: Low
Drought Tolerance: Low
Soil Requirements: Widely adaptable
Light Requirements: Moderate
Nutritional Requirements: Moderate
Uses: Foliage plant, specimen shrub
Propagation: Seed, germinating in two to three months; division; adjacent germination
Human Hazards: None
Pest Problems: None reported
Disease Problems: None reported

Morphology (Identifying Characteristics)

Habit: Clustering; each stem with five to six leaves
Trunk or Stem: Slender, yellowish-green, smooth with light brown ring scars
Leaf: Pinnately compound, reduplicate; with a few broad leaflets, the lower ones coming to a curved point, the upper with truncated, toothed tips
Foliage Color: Light green; emerging leaves often pink
Leaf Size: 3-5' (.9-1.5 m) long
Petiole: Approximately 1.5' (46 cm) long; unarmed; with brown woolly scales
Crownshaft: Green; inconspicuous
Inflorescence: 1' (30 cm) long from below the crownshaft
Gender: Separate male and female flowers on the same inflorescence
Flower Color: Cream to pink
Fruit Size: 1/2" (1.3 cm)
Fruit Color: Red

Comments: This palm has been widely grown as *Pinanga kuhlii* but this name is no longer taxonomically correct. This species represents the hardiest member of a large Asian genus of beautiful rain forest understory palms. The attractive color of emerging leaves makes an eye-catching accent in the shade garden, where *P. coronata* can be combined with various *Chamaedorea* and *Licuala* species to create a palm understory in the established garden. Sites subject to strong winds, especially cold, drying breezes in winter, should be avoided. The pinangas as a group deserve to be more widely trialed as interior subjects.

Scientific Name: *Pritchardia pacifica* (prit-CHAHRD-ee-a pa-SIF-i-ka)

Common Name(s): Fiji fan palm, Fijian fan palm, Pacific fan palm

Classification: Coryphoideae - Corypheae
Height: 25' (7.6 m)
Growth Rate: Slow

Origin: Tonga (but introduced by Polynesians to Fiji)
USDA Hardiness Zone: 10B-11; severely damaged or killed at 26° F (-3.3° C)

Geoff Stein

Horticultural Characteristics

Salt Tolerance: High
Drought Tolerance: Moderate
Soil Requirements: Widely adaptable
Light Requirements: Moderate; high
Nutritional Requirements: Moderate
Uses: Specimen tree
Propagation: Seed, germinating in two to three months; remote germination
Human Hazards: None
Pest Problems: Scales, palm leaf skeletonizer
Disease Problems: Highly susceptible to lethal yellowing

Morphology (Identifying Characteristics)

Habit: Solitary; canopy of about three dozen leaves
Trunk or Stem: Brown, corky, ringed, about 1' (30 cm) in diameter; canopy of three dozen leaves
Leaf: Costapalmate, induplicate, cupped upward; divided about 1/4 into many stiff, tapering segments that split at the tip
Foliage Color: Bright green
Leaf Size: 4-8' (1.8-2.4 m) wide
Petiole: 2.5' (76 cm) long, unarmed, waxy white
Crownshaft: None
Inflorescence: 1-3' (.3-.9 m) long, much branched
Gender: Bisexual flowers
Flower Color: Yellow
Fruit Size: 1/2" (1.3 cm) diameter
Fruit Color: Blue-black

Comments: The Pacific fan palms consists of three dozen beautiful species, 2/3 of which are found only on the Hawaiian Islands. Not surprisingly, it is there that most can be grown to perfection. It is unfortunate that they have proven to be highly susceptible to lethal yellowing disease. Fiji fan palm is well adapted to coastal tropical zones, and performs well in full sun as long as it is never starved for water. Both cold and dry winds will burn the very lovely leaves. Fiji fan palm has a thicker trunk, a denser canopy, and a much shorter flowerstalk than Thurston palm (*P. thurstonii*).

Scientific Name: *Pritchardia thurstonii* (prit-CHAHRD-ee-a thur-STO-nee-eye)

Common Name(s): Thurston palm

Classification: Coryphoideae - Corypheae
Height: 25' (7.6 m)
Growth Rate: Slow

Origin: Fiji
USDA Hardiness Zone: 10B-11; severely damaged or killed at 26° F (-3.3° C)

Timothy K. Broschat

Horticultural Characteristics

Salt Tolerance: High
Drought Tolerance: Moderate
Soil Requirements: Widely adaptable
Light Requirements: Moderate; high
Nutritional Requirements: Moderate
Uses: Specimen tree
Propagation: Seed, germinating in two to three months; remote germination
Human Hazards: None
Pest Problems: Scales, palm leaf skeletonizer
Disease Problems: Highly susceptible to lethal yellowing

Morphology (Identifying Characteristics)

Habit: Solitary; canopy of two dozen leaves
Trunk or Stem: Brown, vertically fissured, ringed, sometimes slightly swollen at base
Leaf: Costapalmate, induplicate, slightly folded upward; divided less than 1/2 into 50 or so stiff, tapering segments that split at the tips
Foliage Color: Bright green
Leaf Size: 4-8' (1.2-2.4 m) wide
Petiole: 3' (.9 m) long, unarmed
Crownshaft: None
Inflorescence: 6-10' (1.8-3 m) long, arching out and down from among the leaves, branched at the tip
Gender: Bisexual flowers
Flower Color: Yellow
Fruit Size: 1/4" (.64 cm) diameter
Fruit Color: Red

Comments: *Pritchardia thurstonii* is well adapted to coastal tropical zones, and performs well on alkaline soils. Though easily cold-damaged, Thurston palm accepts full sun and considerable salt exposure. Young specimens of this beautiful fan palm can be enjoyed for many years as container plants. The high susceptibility to lethal yellowing limits its use to tropical areas not known to harbor the disease.

Scientific Name: *Pseudophoenix sargentii* (soo-doe-FEE-nix sahr-JEN-tee-eye)

Common Name(s): buccaneer palm, cherry palm, kuka

Classification: Ceroxyloideae - Cyclospatheae
Height: 10' (3 m)
Growth Rate: Slow

Origin: Florida Keys and Caribbean region
USDA Hardiness Zone: 10B-11; severely damaged or killed at 26° F (-3.3° C)

Horticultural Characteristics

Salt Tolerance: High
Drought Tolerance: High
Soil Requirements: Widely adaptable
Light Requirements: Moderate; high
Nutritional Requirements: Low
Uses: Small tree
Propagation: Seed, germinating in two to four months; remote germination
Human Hazards: None
Pest Problems: None reported
Disease Problems: None reported
Cultivars: Several variants have been described on the basis of ultimate height or other minor characteristics

Morphology (Identifying Characteristics)

Habit: Solitary; canopy of 10 leaves
Trunk or Stem: Gray-green with light brown rings when young; older trunks dark gray, variably swollen at some point along length
Leaf: Pinnately compound, reduplicate, stiff, twisted, with well over a hundred pointed narrow leaflets
Foliage Color: Blue-green
Leaf Size: 9' (2.7 m) long; leaflets 2' (.6 m) long, 2" (5 cm) wide
Petiole: 2' (.6 m) long, unarmed
Crownshaft: Short, wide, blue-green
Inflorescence: 3' (.9 m) long, from among the leaves
Gender: Separate male and female or bisexual flowers on same inflorescence
Flower Color: Yellow
Fruit Size: 3/4" (1.9 cm) diameter
Fruit Color: Red

Comments: This native of the Florida Keys and Caribbean Islands is one of the most durable palms for seaside landscaping. It is considered endangered in Florida (though is common in Cuba and other Caribbean islands). Pest-free and highly drought tolerant to boot, the wider use of buccaneer palm has been limited only by its extremely slow rate of growth. No two specimens look alike due to the variable bulging of the trunk.
Other Species: *P. vinifera* (Haiti), the cherry palm, has a thicker trunk and longer leaves on silvery petioles. A wine is made from the sweet juice of the fruit.

Scientific Name: *Ptychosperma elegans* (ty-ko-SPUR-ma EL-e-ganz)

Common Name(s): solitaire palm, Alexander palm

Classification: Arecoideae - Areceae
Height: 20' (6.1 m)
Growth Rate: Moderate

Origin: Australia
USDA Hardiness Zone: 10B-11; severely damaged or killed at 26° F (-3.3° C)

Ripening fruit

Flower stems

Horticultural Characteristics

Salt Tolerance: Low
Drought Tolerance: Moderate
Soil Requirements: Widely adaptable
Light Requirements: Moderate; high
Nutritional Requirements: Moderate
Uses: Specimen tree, interiorscape
Propagation: Seed, germinating in two to three months; adjacent germination
Human Hazards: None
Pest Problems: Scale, mites (interior)
Disease Problems: Ganoderma

Morphology (Identifying Characteristics)

Habit: Solitary, bearing 10-12 leaves in the canopy
Trunk or Stem: Slender, gray, swollen base, ridged leaf scars
Leaf: Pinnately compound, reduplicate; with four to five dozen pleated leaflets that are bluntly jagged at their tips
Foliage Color: Green; leaflets grayish below
Leaf Size: 6-8' (1.8-2.4 m) long; leaflets 2.5' (.76 m) long, 3-5" (7.6-12.7 cm) wide
Petiole: 1' (30 cm) or less long, with dark brown scaly hairs, unarmed
Crownshaft: Smooth, waxy
Inflorescence: 2-3' (.6-.9 m) long, branched, yellow; borne below the crownshaft
Gender: Separate male and female flowers on the same inflorescence
Flower Color: White
Fruit Size: 3/4" (1.9 cm)
Fruit Color: Red

Comments: Solitaire palm is one of the most common landscape palms for tropical landscaping. Its small stature fits well into scaled down residential yards. It is often grown as a multiple specimen, though the species is solitary by nature. It thrives in a site protected from cold and drying winds. Large acclimated specimens are durable interiorscape plants.

Scientific Name: *Ptychosperma macarthurii* (ty-ko-SPUR-ma mak-AHRTH-er-ree-eye)

Common Name(s): Macarthur palm

Classification: Arecoideae - Areceae
Height: 25' (7.6 m)
Growth Rate: Moderate

Origin: Australia, New Guinea
USDA Hardiness Zone: 10B-11; severely damaged or killed at 26° F (-3.3° C)

Horticultural Characteristics

Salt Tolerance: Low
Drought Tolerance: Moderate
Soil Requirements: Widely adaptable
Light Requirements: Moderate; high
Nutritional Requirements: Moderate
Uses: Multi-trunked specimen tree, interiorscape
Propagation: Seed, germinating in two to three months, division; adjacent germination
Human Hazards: Irritant
Pest Problems: Palm aphid
Disease Problems: Sooty mold (usually accompanying palm aphid infestation), ganoderma, phytophthora bud rot
Cultivars: Finer-leaved form said to occur

Morphology (Identifying Characteristics)

Habit: Clustering; each stem bearing 8-10 leaves
Trunk or Stem: Very slender, light gray, ridged leaf scars
Leaf: Pinnately compound, reduplicate, with four to five dozen leaflets bluntly notched at the tip
Foliage Color: Green on both sides
Leaf Size: 3-6' (.9-1.8 m) long; leaflets 2.5' (.76 m) long, 2-3" (5-7.6 m) wide
Petiole: 1' (30 cm) long, unarmed
Crownshaft: Smooth, green, waxy especially when young
Inflorescence: 2' (.6 m) long, branched, borne below the crownshaft
Gender: Separate male and female flowers on the same inflorescence
Flower Color: White
Fruit Size: 1/2" (1.3 cm) long
Fruit Color: Red
Fruit: Irritant; contains calcium oxalate crystals

Comments: Macarthur palm is a naturally clumping species, with smaller leaves and skinnier trunks than solitaire palm. It is not used as widely as the latter, but makes an equally fine specimen under the same conditions, though requiring additional space to accommodate its multiple stems.

Scientific Name: *Ravenea rivularis* (rav-e-NAI-a riv-yoo-LAR-iss)

Common Name(s): majesty palm, bakaly, gora, malio, majestic palm

Classification: Ceroxyloideae - Ceroxyleae
Height: 60-80' (18.3-24.4 m)
Growth Rate: Fast in first years; slows after trunk development

Origin: Madagascar
USDA Hardiness Zone: 10A-11; damaged but recovered at 26° F (-3.3° C)

Horticultural Characteristics

Salt Tolerance: Moderate
Drought Tolerance: Moderate
Soil Requirements: Widely adaptable, slightly acid is best
Light Requirements: Moderate; high
Nutritional Requirements: Moderate to high
Uses: Small specimen tree, interiorscape
Propagation: Seed, germinating in two to three months; adjacent germination
Human Hazards: None
Pest Problems: Rotten sugar cane borer
Disease Problems: None reported

Morphology (Identifying Characteristics)

Habit: Solitary, robust; canopy of 10-15 leaves
Trunk or Stem: Gray, swollen at base and gradually tapering upward, attractively ringed
Leaf: Pinnately compound, reduplicate, erect at first, then arching, twisted near apex; with numerous, crowded, narrow, ribbed leaflets
Foliage Color: Green
Leaf Size: 6-8' (1.8-2.4 m) long; leaflets 1.5-2' (46-60 cm) long, 1" (2.5 cm) wide
Petiole: Unarmed, fibrous margined
Crownshaft: None
Inflorescence: Short, borne from among the lower leaves
Gender: Separate male and female plants
Flower Color: White
Fruit Size: 1/2" (1.3 cm) diameter
Fruit Color: Red

Comments: Majesty palm is currently finding its widest use as an interior plant. An initial flurry of excitement over its landscape possibilities weakened when it was found to require frequent fertilization or else moderate shade in order to maintain a healthy green color. Majesty palm very quickly reaches about 10' (3 m) of height, at which point growth seems to slow considerably. Its interesting trunk and shade tolerance make it a fine addition to tropical landscapes where it can be situated at the edge of the canopy of tall trees to good effect. In the landscape, majesty palm performs well in full sun only on fertile, moist soils with regular fertilization. It is more dependable as a landscape plant in southern California.

Scientific Name: *Reinhardtia gracilis* (ryn-HART-tee-a GRAS-i-lis)

Common Name(s): window pane palm, window palm

Classification: Arecoideae - Areceae
Height: 5' (1.5 m)
Growth Rate: Slow to moderate

Origin: Central America
USDA Hardiness Zone: 10B-11; killed at 26° F (-3.3° C)

Geoff Stein

Horticultural Characteristics

Salt Tolerance: Low
Drought Tolerance: Low
Soil Requirements: Organic-rich, well-drained
Light Requirements: Low
Nutritional Requirements: Moderate
Uses: Understory palm or container plant
Propagation: Seed or careful division; fresh seed that has not been allowed to dehydrate may germinate in 45 days, otherwise erratic; remote germination
Human Hazards: None
Pest Problems: None reported
Disease Problems: Root diseases if soil stays sodden
Cultivars: Four varieties (var. *gracilior*, var. *rostrata*, var. *tenuissima* as well as var. *gracilis*) have been recognized on the basis of flower characteristics and leaf size.

Morphology (Identifying Characteristics)

Habit: Clustering (rarely solitary) with leaves clothing the upper third of each stem
Trunk or Stem: Very slender
Leaf: Pinnately compound with two to four pairs of wedge-shaped leaflets (the upper large and with "windows" at the base), reduplicate
Foliage Color: Dark green
Leaf Size: 2-3' (.6-.9 m) long, leaflets 3-6" (7.5-15 cm) long
Petiole: 3-24" (7.5-60 cm) long, slender
Crownshaft: None
Inflorescence: Borne from among the leaves, 2' (.6 m) long, with 3-11 branches
Gender: Separate male and female flowers on the same inflorescence
Flower Color: Creamy white
Fruit Size: 1/2" (1.3 cm) long
Fruit Color: Purple-black, on a red, branched stalk

Comments: Window pane palm is a choice specimen for the foreground of bright, shady spots in which the unusual "windows" at the base of the wide upper leaflets can be observed. *R. gracilis* can be finicky unless the right balance of moisture, soil and light is provided. High humidity and a rich, organic, moist soil are essential.

Scientific Name: *Rhapidophyllum hystrix* (rap-i-doe-FYL-lum HISS-trix)

Common Name(s): needle palm, porcupine palm, creeping palmetto, spine palm, hedgehog palm

Classification: Coryphoideae - Corypheae
Height: 5' (1.5 m)
Growth Rate: Slow

Origin: Southeastern United States
USDA Hardiness Zone: 7A-10B; no damage at 5° F (-15° C), considered to be hardy to -5° F (-20.6° C) once established

Horticultural Characteristics

Salt Tolerance: Low
Drought Tolerance: Moderate
Soil Requirements: Widely adaptable
Light Requirements: Moderate; high
Nutritional Requirements: Moderate
Uses: Shrub
Propagation: Seed, germinating in six months or more; division
Human Hazards: Spiny
Pest Problems: None reported
Disease Problems: None reported

Comments: Though usually found in the understory of rich, hardwood forests, needle palm can be adapted to full sun and makes an interesting specimen plant for accent. Nowhere abundant throughout its broad range, wild populations have been heavily collected in some areas for horticultural production by division of the clumps, largely because the seed is difficult to collect and slow and uneven in germination. Fortunately, nursery seed production is increasing. It is one of the hardier palm species, though growth will be slowest at the northern end of its range.

Morphology (Identifying Characteristics)

Habit: Clustering, essentially trunkless; stem prostrate or erect; 6-18 leaves
Trunk or Stem: Trunkless, fiber-matted crown occasionally elongating to 5' (1.5 m); covered with needle-like fibers from decayed leaf bases
Leaf: Palmate, induplicate, divided deeply into 15-20 blunt and jagged-tipped segments
Foliage Color: Dark green above, silvery below
Leaf Size: 4' (1.2 m) wide; segments 2' (60 cm) long, 3/4" (1.9 cm) wide
Petiole: 2' (60 cm) long, unarmed
Crownshaft: None
Inflorescence: 1' (30 cm) long, held among the crown fibers and leaves, shortly branched
Gender: Separate male and female plants; occasionally both sexes on same plant
Flower Color: Yellow, purple
Fruit Size: 1" (2.5 cm)
Fruit Color: Purple-brown, wooly

Scientific Name: *Rhapis excelsa* (RAP-is ek-SEL-sa)

Common Name(s): lady palm

Classification: Coryphoideae - Corypheae
Height: 7' (2.1 m)
Growth Rate: Moderate

Origin: China
USDA Hardiness Zone: 9A-11; no damage at 25° F (-3.9° C); damage increases at lower temperatures down to 15-18° F (-9.4 to -7.8° C) at which point stems may be killed

Horticultural Characteristics

Salt Tolerance: Low
Drought Tolerance: Moderate
Soil Requirements: Widely adaptable
Light Requirements: Moderate; low
Nutritional Requirements: Moderate
Uses: Shrub, hedge, specimen plant, interiorscape
Propagation: Seed, germinating over several months with heat; division; remote germination
Human Hazards: None
Pest Problems: Scales, mealybugs
Disease Problems: Iron deficiency; manganese deficiency on alkaline soils
Cultivars: A large number of named variegated forms, propagated by division, are popular in Japan.

Morphology (Identifying Characteristics)

Habit: Clustering densely; up to several hundred stems, each with 4-10 leaves
Trunk or Stem: Slender, covered with brown matted fiber and protruding leaf bases; eventually black with tan leaf scars
Leaf: Palmate, appearing reduplicate, deeply divided into 4-10 wide segments, bluntly toothed at the tip
Foliage Color: Shiny green
Leaf Size: 2.5' (.76 m) wide; segments 1/2-1" (1.3-2.5 cm) wide
Petiole: 15-18" (38-46 cm) long, unarmed
Crownshaft: None
Inflorescence: Slender, short, less than 1' (30 cm) long, branched, pinkish; borne from among the upper leaves
Gender: Separate male and female plants; occasionally both sexes on same plant
Flower Color: White
Fruit Size: 1/2" (1.3 cm) diameter
Fruit Color: White

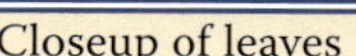

Closeup of leaves

Female flower stems

Detail of stem

Variegated *Rhapis excelsa*

Developing fruits

Comments: Lady palm is best suited for use in partial shade where the leaves remain dark, shiny green. In full sun, leaves tend to yellow and will burn if the roots are allowed to become too dry. Lady palm makes a very effective low screen, but is equally effective as a single specimen shrub (though removal of stems may be necessary in time to keep the plant in bounds). Well-grown, leaves in good condition will clothe the matted stems almost to the base; these can be trimmed up to accent the interesting slender stems. Lady palm has enjoyed great success as an interior plant and can be maintained in a container for some time. The variegated forms, so popular in Japan, fetch very high prices.

Scientific Name: *Rhapis humilis* (RAP-is HYOO-mi-lis)

Common Name(s): slender lady palm, reed rhapis

Classification: Coryphoideae - Corypheae
Height: 7' (2.1 m)
Growth Rate: Slow

Origin: Southern China, but known only in cultivation
USDA Hardiness Zone: 9A-11; no damage at 22° F (-5.6° C); damage increases with lower temperature, and below 20° F (-6.7° C), stems may be killed; prefers cool summer areas

Horticultural Characteristics

Salt Tolerance: Low
Drought Tolerance: Moderate
Soil Requirements: Widely adaptable
Light Requirements: Moderate; low
Nutritional Requirements: Moderate
Uses: Shrub, hedge, foliage plant
Propagation: Division; remote germination
Human Hazards: None
Pest Problems: Scales, mealybugs
Disease Problems: None reported

Morphology (Identifying Characteristics)

Habit: Clustering tightly; stems with 4-10 leaves
Trunk or Stem: Slender, covered with very closely woven, light brown fibers and protruding leaf bases
Leaf: Palmate, appearing reduplicate; divided deeply into 15-20 narrow, drooping segments that are almost pointed at the tip
Foliage Color: Green, slightly shiny
Leaf Size: 2-3' (.6-.9 m) wide; segments 1/2-1" (1.3-2.5 cm) wide
Petiole: 1' (30 cm) long, thin
Crownshaft: None
Inflorescence: 2' (60 cm) long, branched, whitish
Gender: Only male plant known; all material in cultivation divided from this one
Flower Color: White
Fruit Size: Unknown
Fruit Color: Unknown

Comments: Slender lady palm has smaller stems and leaves than *R. excelsa*, but larger flowerstalks. It is rare as a landscape plant, no doubt due to its slow increase. All material in cultivation is derived from a single male plant known only from cultivation in China. Additional species of *Rhapis*, some quite dwarf, are occasionally offered by nurseries.

Scientific Name: *Rhopaloblaste augusta* (rop-a-lo-BLAS-tee aw-GUS-ta)

Common Name(s): Nicobar majestic palm

Classification: Arecoideae - Areceae
Height: 50' (15.2 m), to 100' (30.5 m) in the wild
Growth Rate: Moderate

Origin: Nicobar Islands
USDA Hardiness Zone: 10B-11

Inflorescence and developing fruit

Horticultural Characteristics

Salt Tolerance: Low
Drought Tolerance: Moderate
Soil Requirements: Moist, well-drained, slightly acid
Light Requirements: High
Nutritional Requirements: Moderate
Uses: Specimen, containers
Propagation: Seed, germinating in over six months; adjacent germination
Human Hazards: None
Pest Problems: None reported
Disease Problems: None reported

Morphology (Identifying Characteristics)

Habit: Solitary, with a canopy of about 10 leaves
Trunk or Stem: Medium-heavy, about 12" (25 cm) diameter, swollen at base, light brown with darker ring scars
Leaf: Pinnately compound with numerous long, narrow, hanging leaflets, reduplicate
Foliage Color: Dark green, glossy
Leaf Size: 8' (2.4 m) long; leaflets 2' (60 cm) long
Petiole: 3-4" (7.6-10.2 cm) long
Crownshaft: 2' (60 cm) long, bulging in the middle, covered with velvety grayish-brown hairs
Inflorescence: Borne below the crownshaft, 2' (60 cm) long, branched close to the base, the branches pendulous
Gender: Male and female flowers separate but in the same inflorescence
Flower Color: Greenish
Fruit Size: Ovoid, about 2" (5 cm) across
Fruit Color: Showy, orange to red

Comments: *Rhopaloblaste augusta* is a robust but elegant palm with a graceful, spreading canopy of leaves with pendant leaflets. It has performed well in a variety of climates as long as adequate moisture is provided along with protection from drying winds.

Scientific Name: *Roystonea regia* (roy-STON-ee-a REE-jee-a)

Common Name(s): royal palm, Cuban royal palm, Florida royal palm

Classification: Arecoideae - Areceae
Height: 50-70' (15.2-21.3m)
Growth Rate: Moderate

Origin: Cuba, Florida
USDA Hardiness Zone: 10A-11; damage below 28° F (-2.2° C)

Closeup of fruit

Horticultural Characteristics

Salt Tolerance: Moderate
Drought Tolerance: Moderate to high
Soil Requirements: Widely adaptable
Light Requirements: Moderate; high
Nutritional Requirements: Moderate
Uses: Specimen tree, street tree, border
Propagation: Seed, germinating in two to three months (sometimes longer); adjacent germination
Human Hazards: Irritant fruit
Pest Problems: Royal palm bug, rotten sugar cane borer
Disease Problems: Fungal leaf spots, potassium deficiency (Florida), ganoderma, phytophthora bud rot

Morphology (Identifying Characteristics)

Habit: Solitary, canopy of about 15 leaves
Trunk or Stem: Light gray, smooth, closely ringed, swollen at base and again at middle or just below crownshaft
Leaf: Pinnately compound, reduplicate; several hundred multi-ranked leaflets, often with conspicuous secondary ribs on either side of midrib
Foliage Color: Bright green
Leaf Size: 10' (3 m) long; leaflets 3' (.9 m) long, 2" (5 cm) wide
Petiole: Short, stout, unarmed
Crownshaft: Long, smooth, deep glossy green
Inflorescence: 3' (.9 m) long, borne just below the crownshaft, tightly branched, the branches straight
Gender: Separate male and female flowers on the same inflorescence
Flower Color: Yellow
Fruit Size: 1/4" (.64 cm) long
Fruit Color: Reddish-purple
Fruit: Irritant; contains calcium oxalate crystals

Comments: The Florida royal palm (formerly *R. elata*) is no longer considered distinct from the Cuban royal (*R. regia*). Few palms perform as distinctively for lining avenues and boulevards as do royal palms. The majority of the old, large royal palms in south Florida are specimens of this species, brought from Cuba during the 1930's. Royal palms are best avoided when landscaping around modestly-sized homes; their stature makes a small house look even smaller. Royal palm bug, which destroys young leaves, can be a persistant problem in Florida, especially after a mild winter. **Related Species:** *R. borinqueana* (Puerto Rico) resembles *R. regia* but has shiny surfaced leaves. *R. oleracea* (Venezuela, southern Caribbean) holds its leaflets in only one plane and lacks trunk bulges. *R. princeps* (Jamaica) has a fairly slender trunk and a sparser canopy than most royals. Even large specimens will decline from nutrient deficiencies on nutrient-poor soils if not adequately fertilized.

Scientific Name: *Sabal causiarum* (SAI-bahl kow-see-AHR-um)

Common Name(s): hat palm, Puerto Rican hat palm, palma cana
Panama hat palm, yarey, palma de sombrero

Classification: Coryphoideae - Corypheae
Height: 50' (15.2 m)
Growth Rate: Slow

Origin: Puerto Rico
USDA Hardiness Zone: 9A-11; no damage at 21° F (-6.1° C); thought to be hardy to at least 20° F (-6.7° C); reports exist of old specimens surviving 10° F (-12.2° C)

Horticultural Characteristics

Salt Tolerance: Moderate
Drought Tolerance: High
Soil Requirements: Widely adaptable
Light Requirements: High
Nutritional Requirements: Low
Uses: Specimen tree
Propagation: Seeds, germinating in two to three months; remote germination
Human Hazards: None
Pest Problems: None reported
Disease Problems: Ganoderma

Morphology (Identifying Characteristics)

Habit: Solitary, massive; canopy of about 40 leaves
Trunk or Stem: Large diameter; leaf bases shed relatively quickly; gray, smooth and closely ringed
Leaf: Costapalmate, induplicate; twisted; divided for about 2/3 of length into numerous segments
Foliage Color: Green
Leaf Size: 6' (1.8 m) or more wide; segments 4' (1.2 m) long, 2" (5 cm) wide
Petiole: 6' (1.8 m) or more long, extending far into leaf blade; unarmed
Crownshaft: None
Inflorescence: Long, much branched, extending past leaves
Gender: Bisexual flowers
Flower Color: White
Fruit Size: 1/3" (84 mm)
Fruit Color: Dark brown to black

Closeup of fruit

Comments: This relative of our native *S. palmetto* makes an imposing specimen plant on the weight of its massive trunk which achieves nearly 4' (1.2 m) in diameter. Despite its hardiness (large specimens in Gainesville, Florida attest to a surprising degree of frost resistance for a palm from Puerto Rico), *S. causiarum* has not been widely available from nurseries and is not frequently seen in landscapes, probably because of its slow rate of growth. As with all *Sabal* species, a great deal of underground elaboration of the stem takes place before much top growth is apparent. Even before much trunk development occurs, the canopy of large leaves requires ample room for its spread.

Scientific Name: *Sabal mauritiiformis* (SAI-bahl maw-rit-tee-eye-FOR-mis)

Common Name(s): bay leaf palm, savannah palm, botán, palma amarga, palma de guagara, carata, palma redonda, palma de vaca

Classification: Coryphoideae - Corypheae
Height: 30-60' (9-18.3 m)
Growth Rate: Slow

Origin: Mexico to northern South America
USDA Hardiness Zone: 10A-11, 9B with protection; variable damage at 25° F (-3.9° C)

Geoff Stein

Horticultural Characteristics

Salt Tolerance: Low
Drought Tolerance: Moderate
Soil Requirements: Widely adaptable, prefers slightly alkaline soil
Light Requirements: High
Nutritional Requirements: Moderate
Uses: Specimen tree
Propagation: Seed, germinating in one to several months; remote germination
Human Hazards: None
Pest Problems: Palm leaf skeletonizer, giant palm weevil
Disease Problems: None reported

Morphology (Identifying Characteristics)

Habit: Solitary, very broad canopy of 10-25 leaves
Trunk or Stem: 1' (30 cm) in diameter, columnar, swollen at base, emerald green towards the crown, light gray and darkly ringed
Leaf: Costapalmate, induplicate, deeply divided into 90-150 segments that are pendant at their tips, those on young palms are pleated and more coarsely, unevenly and widely segmented
Foliage Color: Deep green above, whitish to blue-green below
Leaf Size: 6-7' (1.8-2.1 m) in diameter
Petiole: 6-10' (1.8-3 m) long, unarmed
Crownshaft: None
Inflorescence: Borne from among the leaves, suberect and then arching, 6-8' (1.8-2.4 m)
Gender: Bisexual flowers
Flower Color: White
Fruit Size: 1/2" (1.3 cm)
Fruit Color: Black

Comments: One of the most beautiful of the *Sabal* species, *S. mauritiiformis* is named for the resemblance of its leaves to those of the buriti palm, *Mauritia flexuosa*. Leaves of young palms are particularly attractive in silhouette, almost suggesting a licuala palm because of their broad, wedge-shaped segments. The best forms have striking blue-green coloration on the leaf underside.

Scientific Name: *Sabal minor* (SAI-bahl MY-nor)

Common Name(s): dwarf palmetto, little blue stem, scrub palmetto swamp palmetto, bush palmetto

Classification: Coryphoideae - Corypheae
Height: 6' (1.8 m)
Growth Rate: Slow

Origin: Southeastern United States
USDA Hardiness Zone: (6B-)7-10B; no problem at 15° F (-9.4°C); thought to be hardy to at least 5° F (-15° C)

Horticultural Characteristics

Salt Tolerance: Moderate
Drought Tolerance: Moderate
Soil Requirements: Widely adaptable
Light Requirements: Moderate; low
Nutritional Requirements: Low
Uses: Shrub
Propagation: Seed, germinating in two to three months; remote germination
Human Hazards: None
Pest Problems: None reported
Disease Problems: Graphiola false smut
Cultivars: *Sabal minor* 'Louisiana'. This is believed to be a faster-growing form of the species that also forms a short above-ground trunk. It apparently comes true from seed and is found locally in Louisiana. It frequently holds more leaves in its canopy than the typical forms of the species, and has larger leaves as well. It is not hardy beyond USDA Hardiness Zone 7B.

Morphology (Identifying Characteristics)

Habit: Solitary, essentially trunkless, with 8-20 leaves
Trunk or Stem: Straight or curved underground, very rarely forming a short trunk
Leaf: Costapalmate (but shortly), induplicate, flat to slightly folded; divided about halfway into 16-40 stiff, unsplit segments
Foliage Color: Green to blue-green
Leaf Size: 2-5' (.6-1.5 m) wide; segments 2' (.6 m) long, 1.75" (4.4 cm) wide
Petiole: 2-3' (.6-.9 m) long, unarmed
Crownshaft: None
Inflorescence: 3-6' (.9-1.8 m) long, erect, rising up above and from among the leaves, much branched
Gender: Bisexual flowers
Flower Color: White
Fruit Size: 3/8" (95 mm) diameter
Fruit Color: Black

Sabal x *texensis* is a name without any botanical validity applied to variants that are allegedly hybrids of *S. minor* and *S. mexicana*. These forms, whatever their genesis, are known as Brazoria County palm, after the area in Texas where they are common. Other growers are comfortable placing them in among the natural variation of the 'Louisiana' form of *S. minor*. Dwarf palmettos in this group tend to form trunks at least 4-5' (1.2-1.5 m) in height. The leaves are more noticeably costapalmate than those of typical *S. minor*. These forms do not perform well in containers. Expected hardiness is through USDA Hardiness Zone 8.

Continued on next page

Michael Richard, Jr.

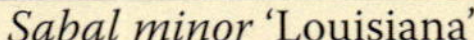

Sabal minor 'Louisiana'

Flowers

Developing fruit

Sabal etonia

Comments: Dwarf palmetto occurs in the understory of woods across a broad swath of the southeastern U. S. It makes an interesting specimen plant in partial shade in areas where few palms could otherwise be grown. There are a fair number of reports of survival after sub-zero° F (below -17.8° C) temperatures. Ultimate hardiness is undoubtedly related to seed source.

Related species: *Sabal etonia*, the scrub palmetto, occurs only in peninsular Florida, from north-central to southeastern Florida on very sandy soils along the highlands ridge, where it occurs in the characteristic oak-pine scrub forests. One small disjunct population is known from western Florida. It occurs on drier soil than *S. minor*, and has smaller, more deeply folded leaves. It is an excellent palm for naturalistic landscapes and adapts equally well to full sun as to partial shade.

Scientific Name: *Sabal palmetto* (SAI-bahl pahl-MET-toe)

Common Name(s): cabbage palm, sabal palm, palmetto palm, blue palmetto cabbage palmetto, cabbage tree, common palmetto

Classification: Coryphoideae - Corypheae
Height: 40' (12.2 m)
Growth Rate: Slow

Origin: Southeastern United States
USDA Hardiness Zone: (7B)8-11; no damage at 15° F (-9.4° C); thought to be hardy to at least 10° F (-12.2° C)

Flower stem

Horticultural Characteristics

Salt Tolerance: High
Drought Tolerance: High
Soil Requirements: Widely adaptable
Light Requirements: High
Nutritional Requirements: Low
Uses: Specimen tree
Propagation: Seed, germinating in two to three months; stems developed deeply in soil
Human Hazards: None
Pest Problems: Palmetto weevils
Disease Problems: Ganoderma, graphiola false smut
Cultivars: *Sabal palmetto* 'Lisa' was described by Robert Riefer, a southwest Florida nurseryman, from a stand of three mature palms that appeared to be the remnant of a once larger natural population. These three palmettos were characterized by a more compact crown, shorter petioles, thicker and more rigid leaves that were less twisted than those of the typical cabbage palm. It was tentatively concluded that the three palms represented a colony of *Sabal palmetto* that has twice the usual number of chromosomes. Seedlings from these three plants are now in production.

Morphology (Identifying Characteristics)

Habit: Solitary; canopy of several dozen leaves
Trunk or Stem: Gray, smooth; frequently covered with a criss-cross of persistant, split leaf bases
Leaf: Costapalmate, induplicate, strongly twisted downward at middle; divided to about 1/2 into numerous segments, some stiff, some drooping
Foliage Color: Dull green
Leaf Size: To 6' (1.8 m) wide; segments 3-4' (.9-1.2 m) long, 2-3" (5-7.6 cm) wide
Petiole: 4-6' (1.2-1.8 m) long, unarmed; leaf base split
Crownshaft: None
Inflorescence: 6-8' (1.8-2.4 m) long, openly branched, borne among the leaves
Gender: Bisexual flowers
Flower Color: White
Fruit Size: 1/2" (1.3 cm) diameter

Continued on next page

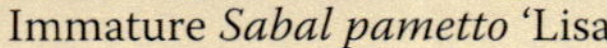

Immature *Sabal pametto* 'Lisa'

Sabal mexicana

Comments: The state tree of both Florida and South Carolina, cabbage palm is one of the most common native palms in the United States, and is widely used for landscaping, adapting well to many different soils and situations. Trees are harvested from wild stands at a fraction of the cost of a similarly sized nursery-grown palm. Sabal palms transplant well, but cut roots do not branch as they do in all other palms examined, and the palm must therefore produce new roots from the base of the trunk. It has been found that removing all leaves from these palms at the time of digging significantly increases survival rate after installation. Cabbage palms vary in the persistence of their leaf bases. Some remain "booted" for many years; others shed the leaf bases fairly quickly.

Similar Species: *S. mexicana*, occurring along the Rio Grande valley in Texas and Mexico, is similar to *S. palmetto*, but has a slightly more robust trunk. It is cultivated primarily in south Texas.

Scientific Name: *Satakentia liukiuensis* (saht-a-KENT-ee-a lee-ook-ee-EN-sis)

Common Name(s): satake palm

Classification: Arecoideae - Areceae
Height: 30-40' (9.1-12.2 m)
Growth Rate: Moderate

Origin: Ryukyu Islands
USDA Hardiness Zone: 10B-11; killed at 26° F (-3.3° C); slight damage at 32° F (0° C)

Horticultural Characteristics

Salt Tolerance: Low
Drought Tolerance: Moderate
Soil Requirements: Widely adaptable
Light Requirements: High (some shade when young is beneficial)
Nutritional Requirements: Moderate
Uses: Specimen tree
Propagation: Seed, germinating in a few months when fresh; should not dry out before sowing; adjacent germination
Human Hazards: None
Pest Problems: None reported
Disease Problems: None reported

Morphology (Identifying Characteristics)

Habit: Solitary with a canopy of 12-14 arching leaves
Trunk or Stem: 1' (30.4 cm) diameter, light brown with closely spaced ring scars
Leaf: Pinnately compound, reduplicate, with many, narrow leaflets regularly spaced in a single plane but eventually drooping
Foliage Color: Deep green
Leaf Size: 8-10' (2.4-3 m) long, leaflets 18-24" (46-60 cm) long
Petiole: 4" (10.2 cm) long (longer on younger palms)
Crownshaft: 2.5' (.76 m) long, largely cylindrical, sometimes swollen at the base, dark green, brown or purple-brown
Inflorescence: Carried horizontally below crownshaft, pinkish-purple when first produced, with several stiffly spreading branches
Gender: Separate male and female flowers on the same inflorescence
Flower Color: Greenish
Fruit Size: Elongated, ovoid, 1/2" (1.3 cm) long
Fruit Color: Black

Comments: The appearance of satake palm has been likened to a coconut, but many would argue that this beautiful and sturdy palm from Japan's southern offshore islands can stand on its own merits. The smooth, often burnished, crownshaft and the graceful deep green canopy are *Satakentia's* most abidingly attractive features. Slow growing at first, but speeding up once established, satake palm is best on rich and evenly moist soil.

Scientific Name: *Serenoa repens* (ser-e-NO-a RE-pens)

Common Name(s): saw palmetto, scrub palmetto

Classification: Coryphoideae - Corypheae
Height: 3-6' (.9-1.8 m)
Growth Rate: Slow

Origin: Southeastern United States
USDA Hardiness Zone: 8A-11; thought to be hardy to at least 15° F (-9.4° C)

Flower stems

Horticultural Characteristics

Salt Tolerance: High
Drought Tolerance: High
Soil Requirements: Widely adaptable
Light Requirements: Moderate; high
Nutritional Requirements: Low
Uses: Shrub, groundcover
Propagation: Seed, germinating in several months; remote germination
Human Hazards: Spiny
Pest Problems: Palmetto weevils
Disease Problems: Ganoderma
Cultivars: Blue-green leaved forms occur naturally along the southern east coast of Florida.

Morphology (Identifying Characteristics)

Habit: Clumping, essentially trunkless; each stem with 12-30 leaves
Trunk or Stem: Mostly underground, sometimes growing prostrate along the ground or rarely erect; covered with leaf bases and fiber
Leaf: Palmate, induplicate; slightly folded, stiff; divided deeply into several dozen segments that split at the tip
Foliage Color: Green or blue-green, waxy
Leaf Size: 3-4' (.9-1.2 m) wide; segments about 2' (60 cm) long, 1" (2.5 cm) wide
Petiole: 3-5' (.9-1.5 m) long, saw-toothed at margins
Crownshaft: None
Inflorescence: 2-3' (60-91 cm) long, much-branched, borne among the leaves
Gender: Bisexual flowers
Flower Color: White
Fruit Size: 1" (2.5 cm)
Fruit Color: Blue-black
Fruit: Smell like rancid butter as they age

Comments: Saw palmetto forms a conspicuous groundcover in pinelands along the southern coastal plain. With the growing interest in native plants, nursery production of saw palmetto has steadily increased. The blue-green forms are particularly prized for naturalistic landscapes. Large specimens do not transplant easily, and the plants are best established from containers. The fruits are the source of a prostate medicine widely used in Mexico and Europe and are often sold dry as an herbal remedy in health food stores. The flowers produce a fine honey, and beekeepers frequently move hives onto the pinelands when the saw palmettos begin to flower.

Scientific Name: *Syagrus botryophora* (sy-AG-rus bo-tree-o-FOR-a)

Common Name(s): sumuqué, Bahia palm, patioba, pati

Classification: Arecoideae - Cocoeae
Height: 40-60' (12.2-18.3 m), shorter in cultivation
Growth Rate: Fast

Origin: Brazil
USDA Hardiness Zone: 10A-11

Horticultural Characteristics

Salt Tolerance: Low
Drought Tolerance: Low
Soil Requirements: Moist, well-drained, acid
Light Requirements: Moderate; high
Nutritional Requirements: Moderate
Uses: Specimen tree, grove planting
Propagation: Seed, germinating in two to three months; water soak may be beneficial
Human Hazards: None
Pest Problems: None reported
Disease Problems: None reported

Morphology (Identifying Characteristics)

Habit: Solitary, canopy of 10-15 leaves
Trunk or Stem: 6-10" (15-25 cm) in diameter, columnar, green above, tan to gray below, with conspicuous dark ring scars
Leaf: Pinnately compound, reduplicate, strongly arching towards the tip, with 100-150 pairs of regularly arranged rigid leaflets that form an upward V-shape
Foliage Color: Deep green
Leaf Size: 10-12' (3-3.7 m) long; leaflets 2' (60 cm) long
Petiole: 12-18" (30-46 cm) long, unarmed
Crownshaft: None
Inflorescence: 3-4' (.9-1.2 m) long, borne from among the leaves, with a thick, woody, grooved bract at the base; 30-50 semi-pendulous branches
Gender: Male and female flowers on the same flowerstem
Flower Color: Cream
Fruit Size: 1.5" (3.8 cm) long, 1" (2.5 cm) wide
Fruit Color: Yellowish-green

Comments: At least as fast growing as its cousin, the queen palm (*S. romanzoffiana*), the pati palm is found in the Atlantic coastal rain forests of northeastern Brazil, and is now considered threatened in the wild due to habitat destruction. Height increases of as much as 6' (1.8 m) per year have been reported. The trunk is more slender than that of the queen palm, and the leaves curl back towards the trunk gracefully. It prefers rich soil and ample moisture.

Scientific Name: *Syagrus coronata* (sy-AG-rus kor-o-NAHT-a)

Common Name(s): licuri palm, licury palm, ouricuri, nicury, licuryseiro

Classification: Arecoideae - Cocoeae
Height: 15-30' (4.6-9.1 m)
Growth Rate: Moderate

Origin: Northeastern Brazil
USDA Hardiness Zone: 10B-11; moderate to severe damage at 26° F (-3.3° C), slight damage at 32° F (0° C)

Horticultural Characteristics

Salt Tolerance: Not known
Drought Tolerance: Moderate
Soil Requirements: Wide tolerance
Light Requirements: High
Nutritional Requirements: Moderate
Uses: Specimen
Propagation: Seed, germinating in a few months
Human Hazards: None
Pest Problems: None reported
Disease Problems: None reported

Morphology (Identifying Characteristics)

Habit: Solitary with a crown of 15-25 leaves
Trunk or Stem: Medium-stout, 10-12" (25-30 cm) diameter, the upper part covered with leaf bases in five, slightly twisting rows
Leaf: Pinnately compound with 40-60 pairs of somewhat widely- and unevenly-spaced leaflets, reduplicate
Foliage Color: Blue-green, whitish-waxy on the lower surface
Leaf Size: 10-12' (3-3.7 m) long
Petiole: Medium-length, unarmed
Crownshaft: None
Inflorescence: Borne between the leaves, arching, much-branched
Gender: Male and female flowers separate but in the same inflorescence
Flower Color: Yellow
Fruit Size: Ellipsoid, about 1" (2.5 cm) long
Fruit Color: Yellow-green to orange, with brown, hairy surface
Fruit: Edible

Distinctive leaf scars

Comments: This handsome palm makes a striking effect with its arching, blue-green foliage and the five-ranked disposition of the persistent leaf bases. When the leaf bases finally fall, an equally unusual leaf scar pattern is left behind. It is found in the dry vegetation called "caatinga" in Brazil, but extends into moister environments as well. Both the fruit and seed are edible. The seed kernal (hardened endosperm) tastes like coconut. The endosperm also contains commercially exploitable levels of oil. The wax on the underside of the leaves is also sometimes used as a substitute for Carnauba wax (*Copernicia prunifera*). The seeds are also the sole breeding season food source of the endangered Lear's macaw, a large blue parrot found only in the state of Bahia. The licury palm is known to hybridize in nature with at least five other *Syagrus* species.

Scientific Name: *Syagrus romanzoffiana* (sy-AG-rus ro-man-zof-ee-AHN-a)

Common Name(s): queen palm, Cocos plumosa, Arecastrum, chiriva, jeriba, pindo

Classification: Arecoideae - Cocoeae
Height: 40' (12.2 m)
Growth Rate: Moderate to fast

Origin: Southern Brazil to Argentina
USDA Hardiness Zone: 9B-11; damaged but recovered at 24° F (-4.4° C)

Horticultural Characteristics

Salt Tolerance: Moderate
Drought Tolerance: Moderate
Soil Requirements: Slightly acid best, but fairly adaptable
Light Requirements: Moderate; high
Nutritional Requirements: High
Uses: Specimen tree
Propagation: Seed, germinating in three to six months
Human Hazards: None
Pest Problems: None reported
Disease Problems: Manganese and potassium deficiency, ganoderma, gliocladium blight (California), phytophthora bud rot, thielaviopsis rot or blight. A new fatal decline disease, believed to be fungal but so far unidentified, is currently affecting this species in Florida.
Cultivars: 'Robusta' or 'Australis' sometimes ascribed to particularly robust forms.

Morphology (Identifying Characteristics)

Habit: Solitary; canopy of 15 or so leaves
Trunk or Stem: Gray, smooth, sometimes bulging at some point, smooth, widely spaced rings
Leaf: Pinnately compound, reduplicate, arching; with several hundred many ranked, drooping leaflets in groups of two to seven
Foliage Color: Dark green
Leaf Size: 10-15' (3-4.6 m) long; leaflets 3' (.9 m) long, 1.75" (4.5 cm) wide
Petiole: 6' (1.8 m) long, fibrous margined on the broad, sheathing base; unarmed
Crownshaft: None
Inflorescence: 4-8' (1.2-2.4 m) long, with conspicuous bract, borne from among the leaves, branched densely, the branches pendulous
Gender: Separate male and female flowers on the same inflorescence
Flower Color: White
Fruit Size: 1.25" (3.2 cm) diameter
Fruit Color: Yellow to orange

Continued on next page

Developing fruit

Byron Keith

Closeup of flower stem

Ripe fruit

Comments: Formerly known as *Arecastrum romanzoffianum*, queen palm has become the standard urban palm throughout South Florida and is grown in southern California where supplementary water can be provided. The species is somewhat weak-rooted and can topple in strong winds. It transplants easily, grows quickly, and is bothered by few pests, though plagued by several disease or deficiency problems. Most recently in Florida, queen palms have begun to suffer a so far irreversible decline that is believed to be fungal in origin. The canopy of large leaves is very graceful in appearance. "Frizzletop," caused by manganese deficiency, is frequently a problem if fertilizer is not provided periodically and especially on alkaline soils. Young specimens often carry widely-spaced leaves almost to the base of the stem. The queen palm produces copious quantities of fruit which some consider messy. Unripe fruit is suspected of scouring and death of livestock.

Other Species: *S. amara* (Lesser Antilles), the overtop palm, is a salt tolerant species with a tall slender trunk and a broad canopy of coconut-like leaves.

Scientific Name: *Syagrus schizophylla* (sy-AG-rus skits-o-FYL-la)

Common Name(s): arikury palm, aricuriroba, licurioba

Classification: Arecoideae - Cocoeae
Height: 15' (4.6 m)
Growth Rate: Slow

Origin: Brazil
USDA Hardiness Zone: 10A-11; severely damaged or killed at 26° F (-3.3° C)

Geoff Stein

Detail of stems

Horticultural Characteristics

Salt Tolerance: Moderate
Drought Tolerance: High
Soil Requirements: Widely adaptable
Light Requirements: Moderate; high
Nutritional Requirements: Moderate
Uses: Small tree, interiorscape
Propagation: Seed, germinating in one to two months
Human Hazards: Spiny
Pest Problems: None reported
Disease Problems: Slightly susceptible to lethal yellowing; ganoderma

Morphology (Identifying Characteristics)

Habit: Solitary; canopy of several dozen crowded leaves
Trunk or Stem: Dark brown, clothed with old leaf stem bases in distinctive spiral pattern with fiber in between
Leaf: Pinnately compound, reduplicate, arching; with about 80 pointed, lax leaflets in one plane
Foliage Color: Green
Leaf Size: 6' (1.8 m) long; leaflets 2' (60 cm) long, 1" (2.5 cm) wide
Petiole: 2-3' (60-91 cm) long, narrow, purple-black, with spiny fibers at the margins
Crownshaft: None
Inflorescence: 2-3' (60-91 cm) long, borne from among the lower leaves, pendulous, once-branched
Gender: Separate male and female flowers on the same inflorescence
Flower Color: White
Fruit Size: 1" (2.5 cm) diameter
Fruit Color: Orange
Fruit: Edible (but insipid)

Comments: The arikury palm grows well in and may even prefer partial shade. Its small stature and interesting leaf stem base pattern on the trunk make it a striking specimen plant that will not outgrow its situation. Young plants are very attractive and are starting to be offered as indoor plants.

Scientific Name: *Thrinax excelsa* (THRY-nax ek-SEL-sa)

Common Name(s): giant thatch palm, Jamaican thatch palm, broad thatch silver thatch, John Crow thatch palm

Classification: Coryphoideae - Corypheae
Height: 10-30' (3-9.1 m)
Growth Rate: Moderate

Origin: Jamaica
USDA Hardiness Zone: 10B-11

Horticultural Characteristics

Salt Tolerance: Low
Drought Tolerance: Moderate
Soil Requirements: Widely adaptable
Light Requirements: High
Nutritional Requirements: Moderate
Uses: Specimen
Propagation: Seed, germinating in a few months; remote germination
Human Hazards: None
Pest Problems: None reported
Disease Problems: None reported

Morphology (Identifying Characteristics)

Habit: Solitary with a canopy of 25-30 leaves
Trunk or Stem: Slender, 6-8" (15.2-20.3 cm) diameter
Leaf: Palmate, circular in outline, split to halfway into 50-60 divisions
Foliage Color: Deep green above, gray-waxy on the lower surface
Leaf Size: 5-6' (1.5-1.8 m) across
Petiole: 4-6' (1.2-1.8 m) long, sometimes longer, unarmed
Crownshaft: None
Inflorescence: Borne between and shorter than the leaves, arching
Gender: Flowers perfect (bisexual)
Flower Color: Pinkish-purple, fragrant
Fruit Size: Globose, less than 1/2" (1.3 cm) across
Fruit Color: White

Closeup of flower stems

Comments: A striking palm with larger than typical leaves for the genus. The attractive flowers have a rich fragrance. It is faster-growing than other thatch palm species, and does not grow well if repeatedly drought-stressed.

Scientific Name: *Thrinax morrisii* (THRY-nax mor-RIS-ee-eye)

Common Name(s): Keys thatch palm, peaberry palm, brittle thatch, silver thatch, buffalo top, key palm, buffalo thatch

Classification: Coryphoideae - Corypheae
Height: 20' (6.1 m) but often smaller
Growth Rate: Slow

Origin: Florida Keys and Caribbean Islands
USDA Hardiness Zone: 10A-11; no problem at 26° F (-3.3° C)

Horticultural Characteristics

Salt Tolerance: High
Drought Tolerance: High
Soil Requirements: Widely adaptable, but high tolerance of alkalinity
Light Requirements: Moderate; high
Nutritional Requirements: Low
Uses: Small tree
Propagation: Seed, germinating in two to three months; remote germination
Human Hazards: None
Pest Problems: None reported
Disease Problems: None reported
Cultivars: None, but individuals vary in the degree of silver wax on the leaf underside

Morphology (Identifying Characteristics)

Habit: Solitary; canopy of 20-30 leaves
Trunk or Stem: Slender, gray, inconspicuously ringed; split leaf bases and unruly fiber persist for some time; root mass at swollen base
Leaf: Palmate, induplicate, irregularly folded; split about halfway into 40-50 segments, some lax, others stiff; rounded hastula
Foliage Color: Shiny green above, silver below
Leaf Size: 4-5' (1.2-1.5 m) wide; segments 3' (91 cm) long, 1.5-2" (3.8-5 cm) wide
Petiole: 4-6' (1.2-1.8 m) long, narrow, unarmed
Crownshaft: None
Inflorescence: 3-6' (.9-1.8 m) long, openly branched; erect at first, than arching or drooping
Gender: Bisexual flowers
Flower Color: White
Fruit Size: 1/4" (.64 cm) diameter
Fruit Color: White

Comments: This beautiful thatch palm is perfectly adapted to alkaline sands or limestone outcrops and takes full coastal exposure as well. Inland from the shore, it is just as amenable to garden use, but should be situated where drainage is fast. The nicest specimens have leaves deeply overlaid with silver on the underside. These catch the bright sun as they wave in a sea breeze. Keys thatch palm (and all other *Thrinax*) can be separated from silver palms (*Coccothrinax* spp.) by the split leaf bases, very folded leaves, and uniformly white fruits.

Scientific Name: *Thrinax radiata* (THRY-nax ray-dee-AHT-a)

Common Name(s): Florida thatch palm, sea thatch, silk top thatch chit, guanillo, Jamaican thatch, thatch palm

Classification: Coryphoideae - Corypheae
Height: 20' (6.1 m)
Growth Rate: Slow

Origin: Southernmost Florida and Caribbean region
USDA Hardiness Zone: 10B-11; damaged but recovered at 26° F (-3.3° C)

Horticultural Characteristics

Salt Tolerance: High
Drought Tolerance: High
Soil Requirements: Widely adaptable, but very tolerant of alkaline soils
Light Requirements: Moderate; high
Nutritional Requirements: Low
Uses: Small tree
Propagation: Seed, germinating in two to three months; remote germination
Human Hazards: None
Pest Problems: None reported
Disease Problems: None reported

Morphology (Identifying Characteristics)

Habit: Solitary; canopy of 12-20 leaves
Trunk or Stem: Slender, gray, indistinctly ringed, swollen at base; covered with split leaf bases and fiber in upper portions
Leaf: Palmate, induplicate, circular, slightly folded; divided about halfway into 30-50 segments that are split at the tip; pointed hastula
Foliage Color: Green with yellow ribs above; yellowish-green below
Leaf Size: 4-5' (1.2-1.5 m) wide; segments 2.5' (.76 m) long, 2" (5 cm) wide
Petiole: 2-3' (60-91 cm) long, unarmed; base split, fibrous, reddish
Crownshaft: None
Inflorescence: 3-4' (.9-1.2 m) long, erect to arching; borne from among the leaves
Gender: Bisexual flowers
Flower Color: White
Fruit Size: 1/4" (.64 cm) diameter
Fruit Color: White

Ripe fruit

Comments: Florida thatch palm is a carefree if slow-growing small palm with excellent seaside and alkali tolerance. Best in full sun, it will tolerate partial shade as well. It has proven resistant to frost and could be tried with protection in USDA Hardiness Zone 10A.
Similar Species: *T. parviflora* (Jamaica), the broom thatch palm, has a smooth trunk and a denser canopy than Florida thatch palm.

Scientific Name: *Trachycarpus fortunei* (traik-ee-KAHRP-us for-TOON-ee-eye)

Common Name(s): windmill palm, Chusan, Chinese windmill palm, hemp palm

Classification: Coryphoideae - Corypheae
Height: 25' (7.6 m), but can grow as tall as 40' (12.2 m)
Growth Rate: Slow

Origin: China
USDA Hardiness Zone: 7B-10B; variably unscathed or minor damage at 10° F (-12.2° C); thought to be hardy to at least 0° F (-17.8° C)

Horticultural Characteristics

Salt Tolerance: Low
Drought Tolerance: Moderate
Soil Requirements: Widely adaptable
Light Requirements: Moderate; high
Nutritional Requirements: Moderate
Uses: Small tree
Propagation: Seed, germinating in two months; remote germination
Human Hazards: Spiny
Pest Problems: None reported
Disease Problems: Moderately susceptible to lethal yellowing, phytophthora bud rot

Morphology (Identifying Characteristics)

Habit: Solitary; canopy of 20-30 leaves
Trunk or Stem: Slender, covered with unruly dark brown fibers that age to gray and protruding leaf bases
Leaf: Palmate, induplicate; divided almost to the base into about three dozen stiff or drooping segments that shortly split at their tips
Foliage Color: Dark green above, silvery below
Leaf Size: 2-3' (60-91 m) wide; segments 1.5-2' (46-60 cm) long, 1" (2.5 cm) wide
Petiole: 1.5' (46 cm) long, toothed on the margins
Crownshaft: None
Inflorescence: 1.5' (46 cm) long, densely branched
Gender: Separate male and female plants
Flower Color: Yellow, fragrant
Fruit Size: 1/2" (1.3 cm)
Fruit Color: Blue

Comments: Windmill palm is one of the hardiest palms in cultivation, capable of withstanding fairly severe freezes with no damage. In its native habitat, it may even receive a light winter snow cover. Hot tropical climates are not to this species' liking, and specimens tend to be short-lived in those areas. It has also proven at least moderately susceptible to lethal yellowing. Windmill palm is most useful for providing a tropical accent in warm temperate zones, and grows well in cool summer areas such as coastal California and parts of the British Isles that receive the effects of the Gulf Stream. It is tolerant of partial shade.

Scientific Name: *Trachycarpus martianus* (traik-ee-KAHRP-us mahrt-ee-AHN-us

Common Name(s): khasia palm, Martius windmill palm, Martius fan palm

Classification: Coryphoideae - Corypheae
Height: 20-30' (6-9 m)
Growth Rate: Moderate

Origin: Northeastern India, Nepal
USDA Hardiness Zone: 9A-10B; little to no damage at 20° F (-6.7° C)

Horticultural Characteristics

Salt Tolerance: Low
Drought Tolerance: Moderate
Soil Requirements: Slightly acid
Light Requirements: High to moderate
Nutritional Requirements: Moderate
Uses: Small tree
Propagation: Seed, germinating in one to three months; remote germination
Human Hazards: None
Pest Problems: Young plants susceptible to red spider mites
Disease Problems: None reported

Morphology (Identifying Characteristics)

Habit: Solitary; open canopy of 10-20 leaves
Trunk or Stem: 7" (17.8 cm) in diameter; gray, bare of leaf bases and fiber except near crown, ringed with ridged leaf scars in upper portions
Leaf: Palmate, induplicate; circular to semi-circular; divided to 1/2 into 60-80 stiff segments that shortly split at their tips; young leaves often have soft white hairs at their edges and across surface
Foliage Color: Dark green above, bluish-gray below
Leaf Size: 4-5' (1.2-1.5 m) wide; segments 2-3' (60-90 cm), 1" (2.5 cm) wide
Petiole: 4' (1.2 m) long, lightly toothed, covered with white hairs
Crownshaft: None
Inflorescence: 2.5-5' (.8-1.5 m), densely branched
Gender: Separate male and female plants
Flower Color: Yellow to yellow-orange
Fruit Size: 1/2" (1.3 cm)
Fruit Color: Blackish-blue

Comments: *Trachycarpus martianus* grows slightly taller than windmill palm, and has a slimmer trunk that tends to be clean of fiber and leaf bases in its lower portions. It is not as hardy as that species, though many regard it as having superior form and a certain rarefied elegance. It seems to adapt better than windmill palm to subtropical climates. There are hybrids between this species and *T. fortunei* in cultivation, though they are not common.

Scientific Name: *Trithrinax brasiliensis* (try-THRY-nax bra-zil-ee-EN-sis)

Common Name(s): spiny fiber palm, buriti, carandai, Brazilian needle palm

Classification: Coryphoideae - Corypheae
Height: 15' (4.6 m)
Growth Rate: Slow

Origin: Southern Brazil to Paraguay
USDA Hardiness Zone: (8B-)9-11; may have minor damage below 22° F (-5.6° C); thought to be hardy to about 15° F (-9.4° C)

Horticultural Characteristics

Salt Tolerance: Low
Drought Tolerance: High
Soil Requirements: Widely adaptable
Light Requirements: High
Nutritional Requirements: Low
Uses: Specimen plant, small tree
Propagation: Seed, germinating in three or more months
Human Hazards: Spiny
Pest Problems: None reported
Disease Problems: Phytophthora bud rot

Morphology (Identifying Characteristics)

Habit: Solitary; canopy of about 20 leaves
Trunk or Stem: Thick, covered with old leaf bases and spiny brown fibers
Leaf: Palmate, induplicate; divided about halfway into several dozen broad, pointed segments that split at their tips and sometimes droop
Foliage Color: Deep green above, whitish below
Leaf Size: 3-4' (.9-1.2 m) wide; segments 2' (60 cm) long, 2" (5 cm) wide
Petiole: 3' (.9 m) long, unarmed
Crownshaft: None
Inflorescence: 3-4' (.9-1.2 m) long, much-branched, the branches thick and white
Gender: Bisexual flowers
Flower Color: White
Fruit Size: 1" (2.5 cm) diameter
Fruit Color: Yellow-green to white

Comments: About five species comprise the genus *Trithrinax*. They have not been widely cultivated, but deserve to be tried more widely since they appear reasonably hardy. Spiny fiber palm makes a striking specimen plant as long as contact with the fiber spines on the trunk can be avoided. The crown of leaves has a very pleasing symmetrical aspect that fits well into a formal landscape design. It is extremely well-adapted to alkaline soils. In wet, tropical climates, this species is very susceptible to phytophthora bud rot. *T. brasiliensis* flowers when quite small. The white inflorescences and flowers, appearing several at a time, are very showy.
Other Species: *T. campestris* (Argentina) is a clumping species with unusual leaves that are woolly white on the upper side and glossy green below.

Continued on next page

Young specimen

Detail of trunk covered with leaf base fiber

Fruit

Flowers

Martin Gibbons and Tobias Spanner

Scientific Name: *Veitchia arecina* (VEECH-ee-a ar-e-SEE-na)

Common Name(s): arecina palm, Montgomery palm

Classification: Arecoideae - Areceae
Height: 25' (7.6 m)
Growth Rate: Fast

Origin: Vanuatu (formerly New Hebrides Islands)
USDA Hardiness Zone: 10B-11

Horticultural Characteristics

Salt Tolerance: Moderate
Drought Tolerance: Moderate
Soil Requirements: Widely adaptable
Light Requirements: Moderate; high
Nutritional Requirements: Moderate
Uses: Specimen tree
Propagation: Seed, germinating in one to two months; adjacent germination
Human Hazards: None
Pest Problems: None reported
Disease Problems: Slight susceptibility to lethal yellowing

Morphology (Identifying Characteristics)

Habit: Solitary; canopy of 8-10 leaves
Trunk or Stem: Slender, gray, rough, closely ringed, slightly swollen at base
Leaf: Pinnately compound, reduplicate, arching, drooping slightly with age; with about 90 pendulous leaflets that are toothed at their tips
Foliage Color: Green, leaflet scales absent
Leaf Size: About 8' (2.4 m) long; leaflets 2' (60 cm) long, 3" (7.6 cm) wide
Petiole: About 1' (30 cm) long, whitish-green
Crownshaft: Whitish green, with brown scales near top
Inflorescence: About 3' (.9 m) long, much branched, smooth, whitish
Gender: Separate male and female flowers on the same inflorescence
Flower Color: Greenish-white
Fruit Size: 1-2" (2.5-5 cm)
Fruit Color: Red

Comments: Arecina palm was among the lesser statured *Veitchia* species until two taller growing species, *V. mcdanielsii* and *V. montgomeryana*, were lumped with it in a recent revision of the genus. It is useful as a specimen tree in small spaces, yet resistant to lethal yellowing disease. With the exception of Manila palm, the *Veitchia* species treated here are similar in general appearance, differing primarily in ultimate size and by a few relatively inconspicuous foliage characters. All are fine specimen palms for moist tropical landscapes, and function well in group plantings. They are fast growing, attractive in fruit, and generally neat in appearance. Cold traps should be avoided when situating these palms in the landscape. Drying winds will also burn the leaves.

Scientific Name: *Veitchia joannis* (VEECH-ee-a jo-AN-nis)

Common Name(s): joannis palm

Classification: Arecoideae - Areceae
Height: 60' (18.3 m)
Growth Rate: Fast

Origin: Fiji
USDA Hardiness Zone: 10B-11

Closeup of flower stems

Horticultural Characteristics

Salt Tolerance: Moderate
Drought Tolerance: Moderate
Soil Requirements: Widely adaptable
Light Requirements: Moderate; high
Nutritional Requirements: Moderate
Uses: Specimen tree
Propagation: Seed, germinating in one to two months; adjacent germination
Human Hazards: None
Pest Problems: None reported
Disease Problems: None reported

Morphology (Identifying Characteristics)

Habit: Solitary; canopy of 8-10 leaves
Trunk or Stem: Slender, gray-brown, widely ringed, slightly swollen at base
Leaf: Pinnately compound, reduplicate, drooping downward as they age; with 140-160 obliquely-tipped leaflets at a 45° angle from the rachis
Foliage Color: Dark green; leaflets lack scales on underside
Leaf Size: 6-10' (1.8-3 m) long; leaflets 1-2.5' (30-76 cm) long, 2" (5 cm) wide
Petiole: Short, unarmed
Crownshaft: Grayish-green, with pale brown wooly scales at the top
Inflorescence: 2-3' (60-91 cm) long, much branched, borne below the crownshaft, somewhat pendulous, with soft greenish white hairs on ultimate branchlets
Gender: Separate male and female flowers on the same inflorescence
Flower Color: Greenish-white
Fruit Size: 1-1.5" (2.5-3.8 cm)
Fruit Color: Red

Comments: Joannis palm can be distinguished from the other similar *Veitchias* by the habit of the leaves which droop much below the horizontal as they age. It is one of the taller growing *Veitchias* commonly cultivated. Joannis palm makes a beautiful specimen plant in warm tropical regions and lends itself well to grove plantings. The red fruits, borne in quantity over a fairly long period, are also highly ornamental. The leaves can burn if exposed to cold or drying winds.

Scientific Name: *Veitchia winin* (VEECH-ee-a WIN-in)

Common Name(s): winin palm

Classification: Arecoideae - Areceae
Height: 50' (15.2 m)
Growth Rate: Fast

Origin: Vanuatu (formerly New Hebrides Islands)
USDA Hardiness Zone: 10B-11

Geoff Stein

Horticultural Characteristics

Salt Tolerance: Moderate
Drought Tolerance: Moderate
Soil Requirements: Widely adaptable
Light Requirements: Moderate; high
Nutritional Requirements: Moderate
Uses: Specimen tree
Propagation: Seed, germinating in one to two months; adjacent germination
Human Hazards: None
Pest Problems: None reported
Disease Problems: None reported

Morphology (Identifying Characteristics)

Habit: Solitary; canopy of 8-10 leaves
Trunk or Stem: Grayish brown, slender, swollen at base, ringed
Leaf: Pinnately compound, reduplicate, older leaves slightly drooping; about 120 evenly spaced leaflets broadest at the middle and toothed at the tip
Foliage Color: Green, whitish scales on leaflet underside near midrib
Leaf Size: 12-15' (3.7-4.6 m) long; leaflets 2' (60 cm) long, 3" (7.6 cm) wide
Petiole: About 1' (30 cm) long, reddish-brown
Crownshaft: Long; pale green with powdery white scales
Inflorescence: 2' (60 cm) long, borne below crown-shaft, white, branched; fiber tufts present at scar after flowerstem falls off
Gender: Separate male and female flowers on same inflorescence
Flower Color: White
Fruit Size: 1/2" (1.3 cm)
Fruit Color: Red

Comments: Similar in appearance to both joannis and arecina palm, winin palm has a somewhat more open canopy and long leaves that only droop slightly below the hortizontal as they age. The leaf stems are heavily marked with brownish scales.

Scientific Name: *Verschaffeltia splendida* (ver-sha-FELT-ee-a splen-DEED-a)

Common Name(s): stilt palm, Seychelles stilt palm

Classification: Arecoideae - Areceae
Height: 20-30' (6-9.1 m), much taller in native habitat
Growth Rate: Fast

Origin: Seychelles
USDA Hardiness Zone: 11 (10B with protection)

Horticultural Characteristics

Salt Tolerance: Low
Drought Tolerance: Low-moderate
Soil Requirements: Moist, well-drained
Light Requirements: Moderate when young, high with age
Nutritional Requirements: Moderate
Uses: Specimen or container when young
Propagation: Seed, germinating in a few months with heat; adjacent germination
Human Hazards: Sharp black spines on trunk and petioles
Pest Problems: None reported
Disease Problems: None reported

Morphology (Identifying Characteristics)

Habit: Solitary with a small head of upright leaves
Trunk or Stem: Slender, 8-12" (20.3-30 cm) in diameter, black-spiny when young, may develop stilt roots
Leaf: Bifid, almost entire or splitting into pinnate segments
Foliage Color: Deep green
Leaf Size: 5-8' (1.5-2.4 m) long, 3-4' (.9-1.2 m) wide
Petiole: Short, densely black-spiny, particularly on young palms
Crownshaft: None
Inflorescence: 3-6' (.9-1.8 m) long, hanging from between the leaves
Gender: Separate male and female flowers on the same inflorescence
Flower Color: Off-white
Fruit Size: Globular, 1" (2.5 cm) diameter
Fruit Color: Greenish-brown

Comments: Seychelles stilt palm is notable for its entire leaf, black spiny trunk when young, and the development of stilt roots from 2-3' (60-91 cm) above the ground. A sheltered location is recommended since the leaf will split if exposed to wind. It is quite cold tender and requires protection even in USDA Hardiness Zone 10B.

Scientific Name: *Wallichia disticha* (wahl-LIK-ee-a DIS-ti-ka)

Common Name(s): Wallich palm, Wallich's palm

Classification: Coryphoideae - Caryoteae
Height: 15-20' (4.6-6 m)
Growth Rate: Moderate-fast

Origin: Himalayas
USDA Hardiness Zone: 10B-11

Geoff Stein

Geoff Stein

Closeup of trunk fiber

Horticultural Characteristics

Salt Tolerance: Low
Drought Tolerance: Moderate
Soil Requirements: Widely adaptable
Light Requirements: High
Nutritional Requirements: Moderate
Uses: Specimen
Propagation: Seed, germinating erratically over several months even with heat; remote germination
Human Hazards: Irritant fruit
Pest Problems: None reported
Disease Problems: None reported

Morphology (Identifying Characteristics)

Habit: Solitary with a small head of leaves held upright in two rows on opposite sides of trunk
Trunk or Stem: Medium-slender, 6-12" (15-30 cm) diameter, upper part covered with layers of fiber
Leaf: Pinnately compound, induplicate; leaflets narrow
Foliage Color: Dark green above, silvery beneath
Leaf Size: 7-9' (2.1-2.7 m) long, 3-4' (.9-1.2 m) wide; leaflets 8" (20.3 cm) long, slightly wavy along margins with a jagged "fishtail" tip
Petiole: 2' (60 cm) long
Crownshaft: None
Inflorescence: 6-8' (1.8-2.4 m) long, hanging from between the leaves, produced in turn from the top down until tree dies
Gender: Male and female flowers in separate inflorescences on the same tree
Flower Color: Greenish
Fruit Size: Irregularly-oblong, 1/2" (1.3 cm) long
Fruit Color: Dull red
Fruit: Irritant; contains calcium oxalate crystals

Comments: Wallich palm is relatively short-lived since it dies after completing its flowering and fruiting cycle. Flowerstems are produced in turn from the top of the tree downwards over a period of a few years, starting at about 20 years of age. In addition to the unique two-ranked architecture of the crown, layers of fiber at the leaf bases add interest to the trunk.

Scientific Name: *Washingtonia filifera* (wahsh-ing-TO-nee-a fi-LIF-e-ra)

Common Name(s): desert fan palm, California fan palm, petticoat palm cotton palm, California cotton palm, northern washingtonia

Classification: Coryphoideae - Corypheae
Height: 50' (15.2 m)
Growth Rate: Moderate

Origin: California, Arizona
USDA Hardiness Zone: 8A-11; little to no problem at 15° F (-9.4 ° C); thought to be hardy to 0° F (-17.8° C)

Horticultural Characteristics

Salt Tolerance: Moderate
Drought Tolerance: High
Soil Requirements: Widely adaptable
Light Requirements: High
Nutritional Requirements: Moderate
Uses: Specimen tree, street tree
Propagation: Seed, germinating in six weeks to two months; remote germination
Human Hazards: Spiny
Pest Problems: None
Disease Problems: Phytophthora bud rot, pestalotiopsis, diamond scale fungus

Morphology (Identifying Characteristics)

Habit: Solitary, robust; canopy of several dozen leaves
Trunk or Stem: Brown, fairly thick, not swollen at base, closely ringed, fissured; clothed with shag of dead leaves for many years
Leaf: Costapalmate, induplicate; divided at least halfway into 50-70 pointed segments that bend and split at the tips with threads in between
Foliage Color: Grayish-green
Leaf Size: 6-7' (1.8-2.1 m) wide; segments 3-4' (.9-1.2 m) long, 2-3" (5-7.6 cm) wide
Petiole: 4-6' (1.2-1.8 m) long, green, toothed at margin
Crownshaft: None
Inflorescence: 9-15' (2.7-4.6 m) long, branched, hanging down from among the leaves
Gender: Bisexual flowers
Flower Color: White
Fruit Size: 3/8" (95 mm) diameter
Fruit Color: Brownish-black

Comments: The California fan palm does not get as tall as the Mexican washingtonia, nor grow as fast, but the trunk is considerably thicker. In many respects, it makes a more attractive specimen, especially with age. Mixed plantings are not uncommon in California, though probably unintentional, and hybrids between both species (called "filabusta" palm) are common. It is usually short-lived in humid, tropical climates.

Scientific Name: *Washingtonia robusta* (wahsh-ing-TO-nee-a ro-BUS-ta)

Common Name(s): Washington palm, Washingtonian, Mexican fan palm, skyduster, southern washingtonia, Mexican washingtonia, thread palm

Classification: Coryphoideae - Corypheae
Height: 70-100' (21.3-30.4 m)
Growth Rate: Fast

Origin: Mexico
USDA Hardiness Zone: (8B-)9-11; variable damage below 22° F (-5.6° C); hardy to about 20° F (-6.7° C)

Inflorescence

Horticultural Characteristics

Salt Tolerance: Moderate
Drought Tolerance: High
Soil Requirements: Widely adaptable
Light Requirements: High
Nutritional Requirements: Moderate
Uses: Specimen tree, street tree
Propagation: Seed, germinating readily in six weeks to two months; remote germination
Human Hazards: Spiny
Pest Problems: Palmetto weevils, scales
Disease Problems: Phytophthora bud rot, graphiola false smut, ganoderma, pestalotiopsis, fusarium wilt (in Florida)

Morphology (Identifying Characteristics)

Habit: Solitary; canopy of about 30 leaves
Trunk or Stem: Pale gray, closely ringed, fissured; swollen at base; often covered for years with a long shag of dead leaves
Leaf: Costapalmate, induplicate; divided halfway or more into pointed, ribbed, drooping segments with white threads in between on younger plants
Foliage Color: Bright green
Leaf Size: 4-6' (1.2-1.8 m) wide; segments 2-4' (.6-1.2 m) long; 1.5" (46 cm) wide
Petiole: 3-4' (.9-1.2 m) long, orange; sharp teeth on margin; base reddish-brown and split
Crownshaft: None
Inflorescence: 8-12' (2.4-3.7 m) long, white, branched, borne from among the leaf bases and pendulous
Gender: Bisexual flowers
Flower Color: Off-white
Fruit Size: 3/8" (95 mm) diameter
Fruit Color: Brownish-black

Comments: Mexican fan palm has traditionally been more widely grown in Florida than its close relative, the California Washington palm, probably because of its faster growth rate. Hybrids between the two species occur, and many specimens in landscapes in both Florida and California are likely of mixed ancestry. Though a desert palm, the species lives nearby permanent surface or sub-surface water, and fastest growth occurs with periodic irrigation, especially during establishment. In humid, subtropical climates, over-watering can lead to root and bud rots. With age, Mexican fan palm loses some of its appeal as the trunk tapers and thins. In Florida, lightning commonly ends the landscape life of this palm as soon as it begins to tower over surrounding vegetation. It is the tallest growing of the hardier palms.

Scientific Name: *Wodyetia bifurcata* (wod-YET-ee-a by-foor-KAHT-a)

Common Name(s): foxtail palm

Classification: Arecoideae - Areceae
Height: 30' (9.1 m)
Growth Rate: Fast

Origin: Northern Australia
USDA Hardiness Zone: 10B-11; damaged below 29° F (-1.7° C)

Inflorescence

Horticultural Characteristics

Salt Tolerance: Low
Drought Tolerance: Moderate
Soil Requirements: Widely adaptable
Light Requirements: Moderate; high
Nutritional Requirements: Moderate
Uses: Specimen tree
Propagation: Seed, germinating in two to three months; adjacent germination
Human Hazards: None
Pest Problems: Rotten sugar cane borer, banana moth
Disease Problems: Leaf spots with overhead watering

Morphology (Identifying Characteristics)

Habit: Solitary; canopy of 8-10 leaves
Trunk or Stem: Slender, gray, swollen at base, ringed with leaf scars
Leaf: Pinnately compound, reduplicate, arching; several hundred fishtail leaflets attached in several ranks; marginal reins frequent
Foliage Color: Deep green; silvery on underside
Leaf Size: 8-10' (2.4-3 m) long; leaflets about 6" (15 cm) long, 2" (5 cm) wide (widest point at tip)
Petiole: 1/2"-1' (15-30 cm) long, whitish green, with brown scales
Crownshaft: Narrow, green with whitish waxy scales; leaf sheaths with dark brown scales at top
Inflorescence: Branched, borne below the crownshaft, green
Gender: Separate male and female flowers on the same inflorescence
Flower Color: White
Fruit Size: 2" (5 cm)
Fruit Color: Red-orange

Comments: The foxtail palm, little known 12 years ago, has taken the palm world by storm. Plentiful seed has made this attractive Australian species widely available in the nursery trade, and it has already become one of the most popular items for landscaping in moist tropical and subtropical areas. The common name is derived from the very full appearance of the leaves, formed by the circular arrangement of the leaflets around the rachis. Foxtail palm is very fast-growing, and appears adaptable to a broad range of soil conditions. Young plants can be afflicted by leaf spot fungi, though not consistently; this seems to be aggravated by frequent overhead irrigation. Foxtail palm takes full sun even at a young age.

Scientific Name: *Zombia antillarum* (ZAHM-bee-a an-til-LAHR-um)

Common Name(s): zombie palm, latayne pikan

Classification: Coryphoideae - Corypheae
Height: 15' (4.6 m)
Growth Rate: Slow

Origin: Hispaniola
USDA Hardiness Zone: 10B-11; severely damaged or killed below 28° F (-2.2° C)

Detail of trunk

Horticultural Characteristics

Salt Tolerance: High
Drought Tolerance: High
Soil Requirements: Widely adaptable, well-drained
Light Requirements: High
Nutritional Requirements: Low
Uses: Specimen plant, shrub
Propagation: Seed, germinating in two months; division
Human Hazards: Spiny
Pest Problems: None reported
Disease Problems: None reported
Cultivars: A dwarf variety, *gonsalezii*, has been described

Morphology (Identifying Characteristics)

Habit: Clustering tightly; canopy of about 20 leaves per trunk
Trunk or Stem: Slender, covered with burlap-like matting and rings of sharp, spiny fibers
Leaf: Palmate, induplicate, slightly folded; divided to 1/2-2/3 into 30-40 segments that droop and are slightly split at tips; three-pointed hastula
Foliage Color: Bright green above, silver below
Leaf Size: 2-3' (60-91 cm) wide; segments 2' (60 cm) long, 1-2" (2.5-5 cm) wide
Petiole: 4' (1.2 m) long, very thin, unarmed
Crownshaft: None
Inflorescence: 1.5' (46 cm) long, twice-branched
Gender: Bisexual flowers
Flower Color: White
Fruit Size: 1" (2.5 cm) diameter
Fruit Color: White

Comments: This unusual fan palm is closely related to *Coccothrinax* and *Thrinax* and has been known to hybridize with species of the former genus. The tightly clustering stems eventually produce a beautiful specimen plant, on no small account due to the intricate weaving of leaf stem base fibers that envelop the trunk. These should be admired at a comfortable distance, however, since the end of the fibers project outward and upward as sharp spines. The evocative name of the species is derived from the alleged use of these spines as voodoo doll needles. Zombie palm prefers a very well-drained soil and a situation in full sun.

Cocos nucifera 'Fiji Dwarf'

Section III

Use and Care of Landscape Palms

Propagation of Palms

Palms are unique among woody ornamental plants since, with relatively few exceptions, they can only be propagated from seed. Palms are also notorious in the nursery trade for slow and uneven seed germination.

Seed Propagation

Palm seeds are enclosed by a fleshy or fibrous fruit wall (mesocarp) that, with few exceptions, must be removed prior to storage or planting. If only a small number of seeds are to be processed, they can be cleaned by hand, using a knife to cut away the fruit tissue. For large quantities, machine cleaning is advisable. Species that have a relatively thin mesocarp, can be cleaned easily by rubbing seeds across a strong, large mesh screen while rinsing with a hose to remove the mesocarp, or by rubbing off the mesocarp by hand in a bucket of water and rinsing.

A number of palm species have an irritant (calcium oxalate crystals) in the fruit pulp that can make cleaning by hand a painful experience. Gloves should be worn when handling fruits of palms such as *Arenga*, *Caryota* and *Chamaedorea* spp.

Most palm fruits require a soak in water to first soften (ferment) the fleshy mesocarp. The water should be changed daily if possible. The fruits are ready for processing when the mesocarp yields easily to finger pressure, and can be easily removed by hand or mechanically.

With few exceptions, it is best to plant palm seed shortly after cleaning. If this is not possible, the best general storage procedure is to dust cleaned and air-dried seed with fungicide, seal the seed in plastic bags, and store at 65 to 75° F (18 to 24° C). However, it has been noted that retention of powdered fungicide lowered germination in date palms.

A fairly universal recommendation has been to soak palm seed in water for 1 to 5 days. The water should be changed daily and the seed planted immediately after the treatment. There is little published research on the optimum duration for water presoaks. Water soaks may serve to leach water-soluble germination inhibitors from the seed coat, or may simply promote water uptake in species having rather impermeable seed coats.

Scarification of palm seed involves thinning the bony endocarp of the seed that may impede water imbibition. It may be accomplished mechanically, by abrading the surface of the seed until the endosperm becomes visible, or by soaking the seed in concentrated sulfuric acid (H_2SO_4) or nitric acid (HNO_3) for 10 to 30 minutes. Scarification has increased the rate of germination of a number of palm species with hard, water-impermeable seed coats, such as *Butia* spp. The danger in mechanical or acid scarification is damage to the embryo during the process. This practice should be reserved for seeds having hard and impermeable seed coats. Species having slow or uneven germination without scarification should have seed scarified on a trial basis before treating the entire lot of seed.

Palm seed germination media must be well-drained, yet have some moisture holding capacity. An alternating pattern of extreme dryness and wetness is detrimental to palm seeds during germination. Particle size in the substrate should not be excessively large or prone to separation with repeated irrigation. A 1:1 or 2:1 by volume mixture of peat moss and perlite has been successfully used under a wide range of nursery conditions. The mix in a germination substrate should be adjusted depending on the conditions to which the seed will be exposed. For example, seed germinated in full sun will require a substrate with higher water holding capacity than seed germinated under shade, all other conditions being equal. A mix for slowly germinating seeds (six months or longer) should be designed to maintain its physical properties for a longer period of time than can be expected of largely peat-based substrate. Coconut coir dust, for example, is much more resistant to oxidation than either sedge or sphagnum peat and may thus be a better choice in such a situation.

The depth at which palm seed should be sown varies among species. More importantly, the environmental conditions under which seed will be germinated dictates depth of planting. If seed will be germinated in full sun, it is usually necessary to cover the seed with 1/2 to 1" (1 to 2 cm) of substrate so that it will not dry out. However, if the seed is to be germinated under shade, it is usually better to sow it shallowly (1/2" [1 cm] or less). For larger seeds, this means simply pressing them into the soil so that the top of the seed is exposed. Frequency of irrigation will also influence the planting depth. Seed germinated in full sun can be planted more shallowly if irrigation will be frequent enough that the substrate does not dry out.

Virtually all tropical palms require high temperatures for rapid and uniform germination of their seed. Most species germinate best at temperatures of 86 to 95° F (30 to 35° C). Cold-hardy species such as *Chamaerops humilis* and *Trachycarpus fortunei* germinated better at 59 to 77° F (15 or 25° C) than at 95° F (35° C); however, other equally cold-hardy species do not germinate at all at 59° F (15° C). The cold tolerance of seeds does appear to be related to the hardiness of the adult palms, with freeze-tolerant palms having freeze-tolerant seeds and cold-sensitive palms having cold-sensitive seeds. Since most palm seeds require high germination temperatures, it is best to sow seed during the warmer months of the year. If availability of fresh seed makes this difficult, soil temperatures can be increased by using bottom heat below the germination containers or covering the containers with clear plastic. Placing the containers on a heat retaining surface can also increase temperatures by several degrees.

Palm seeds require uniform moisture during the first critical stages of germination when the cotyledonary petiole (remote germinators) or button (adjacent germinators) first emerges from the seed. Alternating periods of extreme wet and dry during this time period usually have deleterious effects on seed germination. If the germination substrate does not receive some type of automatic irrigation, it may be necessary to cover the containers with clear plastic to retain adequate soil moisture. Overwatering can be equally deleterious. At no time should standing water be visible on the surface of the germination substrate.

Palm seeds do not require supplementary fertilization during germination or for the first two months after germination. The endosperm within the seed provides all the nutrition that the seedling needs during this period.

The speed at which palm seed germinates, the uniformity of germination, and the percentage of total germination can vary tremendously from species to species, from seed lots collected from different plants of the same species, and even from seed lots collected in different years from the same plant.

Palm seedlings may be transplanted after either 1 or 2 seedling leaves have formed. The objective is to minimize the degree of root disturbance to the seedlings; thus it is best to transplant before roots begin to circle the container or roots of adjacent seedlings become entangled. If possible, palms should be transplanted in the warmer months of the year, when root growth will be rapid. Seedlings will usually have one long root at the time of transplanting. Seedlings should be first transferred from the germination container to a small but deep pot that accommodates the root system and allows some subsequent root growth. Palm seedlings benefit from the deeper root run, as adventitious roots emerging from the root initiation zone tend to grow markedly downward.

Palms are very intolerant of being planted too deeply, regardless of age or size. For palm seedlings, planting as little as 1/2" (1 cm) too deep can result in severe production setbacks or even death of small seedlings. Palm seedlings should be transplanted so that the point on the seedling stem just above where the root system appears to begin lies at the soil surface. This point is sometimes marked by a noticeable swelling, particularly on older seedlings. On palms with adjacent germination, it is the point at the base of the button. Do not sever the connection of the seed to the seedling palm. If the seed is still attached to the plant by the cotyledonary petiole (remote germination), drape the seed over the edge of the pot or allow it to sit on the soil surface. This may result in the seedling being transplanted slightly higher than it was in the germination container. Pruning palm seedling roots when transplanting is not recommended. If the seedling root is longer than the transplant container, it can be allowed to slightly curve upward or around the inside perimeter of the container. A better solution is use pots large enough to accommodate the full length of the root.

Ideally, newly transplanted seedlings should be placed under light shade (30 to 50%) for several weeks, or until new growth is apparent. If this is not possible, irrigation frequency must be carefully monitored so that the transplants are not water-stressed during establishment.

Vegetative Propagation

Despite the overwhelming reliance on seed propagation for palms, there are several methods of clonal (vegetative) propagation that can be used for some species. Clustering palms that produce new erect shoots from a common base or system of rhizomes, can be divided carefully as a means of increasing stock. Species that produce new shoots at some distance from the parent stems (e.g., *Rhapis* spp.) are the most easily divided. Multi-stemmed palms such as some *Chamaedorea microspadix* and *Acoelorrhaphe wrightii* are also amenable to this type of propagation. Containerized stock is generally easiest to divide. For best results in the field or landscape, it is advisable to separate divisions from the parent plant with a sharp spade in the spring, but leave the divisions in place until new growth is evident. At that time the divisions can be carefully lifted, with as much of the root ball as can be managed. Newly separated divisions are best potted and kept shaded and well-watered until established (at least 1 year), after which they can situated in the ground.

Several date palm species, most notably *Phoenix dactylifera*, produce offshoots or suckers at the base of the trunk. Once these offshoots have produced their own roots, they can be cut from the parent plant and either containerized or planted directly in the ground. If no roots are present when the suckers are cut, the leaves should be reduced in number and/or size. Rooting can be encouraged in offshoots originating slightly above the soil surface by mounding soil around the base of the offshoot.

References:

Broschat, T.K. 1998. "Endocarp removal enhances *Butia capitata* seed germination." HortTechnology 8: 586-587.

Broschat, T. K. and H. Donselman. 1987. "Effects of fruit maturity, storage, presoaking, and seed cleaning on germination in three species of palms." J. Environ. Hort. 5: 6-9.

Broschat, T. K. and A. W. Meerow. 2000. *Ornamental Palm Horticulture*. University Press of Florida, Gainesville.

Carpenter, W. J. 1987. "Temperature and imbibition effects on seed germination of *Sabal palmetto* and *Serenoa repens*." HortScience 22: 660.

Carpenter, W. J. 1988a. "Temperature affects seed germination of four Florida palm species." HortScience 23: 336-337.

Carpenter, W. J. 1988b. "Seed after-ripening and temperature influence *Butia capitata* germination." HortScience 23: 702-703.

Carpenter, W. J. 1989. "Influence of temperature on germination of *Sabal causiarum* seed." Principes 33: 191-194.

Holmquist, J. de Dios and J. Popenoe. 1967. "The effect of scarification on the germination of seed of *Acrocomia crispa* and *Arenga engleri*." Principes 11: 23-25.

Kitzke, E. D. 1958. "A method for germinating *Copernicia* palm seeds." Principes 2: 5-8.

Loomis, H. F. 1958. "The preparation and germination of palm seeds." Principes 2: 98-102.

Meerow, A. W. 1994. "Fungicide treatment of pygmy date palm seeds affects seedling emergence." HortScience 29: 1201.

Odetola, J. A. 1987. "Studies on seed dormancy, viability, and germination in ornamental palms." Principes 31: 24-30.

Wagner, R. I. 1982. "Raising ornamental palms." Principes 26: 86-101.

Transplanting of Palms

Young palms (that is, without visible trunk development) should only be transplanted from containers. Palms are not very tolerant of the extreme root disturbance that accompanies digging from a field nursery or previous landscape site until visible trunk development has taken place. This is most critical for species that characteristically complete a great deal of stem development deeply below ground (for example, *Bismarckia noblilis*, *Latania* spp., *Sabal* spp.). Even if the palms are not killed by premature transplanting, growth setbacks and possibly less than optimum caliper development may occur.

Palms establish most quickly if transplanted during the spring and early summer when soils temperatures are on the increase. Many tropical palms exhibit reduced root function at soils temperatures below 65° F (18.3° C), thus winter planting should be avoided if possible when tropical species are being used in slightly more temperate zones. In the tropics, time of year is not as critical from the perspective of temperature, though planting should coincide with the rainy season in order to reduce the need for supplementary irrigation during the first critical months of establishment.

Preparation for Transplanting

Root Ball Size. From the list of palms whose root regeneration patterns have been studied (Table 1, p. 159), it appears that the most common response is 1) some degree of branching of cut roots, the percentage increasing with the length of the stub (up to a point) accompanied by 2) some variable degree of new root initiation from the trunk base. In general, for single-stemmed palms less than 15 feet (4.6 m) in height, a root ball of shovel width radius from the trunk is a common industry average for size and should provide for adequate root survival in those species exhibiting that response. For clustering or larger solitary specimens, an incrementally larger root ball may be advisable to insure successful establishment under site conditions that may be less than ideal. An obvious concern for the field grower is to minimize loss of soil from the field. A one foot (30 cm) minimum radius (from the trunk) is recommended for these palms. While a larger root ball may well increase transplant success, the additional weight and costs involved in transportation may not justify the slight gains in post transplant survival.

Queen palms will likely survive with a root ball of 6 inch radius (15 cm), but a larger root ball will increase root survival at the landscape site. Root branching in coconut palms (*Cocos nucifera*) does not appear to be dependent on the size of the root ball. In sabal palms (*Sabal palmetto*), virtually all of which are dug from native stands rather than nursery grown, negligible root branching occurs, and new roots must be initiated from the trunk. For these two species, smaller root balls are acceptable.

Root Pruning. Root pruning has generally not been considered necessary for palms, with the exception of Bismarck palm (*Bismarckia nobilis*) and a few others. However, if the species is a particularly high value palm for which replacement costs would be expensive, the extra labor may well be cost effective. For palms that must regenerate new roots from the trunk, root-pruning 2-3 months before digging will provide adequate time for new root growth within the ball.

Lifting From the Field. When moving palms out of the field, they should be well-supported to prevent injury to the tender heart. Some palms (for example, King Alexander, *Archontophoenix alexandrae*) are much more sensitive to heart injury due to rough handling than others, and require extra care in transport. For certain species with slender trunks (for example, Senegal date, *Phoenix reclinata*; Paurotis palm, *Acoelorrhaphe wrightii*), a supporting splint should be tied to each trunk and should extend into the foliage to protect the bud. Palms with very heavy crowns (for example, Canary Island date palm, *Phoenix canariensis*) should be braced similarly to prevent the weight of the crown from snapping the bud. Stems of clustering palms should also be tied together for additional support. A tree crane is usually required to lift large palms out of the field, and the trunk should be protected with burlap or other material wherever ropes, cables, chains or straps will be attached.

Leaf Removal. The greatest loss of water in newly dug palms occurs from transpiration through the leaves. To minimize this, one half or more of the older leaves should be removed at the time of digging. The remaining leaves should be tied together in a bundle around the bud with a biodegradable twine for transport. The twine should be removed after planting. The best method of insuring survival after transplanting to the landscape may be to remove ALL leaves on species like sabal palms that must regenerate all new roots from the trunk. Sabal palms have repeatedly exhibited higher establishment success rates when all leaves are removed when they are dug. Complete leaf removal may also be advisable during installation of any species where normal post-transplant irrigation is impossible. However, many buyers will object to this practice for aesthetic reasons. Where practical, misting or irrigation of the foliage may reduce water loss during the transplant process, though there is an accompanying risk of increasing disease problems in the canopy.

Site Preparation. It is always best to install newly dug specimen palms immediately to minimize stress and possible loss of the palm. If delivered palms cannot be planted immediately upon arrival at the installation site, the palms should be placed out of direct sun and the trunk, root ball and canopy kept moist. Temporarily "heeling in" the root balls under a layer of mulch is advisable, especially if no other means of keeping the roots from drying out is available.

Fig. 3.1. The proper method of supporting a newly installed large palm specimen after transplanting

Installation site conditions also contribute to the establishment success of transplanted palms. A well-drained location is essential; standing water should not appear at the bottom of the planting hole. If drainage is a problem at the site, a berm should be constructed to raise the root ball above the level of water. Though some palm species may adjust to less than optimal drainage after establishment, standing water around a newly dug root ball will have adverse effects on root regeneration.

The planting hole should be wide enough to easily accept the root ball and provide at least several inches of new growth from the ball. It need only be deep enough to situate the palm at the same depth at which it previously grew. The amending of backfill soil from the planting hole is not recommended unless the surrounding site soil has been positively amended, or if the site presents special problems (e.g., rockland soils in South Florida). If the backfill soil differs greatly in structure and texture from the surrounding site soil, new roots will have a tendency to remain within the backfill. If amending the backfill soil is demanded, the volume of amendment should not exceed 25% of the soil removed from the hole.

Planting and Support

Planting Depth. In general, palms should not be transplanted any deeper than they were originally grown. The root initiation zone of most palms (located at the base of the trunk) is sensitive in this regard, and planting too deeply can cause root suffocation, nutritional deficiencies, root rot disease and frequently loss of the palm. Unfortunately, it is still a common practice for installers to situate specimen-sized palms at various depths in order to create a planting of uniform height. The decline of deeply planted palms may take several years to become apparent, especially on very well-drained soils, but it can only be reversed by removing the backfill from the suffocated root initiation zone or replanting the palm.

All air pockets should be tamped out of the backfill as the planting hole is filled. A berm should be mounded up at the periphery of the root ball to retain water during irrigation. The initial irrigation should be deep and thorough. Filling the planting hole with water up to the berm will be necessary 2-3 times to fully wet and settle the soil.

Support. Larger palms will require some form of bracing to maintain stability during the first 6-8 months after installation (Fig. 3.1). Short lengths of 2" x 4" lumber should be banded or strapped to the trunk (a foundation of burlap or asphalt paper can be placed around the trunk under these), and support braces (also 2" x 4", or 4" x 4" on very large specimens) are then nailed into them. Under no circumstances should nails be driven directly into a palm trunk. Such damage is permanent, and provides entryway for pathogens and possibly insect pests as well.

Establishment Care

The root ball and surrounding backfill should remain evenly moist, but never saturated during the first 4-6 months after installation. Supplementary irrigation is necessary unless adequate rainfall is received during this time period. Newly transplanted specimen-sized palms should not be expected to produce a great deal of new top growth during the first year; much of the palm's energy reserves will (and should) be channeled into root growth. Drenching the root zone 2-4 times during the first few months with a fungicide labelled for landscape use on soil borne root fungal pathogens is recommended for high value palms. A light surface application of a partially slow-release "palm special" granular fertilizer can be banded at the margins of the root ball 3-4 months after transplanting. A foliar spray of soluble micronutrients may be beneficial during this period, since root absorption activity is limited. When the appearance of new leaves indicates that establishment has been successful, a regular fertilization program can begin.

Landscape Use and Care of Palms

A well established palm in the landscape is largely a low maintenance item as long as a regular program of fertilization and irrigation suitable to the conditions of the landscape site and the needs of the particular species is received. Overwatering can be detrimental to palms that are adapted for dry conditions, and can lead to various disease problems (see Diseases of Landscape Palms, p. 165), while failure to provide adequate water to a wet rain forest dwelling palm can result in poor growth and even loss of the plant.

Palms are best planted in a situation where turfgrass can be kept away from the trunk. Even a small mulched circle around the base of a palm is better than allowing turf to grow right up to the trunk base. The main reason for this is the prevention of trunk injuries from weed eaters, mowers and other lawn care equipment. Such wounds are permanent, and allow the entrance of disease organisms such as the Ganoderma fungus, and possibly some insect pests as well. Palms from arid regions are often not compatible with turf-oriented irrigation schedules, and such species are best not planted as lawn specimens if irrigation will be frequent and shallow. Turf will also compete for water and nutrients with palms planted within the lawn, and growth may not be optimum when compared to the same palm planted in a large, mulched landscape bed.

Within a landscape bed, consideration must be given to the compatibility of the palms to be used with the other plants that will be included. Will the massing of groundcovers or annual flowers near the base of the palm create difficulty in properly fertilizing the palm? Will the water needs of the shrubs, groundcovers or flowers in the bed prove detrimental to the palm? The high cost of replacing or moving specimen palms necessitates that one ask these questions before installation.

Where to Use Palms in the Landscape. Palms can be used for a variety of purposes in the landscape. While few palms can really provide the same measure of shade relative to a broad-leaved tree, tall growing cluster palms or group plantings of solitary palms can function as shade trees for a small home or for a quiet nook in the backyard. Tall growing palms provide a strong vertical accent in the landscape, and can overpower a small building. For example, royal palms (*Roystonea regia*) planted near a small home, only serve to make the house appear smaller.

Tall, solitary palms make effective border or boundary plantings for lining a long driveway or boulevard, while most tall clustering palms are effective as single accent specimens. The bold aspect of many palms draws attention to the area of the landscape that they inhabit.

Palms combine as well with each other as they do with other types of landscape plants. A well-designed bed of various palm species can be the focal point of a subtropical landscape. Growth rates, habit, and eventual size must be considered carefully when combining species to avoid a helter skelter mix that fails aesthetically. Small groves of the same species can also create an attractive landscape accent. King Alexander (*Archontophoenix alexandrae*), various *Veitchia* species and many other slender or moderate trunked species can be grouped successfully in the landscape. Densely clustering species such as the lady palms (*Rhapis* spp.), some *Chamaedorea* species, and areca (*Dypsis lutescens*) can be used to create a screen. Avoid planting tall growing palms directly under roof overhangs and eaves. A misplaced palm is one that will one day have to be removed.

Pruning Palms. Palms do not require pruning as we associate the term with branching, broad-leaved trees. The only trimming any palm needs is the removal of dead or badly damaged or diseased leaves. There is an unfortunate tendency for landscape maintenance workers to overtrim palms, removing perfectly good, green, functional leaves at the same time as dead or dying fronds are trimmed. The logic behind this practice, no doubt, is an attempt to lengthen the interval before trimming is once again necessary. The removal of healthy leaves is a disservice to the palm, especially those species whose canopy consists of no more than 8-12 leaves. Overtrimming reduces the food manufacturing efficiency of the living palm and can result in sub-optimum caliper development at the point in the crown where diameter increase is currently taking place. There is also some evidence that over trimming makes the palm more susceptible to cold damage.

Table 1. Root system responses of selected palm species to digging after approximately 5 months[1]		
Species	Branching	New root initiation
Cocos nucifera (Coconut)	50% cut roots branch regardless of stub length	Low[2] (20 or less)
Phoenix reclinata (Senegal date)	33% cut roots branch if stubs are at least 2' (60cm) long	Moderate (about 60)
Roystonea regia (Royal palm)	24% cut roots branch if stubs are 1-2' (30-60cm) long; 36% if 2-3' (60-91cm) long	High (about 100)
Sabal palmetto (Cabbage palm)	Negligible	Very high (about 200)
Syagrus romanzoffiana[3] (Queen palm)	41% cut roots branch if stubs are 6"-1' (15-30cm) long	Low (13)
Washingtonia robusta (Mexican fan)	31% cut roots branch if stubs are 1-2' (30-60cm) long; 58% if stubs are 2-3' (60-91cm) long	Very high (about 150)

[1] All data from Broschat and Donselman (1984a and b, 1990b).
[2] May increase with age
[3] Redug after 18 weeks of regrowth

Cold Protection and Treating Cold-Damaged Palms

Cold temperatures slow the growth rate of palms, reduce root activity, and may weaken the plant enough to make it more susceptible to disease. Palms that have received balanced fertilization in the months leading up to the period of coldest temperatures are much more likely to survive and recover from cold damage than nutritionally deficient palms. Frosts and freezing temperatures will kill the foliage of many palm species, and can reduce the function of water conducting tissue in the trunk for many years. For just a small number of valuable palms, and especially if they are not yet too tall, coverage with burlap, sheets, or one of several fabrics available for this purpose may provide adequate protection. Anti-transpiriants applied to the foliage may also help, but current research has not yet indicated that these chemicals provide significant cold protection. Tender palms have also been adeqately protected by tying up the leaves in a bundle over the bud. Icing the plants with overhead irrigation works well if performed properly. The irrigation must be turned on before temperatures reach freezing and should continue until the ice visibly melts from the plant surfaces or temperatures rise above freezing. The weight of the ice can, however, cause breakage of palm leaves.

If the irreplaceable bud or "palm heart" survives exposure to freezing temperatures, the recovery of the plant is possible, but proper care in the first few weeks after damage is essential. Leaves with any amount of green tissue should be left on the plants. It may even be wise to leave completely dead leaves attached until the danger of further cold weather is past, since they will provide some measure of insulation to the growing bud. If all the leaves are dead, they can be trimmed off. The hollow collar of overlapping leaf bases left when the spear leaf pulls out should be pierced just above solid tissue to allow water to drain from it. Application of fungicide to the foliage and bud immediately after damage and again 7 to 10 days later may help reduce further loss to disease. Copper based chemicals have traditionally been used for this purpose, but as none are currently labeled for palms, their use may be illegal. Copper sprays should not be repeated more than twice because of the possibility of copper phytotoxicity.

If healthy leaves are present on the palms, or as soon as new leaves emerge, a foliar fertilization with a soluble micronutrient mix should be applied and repeated at monthly intervals until new growth is well under way. A complete fertilizer should be soil applied if this had not been done recently.

Possible preventative action. The secondary plant pathogens that cause death of the bud soon after freeze damage are, in most cases, bacteria that are present on healthy palm tissue at low levels, but become a problem only after the damage is received. Consequently, there may be value in applying a preventative spray of fungicidal copper BEFORE freezing temperatures are reached in order to reduce these bacteria populations to the lowest levels possible. This strategy has not been tested, however, under controlled conditions.

Cryptic cold damage. Palms that were severely damaged during the winter should be watched carefully during the subsequent spring and summer seasons. Damage to embryonic leaves within the bud may not show up until those leaves emerge (as much as 6 months to 1 year after the freeze). If leaves emerging during the spring and summer months appear deformed, partially browned or otherwise abnormal, this may be indicative of this type of damage. In most cases, the palm will grow out of this later in the season.

Freeze damage to conducting tissue in the trunk may limit the ability of the palm to supply water to the canopy of leaves. Unlike typical broad-leafed trees, palms have no ability to regenerate conducting tissue in the trunk. Sudden collapse of some (or even all) of the leaves in the crown during the first periods of high temperature in the spring or summer after a winter freeze may indicate that this type of trunk damage has occurred. Unfortunately, there is nothing that can be done to remedy this, and loss of the palm may be inevitable.

References:

Broschat, T. K. 1991. "Effects of leaf removal on survival of transplanted sabal palms." Journal of Arboriculture 17: 32-33.

Broschat, T. K. and H. M. Donselman. 1984a. "Root regeneration in transplanted palms." Principes 28: 90-91.

Broschat, T.K. and H.M. Donselman. 1984b. "Regrowth of severed palm roots." Journal of Arboriculture 10: 238-240.

Broschat, T. K. and H. Donselman. 1986. "Factors affecting palm transplant success." Proc. Fl. State Hort. Soc. 100: 396-397.

Broschat, T. K. and H. Donselman. 1990a. "IBA, plant maturity and regeneration of palm root systems." HortScience 25: 232.

Broschat, T. K. and H. Donselman. 1990b. "Regeneration of severed roots in *Washingtonia robusta* and *Phoenix reclinata*." Principes 34: 96-97.

Broschat, T. K. and A. W. Meerow. 2000. *Ornamental Palm Horticulture.* University Press of Florida, Gainesville.

Hodel, D.R., D. R. Pittenger, and A. J. Downer. 2005. "Palm root growth and implications for transplanting." Journal of Arboriculture 31: 171-181

Meerow, A. W. and T. K. Broschat. 1992. "Transplanting Palms." University of Florida Extension Circular 1037.

Pittenger, D. R., D. R. Hodel and A. J. Downer. 2005. "Transplanting specimen palms: A review of common practices and research-based information." HortTechnology 15: 128-132.

Tomlinson, P. B. 1990. *The Structural Biology of Palms.* Clarendon Press, Oxford.

Landscape Palm Fertilization Programs

The frequency with which landscape palms need to be fertilized depends greatly on the type of soil in which they are planted and the amount of rainfall (or irrigation) that they will receive. In Florida, for example, poor, shallow soils coupled with heavy rainfall during the growing season results in a very low natural reservoir of essential plant nutrients. Thus mature palms in the Florida landscape should optimally receive a complete granular fertilizer formulated for palms ("palm special") four to six times per year at a rate of 1.5 lbs. /100 sq. ft. (700 gm/9 m2) of canopy area four times per year or 1 lb./100 sq. ft. (500 gm/9 m2) 6 times per year. Rates and/or frequency of application can be reduced in low rainfall areas or on soils that have a moderately high cation exchange capacity. Fertilizers should be uniformly broadcast under the canopy of the palm, but should not be placed up against the trunk where newly emerging roots may be injured. If granular fertilizers will be used in conjunction with drip irrigation systems, the fertilizer should be banded directly below the drip emitters. "Palm special" fertilizers contain additional magnesium and a complete micronutrient ("trace mineral") amendment. Dropping below a minimum of two applications, even for the most budget conscious maintenance schedules, is not recommended. In California, rainfall is lower, soils are generally of much higher quality, and the nutrient holding capacity of these soils should allow less frequent application of fertilizer. Elsewhere, palms planted on loamy, organic, or clay-based soils may also get by with less fertilizer.

A good balanced fertilizer for palms should provide nitrogen (N), phosphorus (P), potassium (K), and magnesium (Mg) in a 2:1:3:1 ratio. It should contain sulfur (S), 1 to 2% Fe and Mn, and trace amounts of zinc (Zn), copper (Cu) and boron (B). The N, K, and Mg should be present in controlled release form (resin- or sulfur-coating). If an entirely water soluble fertilizer must be used, it should be applied monthly and at a rate of 1/2-3/4 lb/100 sq. ft. (226-340 gm/9m2).

Foliar feeds. Foliar fertilization is an inefficient means for providing macronutrient elements such as nitrogen, phosphorus, potassium, and magnesium because of the relatively large amounts of these elements required by plants, but is very useful for supplying micronutrients such as manganese and iron to the plants when soil conditions prevent adequate uptake of these elements by the roots. Foliar fertilization is best used as a supplement for a normal soil fertilization program, particularly for micronutrients.

Fig. 3.2. Early "flecking" stage of potassium deficiency

Nutritional Disorders in the Landscape

Palms suffer quickly and conspicuously from improper mineral nutrition, whether due to insufficient or incorrect fertilization. They also may exhibit certain nutritional disorders in unique ways compared to other ornamental plants. Some nutritional problems in palms are difficult to diagnose accurately because symptoms of several different mineral deficiencies may overlap. The following are the most common nutritional deficiencies likely to be encountered in the landscape.

Fig. 3.3. Later stages of potassium deficiency on coconut (*Cocos nucifera*)

Nitrogen (N). An overall light green color and decreased vigor of the palm are indicative of N deficiency. It is usually only seen in the landscape on palms planted in infertile soils without supplementary fertilization. Application of any fertilizer containing nitrogen will quickly improve the color of the foliage.

Potassium (K). This deficiency is very common in Florida as soils there are naturally deficient in potassium and are quickly leached of this very soluble mineral element. In California, it is not a conspicuous problem. Symptoms vary among palm species, but always occur first on oldest leaves and affects progessively newer leaves as the deficiency becomes more severe. On many palms, the early symptoms are translucent yellow or orange flecks on the leaflets or segments (Fig. 3.2), with or without necrotic spots. Areas of necrosis soon develop along the margins and tips of the leaf (Fig. 3.3). On some species, marginal necrosis is the typical first sign of deficiency. As the symptoms progress, the entire leaf appears burnt and withered. In date palms (*Phoenix* spp.) symptoms are slightly different in that older leaves show an orange-brown discoloration near the tip), in contrast to the bright yellow of magnesium deficiency (see next section and Fig. 3.4). The leaflet tips, rather than the margins, become necrotic as the deficiency progresses. When all available potassium has been shunted from the older leaves to the new growth, the palm declines. "Pencil-pointing" (an abrupt reduction in trunk diameter) and the emergence of small, frizzled or chlorotic new leaves indicate that without immediate treatment, the palm will probably die. Potassium deficiency affects most palms, but in Florida the most susceptible species are royal, queen, coconut, areca, and spindle palms. Treatment requires soil applications of potassium sulfate at rates of 3-8 lbs. (1.4-3.6 kg) per tree four times per year plus half as much magnesium sulfate to prevent a potassium-magnesium imbalance (and resulting magnesium deficiency) from occurring. Symptomatic leaves on K-deficient palms will never recover and must be replaced by new, healthy leaves. In severely deficient palms, this means replacing the entire canopy which may take two years or longer. Foliar sprays with K fertilizers are ineffective in correcting the problem since the amount of K supplied by a foliar spray is insignificant compared to the amount needed to correct the problem.

Fig. 3.4. Magnesium deficiency on date palm (*Phoenix dactylifera*)

Magnesium (Mg). Magnesium deficiency is very common in Florida, and anywhere else where palms are planted on poor, infertile soils. Date palms (*Phoenix* spp.) are particularly susceptible. Visible symptoms begin on the oldest leaves and progress upward to the younger foliage, typically a broad light yellow band along the margin of the older leaves with the center of the leaf remaining green (Fig. 3.4). In severe cases, leaflet tips may become necrotic, but Mg deficiency is rarely if ever fatal to palms. Magnesium deficiency is best treated preventatively since treatment of deficient palms takes considerable time. As with K deficiency, symptomatic leaves will never recover and must be replaced by new healthy leaves. Applications of magnesium sulfate (epsom salts) at rates of 2-4 lbs (0.9-1.8 kg) per tree four times per year should correct the problem.

Fig. 3.5. "Frizzletop" caused by manganese deficiency on queen palm (*Syagrus romanzoffiana*)

Manganese (Mn). Manganese deficiency or "frizzletop" is a common problem in palms growing in alkaline soils, because this element is relatively insoluble at high pH. Symptoms occur only on new leaves which emerge chlorotic, weak, reduced in size, and with extensive necrotic streaking in the leaves (Fig. 3.5). As the deficiency progresses, succeeding leaves will emerge completely withered, frizzled, or scorched in appearance and greatly reduced in size. Later, only necrotic petiole stubs will emerge and death of the bud quickly follows.

In some palms such as coconut, which are not normally affected by the problem, cold soil temperatures during the winter and spring months reduce root activity and thus the uptake of micronutrients (especially Mn). Coconut palms appearing deficient in Mn during the winter and spring will usually grow out of the problem without special treatment once soil temperatures warm up in late spring. Other palms such as queen, royal, paurotis, and pygmy date palms, are highly susceptible to Mn deficiency and must be treated with soil or foliar applications of manganese sulfate or they will likely die.

Fig. 3.6. Iron deficiency on lady palm (*Rhapis excelsa*)

Iron (Fe). Iron deficiency is relatively uncommon in landscape palms and is not usually caused by a lack of Fe in the soil, or even by high soil pH, as in many other plants. Iron deficiency usually appears on palms growing in poorly aerated soils or those that have been planted too deeply. Waterlogged soils and deep planting effectively suffocate the roots. Symptoms appear first on the new leaves and in most palms consist of uniformly chlorotic new leaves (Fig. 3.6), with green coloration entirely restricted to the veins of the new leaves. As the deficiency progresses, new leaves will show extensive dead tissue at the tips (necrosis) and reduced leaf size. Iron deficiency symptoms can sometimes be temporarily alleviated by regular foliar applications of iron sulfate or chelates, but long term correction will only occur when the poor soil aeration or improper planting depth that caused the deficiency is corrected.

Boron (B). Boron is highly soluble and easily leached from soils, especially sandy soils. Deficiency manifests on palms in a number of different ways. A common symptom on feather-leaf palms is the failure of a spear leaf to completely open. Often, only leaflets at the tip of the spear will expand. An early symptom observed on many palms is the bending of leaflet or segment tips, which may then later fall off, giving the leaf a stubby, shorter than normal appearance. "Accordian-leaf," the crumbling or unnatural pleating of new leaves is another frequent B-deficiency syndrome (Fig. 3.7). At its most acute stages, B deficiency may cause an abrupt bend in crown of the stem. Treatment with soluble boron sources must be performed with care, as it is not difficult to induce B toxicity with too liberal an application. For most products, to treat a medium-sized to large palm, 2 to 4 oz (56-113gm) should be dissolved in about 5 gallons of water and poured over the root zone under the canopy. Smaller palms can be treated with foliar sprays of soluble boron fertilizers at a rate of 4 to 8 oz (113-227gm) per 100 gallons of water.

Fig. 3.7. "Accordian pleating" of younger leaves on *Heterospathe heterophylla* caused by boron deficiency

Diagnosis of nutrient deficiencies by visual symptoms alone can be difficult, since some of the symptoms overlap considerably in some species. For instance, Mn and late-stage K deficiencies are easily confused on queen and royal palms. Potassium and Mg deficiencies are very similar in pygmy date palms and K and Fe deficiencies can be very similar in royal palms. If complex symptoms defy a simple diagnosis, it is wise to have a diagnostic laboratory perform a leaf nutrient analysis before undertaking any corrective action.

References:

Broschat, T. K. 2000. *Palm Nutrition Guide.* University of Florida Extension Circular SS-ORH-02.

Broschat, T. K. and A. W. Meerow. 2000. *Ornamental Palm Horticulture.* University Press of Florida, Gainesville.

Elliott, M. L., T. K. Broschat, J. Y. Uchida and G. W. Simone. 2004. *Diseases and Disorders of Ornamental Palms.* American Phytopathological Press, St. Paul.

Insect Pests of Landscape Palms

We are fortunate indeed that relative to many other landscape plants, a well-grown palm remains fairly free of debilitating insect pests. Nevertheless, certain insects will occasionally attack landscape palms in sufficient force to warrant control measures.

Palm aphid (*Cerataphis palmae*). This aphid is unusual in that the female becomes sedentary like a scale, and forms a distinctive ring of white wax around its body (Fig. 3.8). These aphids heavily infest young leaves and excrete honeydew upon which sooty mold will grow. They are sometimes tended by ants. Lady beetles are an excellent biological control, and spraying should be avoided if these aphid predators are observed on the infested palm.

Scales, in great variety, do turn up on palm leaves from time to time, including thread scale, magnolia white scale (Fig. 3.9) oyster scale and others. The hard shell of many scales reduces the effectiveness of many chemicals.

Spider mites. Spider mites are particularly problem on greenhouse grown indoor palms, and on many *Chamaedorea* species. The predatory mite species, *Phytoseiulus persimilis* has been very successfully used to control two-spotted mites (*Tetranychus urticae*) on palms in the greenhouse environment and interiorscapes as well. Many chemical miticides work successfully, too.

Coconut mites. This tiny spider feeds on the husk of coconut fruits, causing mostly cosmetic damage (Fig. 3.10) but sometimes premature fruit drop as well.

Banana moth (*Opogona sacchari*). The larvae of this moth has been a destructive pest on a number of palm species in tropical areas. *Chamaedorea* species, arecas and other species. Though more a palm production pest, infestations of landscape palms have occurred. The caterpillar tunnels through the stems of the palms. Parasitic nematodes have been fairly effective in controlling infestations of this insect.

Palm leaf skeletonizer (*Homaledra sabalella*). The caterpillars of this small moth feed on the upper and lower leaf surfaces of many palms, producing large quantities of "frass" (fibrous excrement) that is often the first conspicuous sign of an infestation (Fig. 3.11). The tissue between the veins or ribs is usually their preferred food, but they will also feed on the leaf stems, disrupting the vascular tissue and causing the death of the entire leaf.

Royal palm bug (*Xylastodoris luteolus*, Fig. 3.12) is troublesome pest of royal palms (*Roystonea* spp.) in Florida and the Caribbean. Infestations in South Florida tend to increase in the spring and summer following a particularly mild winter. This tiny bug feeds on the young leaves of the palms (Fig. 3.13), often getting in between the folds of an emerging leaf. When the leaf unfolds it appears scorched and brown, and usually fails to mature.

Giant palm or palmetto weevils (*Rynchophorus cruentatus*) are large beetles that are drawn to stressed palms (Fig. 3.14) in the subtropical deep south. They most frequently attack cabbage palms (*Sabal palmetto*) and Canary Island date palms (*Phoenix canariensis*), but have been reported on Mexican fan palms (*Washingtonia robusta*), Bismarck palms (*Bismarckia nobilis*) and latan palms (*Latania* spp.). Adult females lay eggs in the leaf bases of the crown, and the large larvae (Fig. 3.15) quickly tunnel into the heart, destroying the palm (Fig. 3.16). All efforts should be made to reduce transplant stress on susceptible species. A preventative spray of a recommended insecticide, applied at and again a few weeks after installation, has shown some success in keeping palms free of infestation. A related species, *R. palmarum*, occurs in Central and South America and the Caribbean and spreads a destructive nematode that causes red ring disease in coconuts and African oil palms.

Rotten sugar cane borer (*Metamasius hemipterus*, Fig. 3.17) is a relatively new pest of palms in South Florida. It attacks royal palms (*Roystonea* spp.), foxtail palm (*Wodyetia bifurcata*) majesty palm (*Ravenea rivularis*), spindle palm (*Hyophorbe verschaffeltii*), Mexican fan palm (*Washingtonia robusta*) and possibly others. The larvae of this weevil completely riddle the stems of the palms (Fig. 3.18) which then succumb to various secondary disease organisms.

Various caterpillars and some grasshoppers feed on the leaves of palms from time to time. Small infestations can be dealt with mechanically without recourse to pesticides; however, if these insects are on palm foliage in force, they can very quickly do appreciable damage, completely defoliating a young palm in as little as 1-2 days.

References:

Howard, F. W., D. Moore, R. Giblin-Davis and R. Abad. 2001. *Insects on Palms.* CABI Publishing, Cambridge, MA and Oxford, UK.

James De Filippis

Fig. 3.8. Ant tending the scale-like palm aphid

Robin Giblin-Davis

Fig. 3.10. Coconut fruits disfigured by coconut mites

James De Filippis

Fig. 3.9. Magnolia white scale

James De Filippis

Fig. 3.11. Damage caused by palm leaf skeletonizer

James De Filippis

Fig. 3.12. Royal palm bugs

Robin Giblin-Davis

Fig. 3.14. Adult female palmetto weevils

Robin Giblin-Davis

Fig. 3.13. Damage caused by royal palm bug

Robin Giblin-Davis

Fig. 3.15. Larvae of giant palm weevil feeding in the leaf bases of Canary Island date palm (*Phoenix canariensis*)

Robin Giblin-Davis

Fig. 3.16. "Dead-heading" (canopy collapse) of cabbage palm caused by giant palm weevils

Robin Giblin-Davis

Fig. 3.17. Adult rotten sugar cane borer (*Metamasius hemipterus*)

Robin Giblin-Davis

Fig. 3.18. Stem of royal palm (*Roystonea regia*) riddled with damage from rotten sugar cane borers

*D*isease Problems of Landscape Palms

Leaf Spots

A number of leaf spot fungi cause variously shaped lesions on the leaf surface of many palm species. High rainfall or frequent overhead irrigation is often instrumental in their spread. If only a single leaf is affected, removal and disposal of that leaf is a simple and effective control. Some leaf spot fungi move in as secondary problems on palm leaves that are deficient in nutrients or have received some sort of damage.

Leaf spots diseases caused by various *Bipolaris* and *Exserohilum* fungi (often called ***Helminthosporium*-complex** leaf spots) affect a broad range of palms with characteristically round, dark brown lesions (Fig. 3.19) that eventually merge and form large blighted areas. The disease is easily spread by overhead irrigation. *Cercospora* leaf spot is frequently a problem on *Rhapis* palms, and *Cylindricladium* on kentia (*Howea forsteriana*). **Anthracnose** caused by a *Colletotrichum* fungus can affect a large number of palms, particularly where overhead irrigation is used. **Stigmina** (*Exosporium fungus*) **leaf spot** can be a particular problem on date palm (*Phoenix*) species. **Graphiola leaf spot** or **"false smut"** can become a significant problem on landscape palms during periods of high rainfall. The disease becomes conspicuous when the fungus responsible produces its grayish-black fruiting bodies which rupture through both leaf surfaces (Fig. 3.20). ***Pestalotiopsis* leaf spot** affects a number of species. It seems to be a particular problem on date palm (*Phoenix*) species on which lesions often first appear on the rachis tissue (Fig. 3.21). **Tar spot** (*Catacauma* leaf spot) causes elongated, diamond-shaped lesions on the leaf surface. Both copper and a wide range of fungicides have been used to combat this fungal disease. In California and Arizona, **diamond scale** (*Sphaerodothus neowashingtoniae*) attacks California fan palm (*Washingtonia filifera*), causing premature death of the leaves. This fungus produces black, diamond-shaped sporulating structures on the leaf blade and stem. Removing infected leaves is the best control; the effectiveness of fungicides is not reported.

Fig. 3.19. *Helminthosporium*-complex leaf spot

Fig. 3.20. The grayish-black fruiting bodies of graphiola false smut are sometimes mistaken for scale insects

Sooty Mold

This superficial fungal disease (Fig. 3.22), caused by *Capnodium* spp., is more a nuisance than a life-or-death problem on palms. When present, it is always associated with infestations of sucking insects such as palm aphid, scales, or mealybugs. These insects excrete "honeydew," a waste product high in sugars that the sooty mold fungus feeds upon. The fungus appears on the leaf surface (and sometimes the trunk) as a conspicuous black, sooty deposit. Heavy infestations

Fig. 3.21. *Pestalotiopsis* lesion on the rachis of pygmy date palm (*Phoenix roebelenii*)

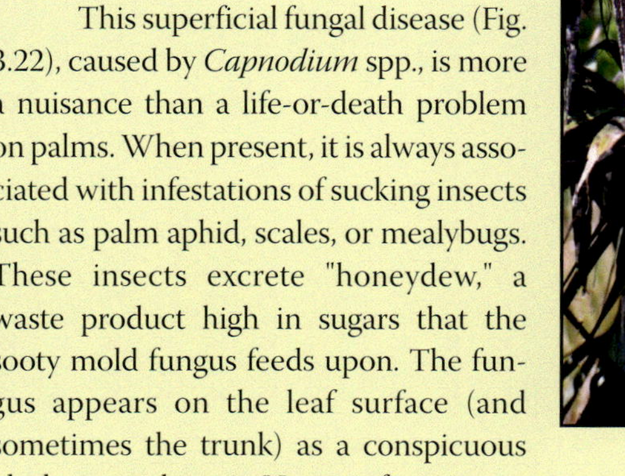

Fig. 3.22. Sooty mold

will interfere with the food-manufacturing efficiency of the leaf. The best control is keep the palm free of honeydew producing insects.

Nigel Harrison

Fig. 3.23. ***Phytophthora*** **bud rot of coconut**

Nigel Harrison

Fig. 3.26. "Conch" of Ganoderma fungus on trunk of affected palm

Bud, Root or Trunk Rots and Wilts

Phytophthora **bud rot** is one of the more common diseases encountered in palms in wet tropical climates (Table 1, p. 168). It is primarily a warm season disease. This soilborne disease causes collapse or brown-out of the younger foliage and emerging leaf (Fig. 3.23). If the bud is cut open, discoloration is evident, often accompanied by a foul smell. Phytophthora can also cause a leafspot and root rot (Fig. 3.24). Overwatering and planting too deeply aggravate incidences of phytophthora. ***Pythium*** **rots** and ***Rhizoctonia*** **root rots** are also occasionally a problem on palms.

Nigel Harrison

Fig. 3.24. Root rot and discoloration of vascular tissue caused by ***Phytophthora***

Pink rot or ***Gliocladium*** **blight**. This fungal disease is a serious problem on *Chamaedorea* species and areca palms in Florida, and queen, date and *Washingtonia* palms in California. The causal agent is not active at temperatures above 85° F (29.4° C), thus it is primarily a winter disease in Florida, while remaining active most of the year in coastal California. Oozing lesions occur on the stems, and leaves turn brown and droop (Fig. 3.25). The fungus produces salmon-pink, powdery fruiting bodies. The disease is easily spread if affected leaves are pulled off the plant prematurely, thus leaving an entrance for new disease inoculum.

Nigel Harrison

Fig. 3.27. Canary Island date palms (*Phoenix canariensis*) with *Fusarium* wilt (left)

Thielaviopsis **trunk** or bud rot is increasing in frequency on palms in Florida, but is not yet terribly common. This soil borne fungus generally enters the palm through wounds, and causes the disintegration of the trunk or bud. It can also infect leaves of young palms. A cross-section through the trunk will reveal blackened fruiting bodies. Affected palms will blow over easily.

Nigel Harrison

Fig. 3.25. Pink rot or *Gliocladium* blight on a queen palm seedling (*Syagrus romanzoffiana*)

Ganoderma butt rot has become a serious and incurable disease of older landscape palms (usually 15 or more years old). The disease progresses from the older leaves upward, which turn brown and droop from the trunk. Wounds on the lower portions of the trunk or roots favor entry of the fungus. The fruiting body of the fungus is a conspicuous bracket or "conch" (Fig. 3.26). The disease spreads rapidly from plant to plant, and the fungus can persist in the soil for many years. Affected palms must be completely removed and destroyed and the soil fumigated. If ganoderma has been diagnosed in a landscape site, it may be best to replant with a broad-leaved tree, as no palm can yet be declared reliably resistant.

Nigel Harrison

Fig. 3.28. Necrotic inflorescence, an early sign of lethal yellowing

Fusarium **wilt**, more common a problem in California, has become more prevalent in Florida. The disease frequently causes an uneven decline in the canopy of an infected palm, with leaflets on only one side of a single leaf dying first. The water and food conducting tissue within the leaves is usually discolored. Date palms have been the worst affected in California (Fig. 3.27), while coconuts and Mexican fan palms have also succumbed to this incurable disease in Florida. Pruning tools are known to transfer the fungus from tree to tree, and should be sterilized before using again on a different tree.

Bacterial bud rot causes a wet blight of the emerging spear leaf which can spread downward to the irreplaceable bud. Affected spear leaves often will pull easily from the bud. A foul odor frequently accompanies the damage. It often follows hard on the heels of recent cold damage to a palm.

Lethal Yellowing (LY)

Lethal yellowing is an incurable disease of many palm species caused by a phytoplasma (a form of life sometimes described as intermediate between a virus and a bacterium) vectored by a leaf hopper bug (*Myndus crudus*). The disease organism is now resident in at least Palm Beach, Broward, Dade, Monroe, Lee and Collier counties of Florida, southern Texas, Mexico, and parts of Central and South America and Africa. The disease often begins with the blackening of young inflorescences on infected palms (Fig. 3.28). On coconuts, developing fruits will suddenly drop off the stems. One by one, mature leaves may begin to yellow on the palm, until all leaves in the canopy wilt and die (Fig. 3.29). On other species (and some varieties of coconut as well) the yellowing may not be conspicuous; instead, leaves collapse and the palm quickly dies (Fig. 3.30). The only practical control is to avoid planting highly LY susceptible palms (Table 2, p. 169). The decline caused by the disease can be temporarily suspended (though not cured) with a program of injections of tetracycline antibiotics (Fig. 3.31), but only on palms with a developed trunk. Injections can be maintained until a resistant replacement palm achieves acceptable size, after which the infected palm is allowed to die.

Nigel Harrison

Fig. 3.29. Coconut palms (*Cocos nucifera*) with lethal yellowing

Nigel Harrison

Fig. 3.30. Christmas palm (*Adonidia merrillii*) with lethal yellowing

Nigel Harrison

Fig. 3.31. Injection of antibiotic into trunk of coconut with lethal yellowing

Miscellaneous Palm Problems

Landscape palms occasionally experience other problems that are not necessarily the consequences of pests, diseases or nutritional deficiency.

Trunk splits or cracks. Some palm species characteristically develop vertical fissures on their trunks. When these appear on palms that normally do not express them, it is usually an indication of water problems. Either too much or too little soil moisture can result in small cracks on the trunk, as can overly deep planting. Large scale trunk splitting is often associated with an over-abundance of water. Trunk cracking can also occur as a consequence of cold damage.

Trunk constrictions. At the point along their length where active growth is taking place, palm stems complete their caliper growth (that is, increase in diameter) before elongating. The optimal caliper that a palm species will achieve is partially determined by the intrinsic character of the species and partially by the quality of the growing conditions at that point in time. If nutrition or water supply is limiting, or if some other type of environmental stress occurs (a freeze, for example), the palm stem may fail to achieve the same increase in diameter as occurred in past years. As conditions improve, the stem will once again reach optimum caliper. The result over the long term will be a constriction in the trunk at the point where the stem was actively growing when the stresses occurred (Fig. 3.32). In older palms, it is sometimes possible to "read" the past history of growing conditions by the patterns of constrictions that appear along the length of the trunk.

Fig. 3.32. Trunk constriction

Fig. 3.33. Lightning strike on coconut palm

Pencil-pointing. This syndrome is often related to that of trunk constriction. "Pencil-pointing" refers to a sudden, unnatural narrowing of the stem towards the crown of the palm. It is often associated with acute nutrient deficiencies, but can also be caused by continuous over-trimming of the canopy. If conditions improve, the palm will return to its normal caliper growth, and a trunk constriction will develop at the point where pencil-pointing was observed.

Lightning strike. A direct lightning hit on a palm is usually fatal. Sudden collapse of the crown (Fig. 3.33), trunk splitting and/or bleeding, and dark streaks on the trunk are all possible symptoms of lightning damage.

Powerline decline. Tall palms that have reached close proximity to high voltage powerlines have been observed with yellowed or necrotic leaves despite regular fertilization and no evidence of pests or disease, suggesting that the electromagnetic fields around these lines can injure them.

Herbicide toxicity. Many herbicides can cause damage to palms. Telltale signs of herbicide injury include distorted and undersized new growth and patches of dead tissue on the leaves. Damage from some pre-emergent herbicides may take months to become apparent. Consequently, special care should taken when using weed-killing chemicals around landscape palms, avoiding any contact of the chemical with new roots, or any green tissue on the palm. Only herbicides labelled for use around palms should be applied.

After-flower decline. Certain palms species (fishtail palms, *Caryota* spp. for example) flower and fruit once and then die. On clustering species with this habit, new stems are produced that continue the growth of the palm, while solitary palms will have to be replaced.

Salt injury. Leaf burn on the windward side of palms planted near the shore is often indicative of salt injury. It usually follows a period of high winds. A sudden intrusion of salt water into the root zone of palms can cause an overall decline and death of the plant. The best way to deal with this problem is to plant in exposed coastal locations only those palms with high salt tolerance.

Table 1. Palms particularly susceptible to *Phytophthora* bud rot

Scientific Name	Scientific Name	Scientific Name
Archontophoenix alexandrae	*Coccothrinax argentata*	*Ptychosperma macarthurii*
Borassus flabellifer	*Coccothrinax crinita*	*Roystonea regia*
Brahea armata	*Cocos nucifera*	*Syagrus romanzoffiana*
Brahea edulis	*Dypsis lutescens*	*Trachycarpus fortunei*
Butia capitata	*Howea forsteriana*	*Trithrinax brasiliensis*
Chamaedorea elegans	*Livistona rotundifolia*	*Washingtonia filifera*
Chamaedorea seifrizii	*Phoenix canariensis*	*Washingtonia robusta*

Table 2. List of relative susceptibility to Lethal Yellowing of some ornamental palms

Scientific Name	Susceptibility	Scientific Name	Susceptibility
Adonidia merrilli	HIGH	*Hyophorbe verschaffeltii*	SLIGHT
Allagoptera arenaria	SLIGHT	*Latania* spp.	MODERATE
Arenga engleri	HIGH	*Livistona chinensis*	MODERATE
Borassus flabellifer	MODERATE	*Livistona rotundifolia*	MODERATE
Caryota mitis	MODERATE	*Nannorrhops ritchiana*	SLIGHT
Caryota rumphiana	MODERATE	*Phoenix canariensis*	MODERATE
Caryota urens	MODERATE	*Phoenix dactylifera*	MODERATE
*Cocos nucifera**	HIGH	*Phoenix reclinata*	SLIGHT
Corypha utan	HIGH	*Pritchardia* spp.	HIGH
Dictyosperma album	MODERATE	*Syagrus schizophylla*	MODERATE
Dypsis cabadae	SLIGHT	*Trachycarpus fortunei*	MODERATE
Dypsis decaryi	SLIGHT	*Veitchia arecina*	SLIGHT

*resistant varieties available

References:

Broschat, T. K. and A. W. Meerow. 2000. *Ornamental Palm Horticulture.* University Press of Florida, Gainesville.

Elliott, M. L., T. K. Broschat, J. Y. Uchida and G. W. Simone. 2004. *Diseases and Disorders of Ornamental Palms.* American Phytopathological Press, St. Paul.

Cryosophila stauracantha
Photo credit: Geoff Stein

Livistona rotundifolia
Photo credit: Geoff Stein

Section IV

Plant Hardiness Zone Maps, Landscape Characteristics Tables, General Index, Glossary, Palm Bibliography, About the Author

Europe - USDA Plant Hardiness Zone Map

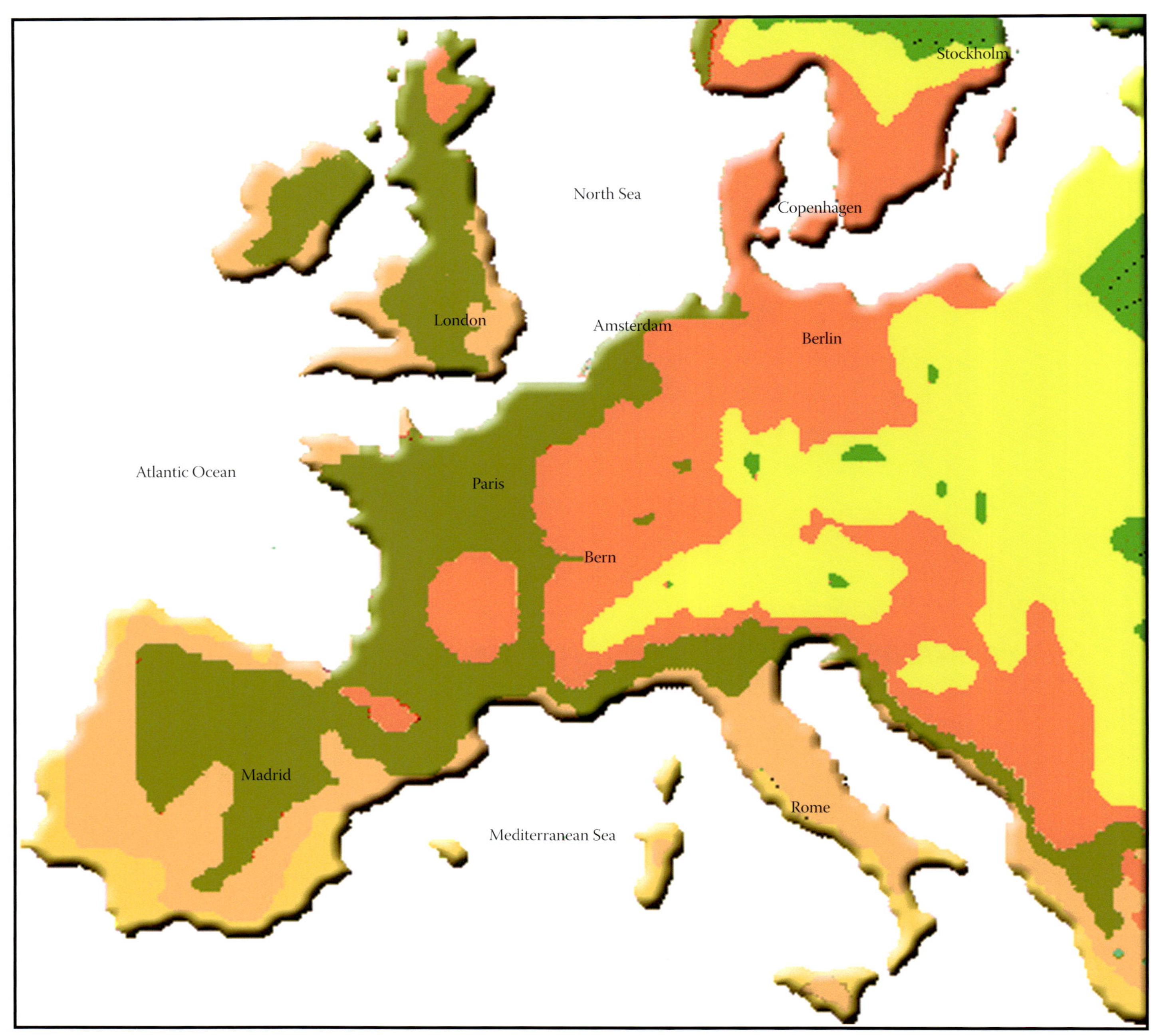

Average Annual Minimum Temperature

°C = 5/9 x (°F - 32) °F = (9/5 x °C) + 32

Zone	°C	°F
Zone 5	-26.2 to -28.8	-20 to -15
Zone 6	-20.6 to -23.3	-10 to -5
Zone 7	-15.0 to -17.7	0 to 5
Zone 8	-9.5 to -12.2	10 to 15
Zone 9	-3.9 to -6.6	20 to 25
Zone 10	1.6 to -1.1	30 to 35

USDA Plant Hardiness Zone Map

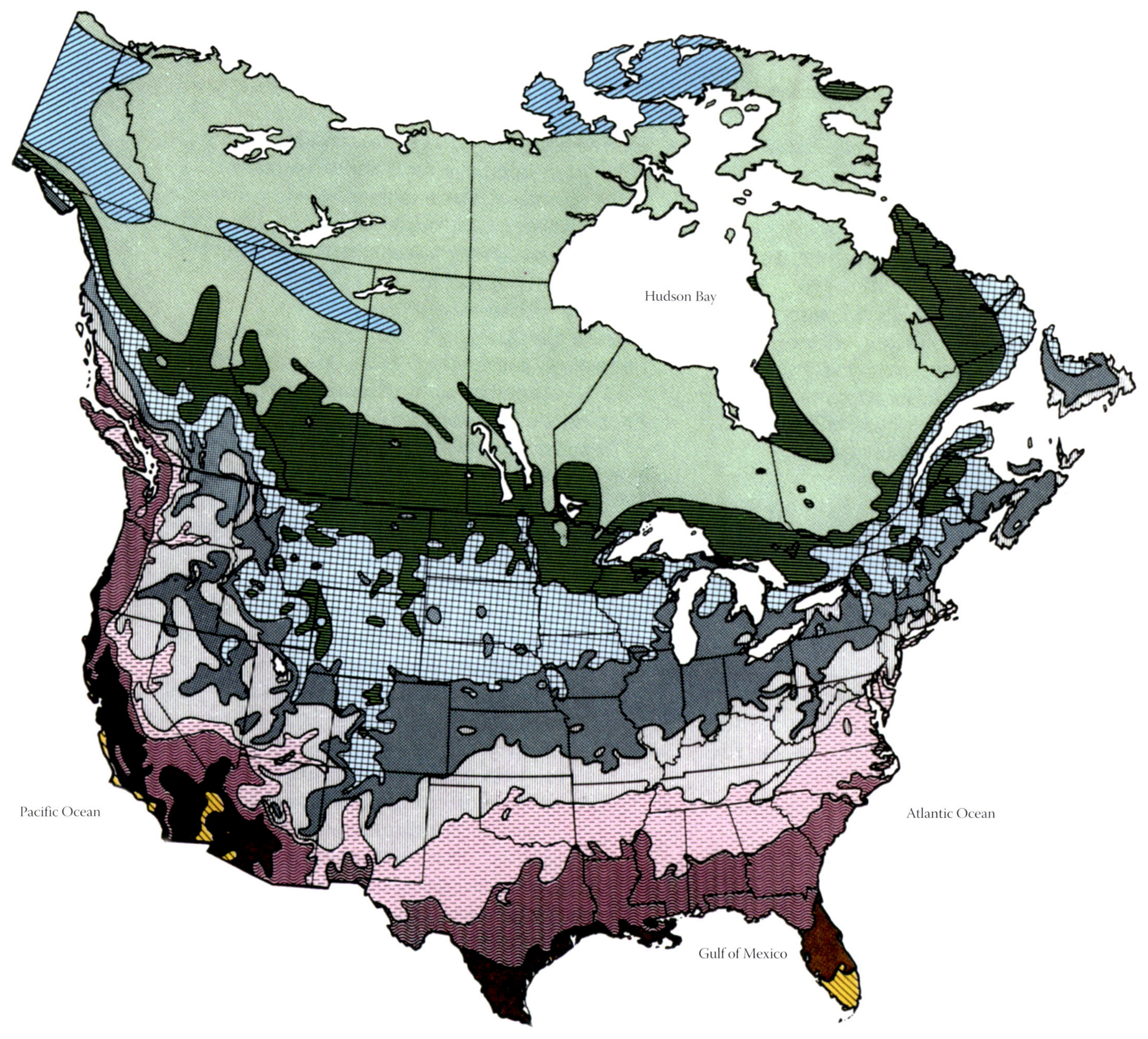

Average Annual Minimum Temperature

	°F	°C
Zone 1	Below -50°	Below -45.6°
Zone 2	-40° to -50°	-40° to -45.5°
Zone 3	-30° to -40°	-34.5° to -39.9°
Zone 4	-20° to -30°	-28.9° to -34.4°
Zone 5	-10° to -20°	-23.4° to -28.8°
Zone 6	0° to -10°	-17.8° to -23.3°
Zone 7	10° to 0°	-12.3° to -17.7°
Zone 8	20° to 10°	-6.7° to -12.2°
Zone 9	30° to 20°	-1.2° to -6.6°
Zone 10	40° to 30°	4.4° to -1.1°

°F = (9/5 x °C) + 32 °C = 5/9 x (°F - 32)

Solitary Palms

Acrocomia aculeata
Adonidia merrillii
Aiphanes aculeata
Archontophoenix alexandrae
Archontophoenix cunninghamiana
Areca catechu
Asterogyne martiana
Bismarckia nobilis
Borassus flabellifer
Brahea armata
Brahea edulis
Butia capitata
Carpenteria acuminata
Caryota gigas
Caryota no
Caryota rumphiana
Caryota urens
Caryota zebrina
Chamaedorea elegans
Chamaedorea metallica
Chamaedorea tepejilote
Chambeyronia macrocarpa
Coccothrinax argentata
Coccothrinax barbadensis
Coccothrinax crinita
Coccothrinax miraguama
Cocos nucifera
Copernicia baileyana
Copernicia hospita
Copernicia macroglossa
Copernicia prunifera
Corypha umbraculifera
Cryosophila stauracantha
Dictyosperma album
Dypsis decaryi
Dypsis leptochilos
Dypsis madagascariensis (clustering forms known)
Elaeis guineensis
Euterpe edulis
Gaussia maya
Heterospathe elata
Howea forsteriana
Hyophorbe lagenicaulis
Hyophorbe verschaffeltii
Hyphaene thebaica (may also be clustering)
Johannesteijsmannia altifrons
Jubaea chilensis
Kentiopsis oliviformis
Kerriodoxa elegans
Latania loddigesii
Latania lontaroides
Licuala grandis
Licuala ramsayi
Livistona australis
Livistona chinensis
Livistona decipiens
Livistona mariae
Livistona rotundifolia
Livistona saribus
Lytocaryum weddellianum
Mauritia flexuosa
Neoveitchia storckii
Normanbya normanbyi
Phoenix canariensis
Phoenix loureiri
Phoenix roebelenii
Phoenix rupicola
Phoenix sylvestris
Pritchardia pacifica
Pritchardia thurstonii
Pseudophoenix sargentii
Ptychosperma elegans
Ravenea rivularis
Rhopaloblaste augusta
Roystonea regia
Sabal causiarum
Sabal mauritiiformis
Sabal minor
Sabal palmetto
Satakentia liukiuensis
Syagrus botryophora
Syagrus coronata
Syagrus romanzoffiana
Syagrus schizophylla
Thrinax excelsa
Thrinax morrisii
Thrinax radiata
Trachycarpus fortunei
Trachycarpus martianus
Trithrinax brasiliensis
Veitchia arecina
Veitchia joannis
Veitchia winin
Verschaffeltia splendida
Wallichia disticha
Washingtonia filifera
Washingtonia robusta
Wodyetia bifurcata

Clustering Palms

Acoelorrhaphe wrightii
Allagoptera arenaria
Areca vestiaria
Arenga hookeriana
Arenga tremula
Bactris gasipaes
Caryota mitis
Chamaedorea cataractarum
Chamaedorea costaricana
Chamaedorea microspadix
Chamaedorea radicalis
Chamaedorea seifrizii
Chamaedorea tepejilote (sometimes solitary)
Chamaerops humilis (solitary forms known)
Cyrtostachys renda
Dypsis cabadae
Dypsis lutescens
Dypsis madagascariensis (solitary forms known)
Euterpe edulis (rarely)
Hyphaene thebaica (solitary forms known)
Licuala spinosa
Nannorrhops ritchiana
Phoenix dactylifera (sometimes solitary)
Phoenix loureiri (solitary forms known)
Phoenix reclinata
Pinanga coronata
Ptychosperma macarthurii
Reinhardtia gracilis
Rhapidophyllum hystrix
Rhapis excelsa
Rhapis humilis
Serenoa repens
Zombia antillarum

Drought Tolerance

High

Acrocomia aculeata
Allagoptera arenaria
Bismarckia nobilis
Borassus flabellifer
Brahea armata
Butia capitata
Chamaerops humilis (once established)
Coccothrinax argentata
Coccothrinax barbadensis
Coccothrinax miraguama
Cocos nucifera
Copernicia baileyana
Copernicia hospita
Copernicia macroglossa
Corypha umbraculifera
Dypsis cabadae
Dypsis lutescens
Hyphaene thebaica
Jubaea chilensis (once established)
Latania loddigesii
Latania lontaroides
Livistona mariae
Livistona saribus
Nannorrhops ritchiana
Phoenix canariensis
Phoenix dactylifera
Phoenix reclinata
Phoenix rupicola
Phoenix sylvestris
Pseudophoenix sargentii
Sabal causiarum
Sabal palmetto
Serenoa repens
Syagrus schizophylla
Thrinax morrisii
Thrinax radiata
Trithrinax brasiliensis
Washingtonia filifera
Washingtonia robusta
Zombia antillarum

Moderate

Acoelorrhaphe wrightii
Adonidia merrillii
Aiphanes aculeata
Archontophoenix alexandrae
Archontophoenix cunninghamiana
Areca vestiaria
Arenga tremula
Bactris gasipaes
Brahea edulis
Caryota mitis
Caryota no
Caryota rumphiana
Caryota urens
Chamaedorea costaricana
Chamaedorea elegans
Chamaedorea metallica
Chamaedorea microspadix
Chamaedorea radicalis
Chamaedorea seifrizii
Chamaedorea tepejilote
Coccothrinax crinita
Copernicia prunifera
Cyrtostachys renda
Dictyosperma album
Dypsis decaryi
Dypsis leptocheilos
Dypsis madagascariensis
Elaeis guineensis
Gaussia maya
Heterospathe elata
Howea forsteriana
Hyophorbe lagenicaulis
Hyophorbe verschaffeltii
Kentiopsis oliviformis
Kerriodoxa elegans
Licuala spinosa
Livistona australis
Livistona chinensis
Livistona decipiens
Livistona rotundifolia
Phoenix loureiri
Phoenix roebelenii
Pritchardia pacifica
Pritchardia thurstonii
Ptychosperma elegans
Ptychosperma macarthurii
Ravenea rivularis
Rhapidophyllum hystrix
Rhapis excelsa
Rhapis humilis
Rhopaloblaste augusta
Roystonea regia
Sabal mauritiiformis
Sabal minor
Satakentia liukiuensis
Syagrus coronata
Syagrus romanzoffiana
Thrinax excelsa
Trachycarpus fortunei
Trachycarpus martianus
Veitchia arecina
Veitchia joannis
Veitchia winin
Verschaffeltia splendida
Wallichia disticha
Wodyetia bifurcata

Low

Aiphanes aculeata
Areca catechu
Arenga hookeriana
Asterogyne martiana
Carpentaria acuminata
Caryota gigas
Caryota zebrina
Chamaedorea cataractarum
Chambeyronia macrocarpa
Cryosophila stauracantha
Euterpe edulis
Johannesteijsmannia altifrons
Licuala grandis
Licuala ramsayi
Lytocaryum weddellianum
Mauritia flexuosa
Neoveitchia storckii
Normanbya normanbyi
Pinanga coronata
Reinhardtia gracilis
Syagrus botryophora
Verschaffeltia splendida

Salt Tolerance

High

Allagoptera arenaria
Coccothrinax argentata
Cocos nucifera
Phoenix dactylifera
Pritchardia pacifica
Pritchardia thurstonii
Pseudophoenix sargentii
Sabal palmetto
Serenoa repens
Thrinax morrisii
Thrinax radiata
Zombia antillarum

Moderate

Acoelorrhaphe wrightii
Acrocomia aculeata
Adonidia merrillii
Areca vestiaria
Bismarckia nobilis
Borassus flabellifer
Chamaerops humilis
Coccothrinax barbadensis
Coccothrinax crinita
Coccothrinax miraguama
Copernicia hospita
Copernicia macroglossa
Copernicia prunifera
Dictyosperma album
Dypsis lutescens
Elaeis guineensis
Hyophorbe lagenicaulis
Hyophorbe verschaffeltii
Hyphaene thebaica
Latania loddigesii
Latania lontaroides
Licuala ramsayi
Livistona australis
Livistona chinensis
Livistona mariae
Livistona saribus
Nannorrhops ritchiana
Phoenix canariensis
Phoenix loureiri
Phoenix reclinata
Phoenix rupicola
Phoenix sylvestris
Ravenea rivularis
Roystonea regia
Sabal causiarum
Sabal minor
Syagrus romanzoffiana
Syagrus schizophylla
Veitchia arecina
Veitchia joannis
Veitchia winin
Washingtonia filifera
Washingtonia robusta

Low

Aiphanes aculeata
Archontophoenix alexandrae
Archontophoenix cunninghamiana
Areca catechu
Arenga hookeriana
Arenga tremula
Asterogyne martiana
Bactris gasipaes
Brahea armata
Brahea edulis
Butia capitata
Carpenteria acuminata
Caryota gigas
Caryota mitis
Caryota no
Caryota rumphiana
Caryota urens
Caryota zebrina
Chamaedorea cataractarum
Chamaedorea costaricana
Chamaedorea elegans
Chamaedorea metallica
Chamaedorea microspadix
Chamaedorea radicalis
Chamaedorea seifrizii
Chamaedorea tepejilote
Chambeyronia macrocarpa
Copernicia baileyana
Corypha umbraculifera
Cryosophila stauracantha
Cyrtostachys renda
Dypsis cabadae
Dypsis decaryi
Dypsis leptocheilos
Dypsis madagascariensis
Euterpe edulis
Gaussia maya
Heterospathe elata
Howea forsteriana
Johannesteijsmannia altifrons
Jubaea chilensis
Kentiopsis oliviformis
Kerriodoxa elegans
Licuala grandis
Licuala spinosa
Livistona decipiens
Livistona rotundifolia
Lytocaryum weddellianum
Mauritia flexuosa
Neoveitchia storckii
Normanbya normanbyi
Phoenix loureiri
Phoenix roebelenii
Pinanga coronata
Ptychosperma elegans
Ptychosperma macarthurii
Reinhardtia gracilis
Rhapidophyllum hystrix
Rhapis excelsa
Rhapis humilis
Rhopaloblaste augusta
Sabal mauritiiformis
Satakentia liukiuensis
Syagrus botryophora
Thrinax excelsa
Trachycarpus fortunei
Trachycarpus martianus
Trithrinax brasiliensis
Verschaffeltia splendida
Wallichia disticha
Wodyetia bifurcata

Growth Rate

Slow

Acoelorrhaphe wrightii
Acrocomia aculeata
Allagoptera arenaria
Bismarckia nobilis
Borassus flabellifer
Brahea armata
Brahea edulis
Butia capitata
Chamaedorea elegans
Chamaedorea metallica
Chamaedorea radicalis
Chamaedorea tepejilote
Chamaerops humilis
Chambeyronia macrocarpa
Coccothrinax argentata
Coccothrinax barbadensis
Coccothrinax crinita
Copernicia baileyana
Copernicia hospita
Copernicia macroglossa
Copernicia prunifera
Cyrtostachys renda
Euterpe edulis
Heterospathe elata
Howea forsteriana
Hyophorbe lagenicaulis
Hyophorbe verschaffeltii
Hyphaene thebaica
Johannesteijsmannia altifrons
Jubaea chilensis
Kentiopsis oliviformis
Kerriodoxa elegans
Latania loddigesii
Latania lontaroides
Licuala grandis
Licuala ramsayi
Licuala spinosa
Livistona australis
Livistona chinensis
Livistona decipiens
Lytocaryum weddellianum
Mauritia flexuosa
Nannorrhops ritchiana
Phoenix canariensis
Phoenix dactylifera
Phoenix roebelenii
Phoenix rupicola
Phoenix sylvestris
Pritchardia pacifica
Pritchardia thurstonii
Pseudophoenix sargentii
Reinhardtia gracilis
Rhapidophyllum hystrix
Rhapis humilis
Sabal causiarum
Sabal mauritiiformis
Sabal minor
Sabal palmetto
Serenoa repens
Syagrus schizophylla
Thrinax morrisii
Thrinax radiata
Trachycarpus fortunei
Trithrinax brasiliensis
Zombia antillarum

Moderate

Adonidia merrillii
Aiphanes aculeata
Archontophoenix alexandrae
Archontophoenix cunninghamiana
Areca catechu
Areca vestiaria
Arenga hookeriana
Arenga tremula
Asterogyne martiana
Bactris gasipaes
Caryota gigas
Caryota mitis
Caryota urens
Caryota zebrina
Chamaedorea cataractarum
Chamaedorea costaricana
Chamaedorea microspadix
Chamaedorea seifrizii
Coccothrinax miraguama
Cocos nucifera
Copernicia prunifera
Corypha umbraculifera
Cryosophila stauracantha
Dictyosperma album
Dypsis cabadae
Dypsis decaryi
Dypsis leptocheilos
Dypsis lutescens
Dypsis madagascariensis
Elaeis guineensis
Gaussia maya
Kerriodoxa elegans
Livistona decipiens
Livistona mariae
Livistona rotundifolia
Livistona saribus
Mauritia flexuosa
Neoveitchia storckii
Normanbya normanbyi
Phoenix loureiri
Phoenix reclinata
Pinanga coronata
Ptychosperma elegans
Ptychosperma macarthurii
Reinhardtia gracilis
Rhapis excelsa
Rhopaloblaste augusta
Roystonea regia
Satakentia liukiuensis
Syagrus coronata
Syagrus romanzoffiana
Thrinax excelsa
Trachycarpus martianus
Wallichia disticha
Washingtonia filifera

Fast

Aiphanes aculeata
Areca vestiaria
Asterogyne martiana
Carpenteria acuminata
Caryota no
Caryota rumphiana
Chamaedorea tepejilote
Ravenea rivularis
Syagrus botryophora
Syagrus romanzoffiana
Veitchia arecina
Veitchia joannis
Veitchia winin
Verschaffeltia splendida
Wallichia disticha
Washingtonia robusta
Wodyetia bifurcata

Light Requirements

Low (< 500 foot candles)

Aiphanes aculeata
Arenga hookeriana
Asterogyne martiana
Chamaedorea cataractarum
Chamaedorea costaricana
Chamaedorea elegans
Chamaedorea metallica
Chamaedorea microspadix
Chamaedorea radicalis
Chamaedorea seifrizii
Chamaedorea tepejilote
Chambeyronia macrocarpa
Howea forsteriana
Johannesteijsmannia altifrons
Licuala grandis
Licuala ramsayi
Lytocaryum weddellianum
Reinhardtia gracilis
Rhapis excelsa
Rhapis humilis
Sabal minor

Moderate

(*indicates moderate to high light)

Acoelorrhaphe wrightii
*Adonidia merrillii**
Aiphanes aculeata (with age)
*Archontophoenix alexandrae**
*Archontophoenix cunninghamiana**
*Areca catechu**
Areca vestiaria
Arenga hookeriana
*Arenga tremula**
*Bactris gasipaes**
*Butia capitata**
*Caryota mitis**
*Caryota rumphiana**
*Caryota zebrina**
Chamaedorea cataractarum
Chamaedorea costaricana
Chamaedorea elegans
Chamaedorea metallica
Chamaedorea microspadix
Chamaedorea radicalis
Chamaedorea seifrizii
Chamaedorea tepejilote
Chamaerops humilis
Chambeyronia macrocarpa
*Coccothrinax argentata**
*Coccothrinax barbadensis**
*Coccothrinax crinita**
*Coccothrinax miraguama**
Cryosophila stauracantha
*Cyrtostachys renda**
*Dypsis cabadae**
*Dypsis decaryi**
*Dypsis lutescens**
*Dypsis madagascariensis**
Euterpe edulis
*Gaussia maya**
*Heterospathe elata**
Howea forsteriana
*Hyophorbe lagenicaulis**
*Kerriodoxa elegans**
Licuala grandis
Licuala ramsayi
Licuala spinosa
*Livistona australis**
*Livistona chinensis**
*Livistona decipiens**
*Livistona rotundifolia**
*Livistona saribus**
Lytocaryum weddellianum
Normanbya normanbyi
*Phoenix loureiri**
*Phoenix roebelenii**
Pinanga coronata
*Pritchardia pacifica**
*Pritchardia thurstonii**
*Pseudophoenix sargentii**
*Ptychosperma elegans**
*Ptychosperma macarthurii**
*Ravenea rivularis**
*Rhapidophyllum hystrix**
Rhapis excelsa
Rhapis humilis
*Roystonea regia**
Sabal minor
*Serenoa repens**
*Syagrus botryophora**
*Syagrus romanzoffiana**
*Syagrus schizophylla**
*Thrinax morrisii**
*Thrinax radiata**
*Trachycarpus fortunei**
*Trachycarpus martianus**
*Veitchia arecina**
*Veitchia joannis**
*Veitchia winin**
Verschaffeltia splendida
*Wodyetia bifurcata**

High

Acrocomia aculeata
Aiphanes aculeata (with age)
Allagoptera arenaria
Bismarckia nobilis
Borassus flabellifer
Brahea armata
Brahea edulis
Carpenteria acuminata
Caryota gigas
Caryota no
Caryota urens
Chamaerops humilis
Cocos nucifera
Copernicia baileyana
Copernicia hospita
Copernicia macroglossa
Copernicia prunifera
Corypha umbraculifera
Dictyosperma album
Dypsis leptocheilos
Elaeis guineensis
*Howea forsteriana**
*only in temperate subtropial climates
Hyophorbe verschaffeltii
Hyphaene thebaica
Jubaea chilensis
Kentiopsis oliviformis
Latania loddigesii
Latania lontaroides
Livistona mariae
Mauritia flexuosa
Nannorrhops ritchiana
Neoveitchia storckii
Phoenix canariensis
Phoenix dactylifera
Phoenix reclinata
Phoenix rupicola
Phoenix sylvestris
Rhopaloblaste augusta
Sabal causiarum
Sabal maritiiformis
Sabal palmetto
Satakentia liukiuensis
Syagrus coronata
Thrinax excelsa
Trithrinax brasiliensis
Wallichia disticha
Washingtonia robusta
Zombia antillarum

Nutritional Requirements

Low

Archontophoenix alexandrae
Borassus flabellifer
Brahea armata
Brahea edulis
Coccothrinax argentata
Coccothrinax barbadensis
Coccothrinax crinita
Coccothrinax miraguama
Copernicia baileyana
Copernicia hospita
Copernicia macroglossa
Copernicia prunifera
Hyphaene thebaica
Nannorrhops ritchiana
Pseudophoenix sargentii
Sabal causiarum
Sabal minor
Sabal palmetto
Serenoa repens
Thrinax morrisii
Thrinax radiata
Trithrinax brasiliensis
Zombia antillarum

Moderate

Acoelorrhaphe wrightii
Acrocomia aculeata
Adonidia merrillii
Aiphanes aculeata
Archontophoenix alexandrae
Archontophoenix cunninghamiana
Areca catechu
Areca vestiaria
Arenga hookeriana
Arenga tremula
Asterogyne martiana
Bactris gasipaes
Bismarckia nobilis
Butia capitata
Carpenteria acuminata
Caryota gigas
Caryota mitis
Caryota no
Caryota rumphiana
Caryota urens
Caryota zebrina
Chamaedorea cataractarum
Chamaedorea costaricana
Chamaedorea elegans
Chamaedorea metallica
Chamaedorea microspadix
Chamaedorea radicalis
Chamaedorea seifrizii
Chamaedorea tepejilote
Chamaerops humilis
Cocos nucifera
Corypha umbraculifera
Cryosophila stauracantha
Cyrtostachys renda
Dictyosperma album
Dypsis cabadae
Dypsis decaryi
Dypsis leptocheilos
Dypsis madagascariensis
Elaeis guineensis
Euterpe edulis
Gaussia maya
Heterospathe elata
Howea forsteriana
Hyophorbe lagenicaulis
Johannesteijsmannia altifrons
Jubaea chilensis
Kentiopsis oliviformis
Kerriodoxa elegans
Latania loddigesii
Latania lontaroides
Licuala ramsayi
Licuala spinosa
Livistona australis
Livistona chinensis
Livistona decipiens
Livistona mariae
Livistona rotundifolia
Livistona saribus
Lytocaryum weddellianum
Mauritia flexuosa
Neoveitchia storckii
Phoenix canariensis
Phoenix dactylifera
Phoenix loureiri
Phoenix reclinata
Phoenix roebelenii
Pinanga coronata
Pritchardia pacifica
Pritchardia thurstonii
Ptychosperma elegans
Ptychosperma macarthurii
Ravenea rivularis
Reinhardtia gracilis
Rhapidophyllum hystrix
Rhapis excelsa
Rhapis humilis
Rhopaloblaste augusta
Roystonea regia
Sabal mauritiiformis
Satakentia liukiuensis
Syagrus botryophora
Syagrus coronata
Syagrus schizophylla
Thrinax excelsa
Trachycarpus fortunei
Trachycarpus martianus
Veitchia arecina
Veitchia joannis
Veitchia winin
Verschaffeltia splendida
Wallichia disticha
Washingtonia robusta
Wodyetia bifurcata

High

Caryota gigas
Caryota zebrina
Hyophorbe verschaffeltii
Licuala grandis
Normanbya normanbyi
Ravenea rivularis
Washngtonia filifera

Palms With Human Hazards

Acoelorrhaphe wrightii
Acrocomia aculeata
Aiphanes aculeata
Areca catechu
Arenga hookeriana
Arenga tremula
Bactris gasipaes
Borassus flabellifer
Brahea armata
Brahea edulis
Butia capitata
Carpenteria acuminata
Caryota gigas
Caryota mitis
Caryota no
Caryota rumphiana
Caryota urens
Caryota zebrina
Chamaedorea cataractarum
Chamaedorea costaricana
Chamaedorea elegans
Chamaedorea metallica
Chamaedorea microspadix
Chamaedorea radicalis
Chamaedorea seifrizii
Chamaedorea tepejilote
Chamaerops humilis
Copernicia baileyana
Copernicia hospita
Copernicia macroglossa
Copernicia prunifera
Corypha umbraculifera
Cryosophila stauracantha
Elaeis guineensis
Gaussia maya
Hyophorbe lagenicaulis
Hyophorbe verschaffeltii
Hyphaene thebaica
Johannesteijsmannia altifrons
Kerriodoxa elegans
Licuala grandis
Licuala ramsayi
Licuala spinosa
Livistona australis
Livistona chinensis
Livistona decipiens
Livistona mariae
Livistona rotundifolia
Livistona saribus
Mauritia flexuosa
Phoenix canariensis
Phoenix dactylifera
Phoenix loureiri
Phoenix reclinata
Phoenix roebelenii
Phoenix rupicola
Phoenix sylvestris
Ptychosperma macarthurii
Rhapidophyllum hystrix
Roystonea regia
Serenoa repens
Syagrus schizophylla
Trachycarpus fortunei
Trithrinax brasiliensis
Verschaffeltia splendida
Wallichia disticha
Washingtonia filifera
Washingtonia robusta
Zombia antillarum

Palms Generally 20' Tall or Less

Acoelorraphe wrightii
Acrocomia aculeata
Adonidia merrillii
Allagoptera arenaria
Areca vestiaria
Arenga hookeriana
Arenga tremula
Asterogyne martiana
Butia capitata
Caryota mitis
Chamaedorea cataractarum
Chamaedorea costaricana
Chamaedorea elegans
Chamaedorea metallica
Chamaedorea microspadix
Chamaedorea radicalis
Chamaedorea seifrizii
Chamaedorea tepejilote
Chamaerops humilis
Coccothrinax argentata
Coccothrinax crinita
Coccothrinax miraguama
Copernicia macroglossa
Cyrtostachys renda
Dypsis lutescens
Hyophorbe lagenicaulis
Hyophorbe verschaffeltii
Johannesteijsmannia altifrons
Kerriodoxa elegans
Licuala grandis
Licuala spinosa
Lytocaryum weddellianum
Nannorrhops ritchiana
Phoenix loureiri
Phoenix roebelenii
Pinanga coronata
Pseudophoenix sargentii
Ptychosperma elegans
Reinhardtia gracilis
Rhapidophyllum hystrix
Rhapis excelsa
Rhapis humilis
Sabal minor
Serenoa repens
Syagrus coronata
Syagrus schizophylla
Thrinax excelsa
Thrinax morrisii
Thrinax radiata
Trithrinax brasiliensis
Wallichia disticha
Zombia antillarum

Palms With Edible Fruit

Bactris gasipaes
Borassus flabellifer
Brahea edulis
Butia capitata
Mauritia flexuosa
Nannorrhops ritchiana
Phoenix canariensis
Phoenix dactylifera

Soil Requirements

**indicates palm listed under more than one requirement*

Alkaline

Brahea armata
Brahea edulis
Cryosophila stauracantha
*Kentiopsis oliviformis (slight)**
Neoveitchia storckii (slight)
*Sabal mauritiiformis (slight)**
*Thrinax morrisii**
*Thrinax radiata**

Moist Soil

Aiphanes aculeata
*Caryota zebrina**
*Johannesteijsmannia altifrons**
Licuala ramsayi
*Lytocaryum weddellianum**
*Mauritia flexuosa**
Normanbya normanbyi
*Reinhardtia gracilis**
*Rhopaloblaste augusta**
*Syagrus botryophora**
*Verschaffeltia splendida**

Well-drained

Areca vestiaria
Arenga hookeriana
*Brahea armata**
*Chamaerops humilis**
*Dypsis decaryi**
*Johannesteijsmannia altifrons**
*Kentiopsis oliviformis**
Kerriodoxa elegans
*Lytocaryum weddellianum**
Nannorrhops ritchiana
Neoveitchia storckii
*Phoenix canariensis**
*Reinhardtia gracilis**
*Rhopaloblaste augusta**
*Syagrus botryophora**
*Verschaffeltia splendida**
*Zombia antillarum**

Acid

Areca catechu
Bactris gasipaes
Caryota gigas
*Caryota zebrina**
Euterpe edulis
*Johannesteijsmannia altifrons**
*Kentiopsis oliviformis (slight)**
*Lytocaryum weddellianum**
*Mauritia flexuosa**
Neoveitchia storckii (slight)
Normanbya normanbyi
*Ravenea rivularis (slight)**
*Rhopaloblaste augusta (slight)**
*Syagrus botryophora**
*Syagrus romanzoffiana**
Trachycarpus martianus (slight)

Rich Soil

*Caryota zebrina**
Chambeyronia macrocarpa
*Johannesteijsmannia altifrons**
*Lytocaryum weddellianum**

Widely Adaptable

Acoelorrhaphe wrightii
Acrocomia aculeata
Adonidia merrillii
Allagoptera arenaria
Archontophoenix alexandrae
Archontophoenix cunninghamiana
Arenga tremula
Asterogyne martiana
Bismarckia nobilis
Borassus flabellifer
Butia capitata
Carpenteria acuminata
Caryota mitis
Caryota no
Caryota rumphiana
Caryota urens
Chamaedorea cataractarum
Chamaedorea costaricana
Chamaedorea elegans
Chamaedorea metallica
Chamaedorea microspadix
Chamaedorea radicalis
Chamaedorea seifrizii
Chamaedorea tepejilote
Chamaerops humilis
Coccothrinax argentata
Coccothrinax barbadensis
Coccothrinax crinita
Coccothrinax miraguama
Cocos nucifera
Copernicia baileyana
Copernicia hospita
Copernicia macroglossa
Copernicia prunifera
Corypha umbraculifera
Cryosophila stauracantha
Cyrtostachys renda
Dictyosperma album
Dypsis cabadae
Dypsis decaryi
Dypsis leptocheilos
Dypsis lutescens
Dypsis madagascariensis
Elaeis guineensis
Gaussia maya
Heterospathe elata
Howea forsteriana
Hyophorbe lagenicaulis
Hyophorbe verschaffeltii
Hyphaene thebaica
Jubaea chilensis
Latania loddigesii
Latania lontaroides
Licuala grandis
Licuala spinosa
Livistona australis
Livistona chinensis
Livistona decipiens
Livistona mariae
Livistona rotundifolia
Livistona saribus
Nannorrhops ritchiana
*Phoenix canariensis**
Phoenix dactylifera
Phoenix loureiri
Phoenix reclinata
Phoenix roebelenii
Phoenix rupicola
Phoenix sylvestris
Pinanga coronata
Pritchardia pacifica
Pritchardia thurstonii
Pseudophoenix sargentii
Ptychosperma elegans
Ptychosperma macarthurii
Ravenea rivularis
Rhapidophyllum hystrix
Rhapis excelsa
Rhapis humilis
Roystonea regia
Sabal causiarum
*Sabal mauritiiformis**
Sabal minor
Sabal palmetto
Satakentia liukiuensis
Serenoa repens
Syagrus coronata
*Syagrus romanzoffiana**
Syagrus schizophylla
Thrinax excelsa
*Thrinax morrisii**
*Thrinax radiata**
Trachycarpus fortunei
Trithrinax brasiliensis
Veitchia arecina
Veitchia joannis
Veitchia winin
Wallichia disticha
Washingtonia filifera
Washingtonia robusta
Wodyetia bifurcata
Zombia antillarum

General Index

Acoelorrhaphe wrightii . . . **14**,155,157
Acrocomia aculeata . . . **15**
Acrocomia totai . . . 15
Adonidia . . . **16**
Adonidia merrillii . . . **16**,167,168
African doum palm . . . **78**
African oil palm . . . **70**
African wild date palm . . . **105**
after-flower decline . . . 168
aguaje . . . **96**
Aiphanes aculeata . . . **17**
Alexander palm . . . **113**
Alexandra palm . . . **19,20**
Allagoptera arenaria . . . **18**,168
Anthracnose . . . 165
Archontophoenix alexandrae . . . **19,20**,157,158,168
Archontophoenix alexandrae 'Kuranda' . . . 19
Archontophoenix cunninghamiana . . . **20**
Archontophoenix purpurea . . . 19
Archontophoenix purpurea 'Mt. Lewis' . . . 19
Areca catechu . . . **21**
areca palm . . . **68**
Areca triandra . . . 21
Areca vestiaria . . . v,**22**
Arecastrum . . . **133**
Arecastrum romanzoffianum . . . 134
arecina palm . . . **143**,145
Arenga caudata . . . 23
Arenga engleri . . . 24,168
Arenga hookeriana . . . **23**
Arenga pinnata . . . 24
Arenga tremula . . . **24**
aricuriroba . . . **135**
arikury palm . . . **135**
assai palm . . . **71**
Australian cabbage tree palm . . . **88**
Australian fan palm . . . **86,88**,91
Australian palm . . . **88**
Bactris gasipaes . . . **26**
Bahia palm . . . **131**
Bailey copernicia . . . **57**
Bailey fan palm . . . **57**
Bailey's palm . . . **57**
bakaly . . . **115**
balai . . . **52**
bamboo palm . . . **44,46**
Banana moth . . . 163
bangalow palm . . . **20**
bay leaf palm . . . **124**
Belmore sentry palm . . . 74,75
betel nut palm . . . **21**
Bipolaris fungi . . . 165
Bismarck palm . . . **27**
Bismarckia nobilis . . . **27**,156,163
black palm . . . **100**
blue fan palm . . . **29**
blue hesper palm . . . **29**,30
blue latan palm . . . **83**
blue palmetto . . . **127**
blushing palm . . . **50**
'Bonetti' . . . 31
'Bonnetii' . . . 31,32
Borassus flabellifer . . . **28**,168,168
Boron (B) . . . 162
botan . . . **124**
bottle palm . . . **76**
Brahea armata . . . **29**,30,168
Brahea edulis . . . **30**,168
Brahea elegans . . . 29
Brazilian needle palm . . . **141**
Brazoria County palm . . . 125
brittle thatch . . . **137**
broad thatch . . . **136**
broom thatch palm . . . 138
buccaneer palm . . . **112**
bud rot . . . 166
buffalo thatch . . . **137**
buffalo top . . . **137**
buriti . . . **96**,124,**141**
Burmese fishtail palm . . . **35**
bush palmetto . . . **125**
Butia capitata . . . 8,10,**31**,**32**,168
Butia eriospatha . . . 31,32
Butia odorata . . . 31,32
Butia yatay . . . 10,31
x*Butiagrus nabonnandii* . . . 31
butterfly palm . . . **68**
cabada palm . . . **65**
cabbage palm . . . **127,128**
cabbage palmetto . . . **127**
cabbage tree . . . **127**
California cotton palm . . . **148**
California fan palm . . . **148**
California Washington palm . . . **149**
cambo . . . **72**
canangucho . . . **96**
Canary date . . . **101**
Canary Island date . . . **101**,108
capoca . . . **25**
carandai . . . **141**
caranday-guazu . . . **96**
carata . . . **124**
carnaday palm . . . 60
carnauba wax palm . . . **60**
Carpentaria palm . . . **33**
Carpenteria acuminata . . . **33**
carpy . . . **33**
Caryota gigas . . . **34**
Caryota mitis . . . **35**,168
Caryota no . . . **36**
Caryota ophiopellis . . . 39
Caryota rumphiana . . . **37**,168
Caryota urens . . . **38**,168
Caryota zebrina . . . **39**
cascade palm . . . **40**
cat palm . . . **40**
Catacauma leaf spot . . . 165
cataract palm . . . **40**
caxando . . . **18**
Central Australian cabbage palm . . . **92**
Central Australian fan palm . . . **92**
Cerataphis palmae . . . 163,164
Cercospora leaf spot . . . 165
Chamaedorea cataractarum . . . **40**
Chamaedorea costaricana . . . **41**
Chamaedorea elegans . . . **42**,43
Chamaedorea ernesti-augusti . . . 43
Chamaedorea metallica . . . **43**

Chamaedorea microspadix . . . 11,**44**,155
Chamaedorea radicalis . . . 44,**45**
Chamaedorea seifrizii . . . 41,44,**46**,168
Chamaedorea tepejilote . . . **47**
Chamaerops humilis . . . 10,**48,49**,155
Chamaerops humilis var. *cerifera* . . . 48
Chamaerops humilis var. *elatior* . . . 48
Chamaerops humilis 'Green Mound' . . . 48,49
Chambeyronia macrocarpa . . . **50**,187
chate . . . **42**
cherry palm . . . **112**
chiate . . . **46**
Chilean wine palm . . . 31,**80**
Chinese fan palm . . . **89**
Chinese windmill palm . . . **139**
chiriva . . . **133**
chit . . . **138**
chonta . . . **26**
Christmas palm . . . **16**
Chrysalidocarpus cabadae . . . 65
Chrysalidocarpus lucubensis . . . 69
Chrysalidocarpus lutescens . . . 68
Chusan . . . **139**
cliff date . . . **107**
clustering fishtail palm . . . **35**
Coccothrinax argentata . . . **51**,52,168
Coccothrinax argentea . . . 51
Coccothrinax barbadensis . . . **52**
Coccothrinax crinita . . . **53**,168
Coccothrinax miraguama . . . **54**
coco de praia . . . **18**
Coconut mites . . . 163,164
Coconut palm . . . **55,56**
Cocos nucifera . . . 11,12,**55,56**,152,156,159,161,167,168,168
Cocos nucifera 'Atlantic Tall' . . . 55
Cocos nucifera 'Fiji Dwarf' . . . 55,56
Cocos nucifera 'Jamaican Tall' . . . 55
Cocos nucifera 'Malayan Dwarf' . . . 55
Cocos nucifera 'Maypan' . . . 55
Cocos nucifera 'Panama Tall' . . . 55
Cocos plumosa . . . **133**
cold protection . . . 159,160
cold-damage treatment . . . 159,160
Colletotrichum fungus . . . 165
common palmetto . . . **127**
Copernicia alba . . . 60
Copernicia baileyana . . . **57**
Copernicia hospita . . . **58**
Copernicia macroglossa . . . **59**
Copernicia prunifera . . . 57,**60**,132
Copernicia rigida . . . 58
coquito palm . . . **80**
cortadera . . . **25**
Corypha umbraculifera . . . **61**
Corypha utan . . . 61,168
Costa Rican bamboo palm . . . **41**
cotton palm . . . **148**
coyol palm . . . **15**
coyure palm . . . **17**
creeping palmetto . . . **117**
Cryosophila stauracantha . . . **62**,169
Cuban petticoat palm . . . **59**
Cuban royal palm . . . **122**
Cylindricladium . . . 165
Cyrtostachys renda . . . **63**
date palm . . . **103**
desert fan palm . . . **148**
diamond joey . . . **79**
diamond scale . . . 165
Dictyosperma album . . . 19,**64**,168
Dictyosperma album var. *aureum* . . . 64
Dictyosperma album var. *furfuraceum* . . . 64
Dictyosperma album var. *rubrum* . . . 64
doub palm . . . **28**
doum palm . . . **78**
duma yaka . . . **24**
dwarf date palm . . . **104,106**
dwarf golden malayan . . . **55**
dwarf palmetto . . . **125**
dwarf royal palm . . . **16**
dwarf sugar palm . . . **24**
Dypsis cabadae . . . **65**,168
Dypsis decaryi . . . **66**,168
Dypsis lastelliana . . . 67
Dypsis leptocheilos . . . **67**
Dypsis lutescens . . . 11,65,**68**,158,168
Dypsis madagascariensis . . . **69**
edible date palm . . . **103**,108
Elaeis guineensis . . . **70**
Elaeis oleifera . . . 70
escoba . . . **62**
establishment care . . . 157
European fan palm . . . **48,49**
Euterpe edulis . . . 26,**71**
Euterpe oleracea . . . 71
everglades palm . . . **14**
Exosporium fungus . . . 165
Exserohilum fungi . . . 165
false smut . . . 165
fan palm . . . **88**
feather palm . . . **95**
fertilizing . . . 160,161,162
Fiji fan palm . . . **110**
filabusta palm . . . 148
flame palm . . . **50**
flame thrower palm . . . **50**
Florida royal palm . . . **122**
Florida silver palm . . . **51**
Florida thatch palm . . . **138**
footstool palm . . . **93**
forster sentry palm . . . **74**
fountain palm . . . **91**
foxtail palm . . . **150**
Franchesi palm . . . 29
frizzeltop . . . 161
Fusarium wilt . . . 166
Ganoderma butt rot . . . 166
Gaussia maya . . . **72**
gebang palm . . . 61
gecko palm . . . **39**
Genera Palmarum . . . 10
giant fishtail palm . . . **34,36,37**
giant palm weevil . . . 163,164
giant thatch palm . . . **136**
gingerbread palm . . . **78**
Gippsland palm . . . **88**
give and take . . . **62**
Gliocladium blight . . . 166

golden cane palm **68**
gora **115**
Graphiola leaf spot 165
grey goddess **29**
gru-gru **15**
guadalupe palm **30**
guanillo **138**
guano **14**
guano barbudo **53**
guano cano **58**
guano petate **53**
guayita de los arroyos **40**
hairy tom palmetto **14**
hardy bamboo palm **44**
hat palm **123**
hedgehog palm **117**
Helminthosporium complex leaf spots 165
hemp palm **139**
herbicide toxicity 168
Heterospathe elata **73**
Heterospathe heterophylla 162
Homaledra sabalella 163,164
Hooker's arenga **23**
hospita palm **58**
houailou red leaf palm **50**
Howea belmoreana 74,75
Howea forsteriana 6,**74,75**,165,168
hurricane palm **64**
Hyophorbe lagenicaulis **76**,77
Hyophorbe verschaffeltii x,**77**,163,168
Hyphaene compressa 78
Hyphaene coriacea 78
Hyphaene dichotoma 78
Hyphaene thebaica **78**
India date palm **107,108**
Indian wine palm **107**
induplicate leaves 9
International Palm Society 11
Iron (Fe) 162
ivory cane palm **109**
ivory crownshaft palm **109**
jaggery palm **38**
Jamaican thatch palm **136,138**
jata de guanabacoa **59**
jata palm 58
jelly palm **31**
jeriba **133**
joannis palm **144**,145
joey palm **79**
Johannesteijsmannia altifrons **79**
Johannesteijsmannia magnifica 79
John Crow thatch palm **136**
Jubaea chilensis 31,32,**80**
juçara palm **71**
juncara palm **71**
kentia palm **74**
Kentiopsis oliviformis **81**
Kerriodoxa elegans **82**
key palm **137**
Key thatch palm **137**
khajuri **108**
khasia palm **140**
King Alexander palm **19**
King palm **19**
kitul palm **38**
kuka **112**
lady palm **118,119**
Latania loddigesii **83**
Latania lontaroides **84**
Latania verschaffeltii 84
latanier **52**
latayne pikan **151**
leaf hopper bug 167
leaf removal 157
leaf spots 165
Lesser Antilles silver thatch **52**
lethal yellowing 167
Licuala gracilis 87
Licuala grandis **85**,87
Licuala lauterbachii 85
licuala palm **85**
Licuala paludosa 85
Licuala ramsayi **86**
Licuala rumphii 87
Licuala spinosa 85,**87**
licuri palm **132**
licurioba **135**
licury palm **132**
licuryseiro **132**
lipstick palm **63**
little blue stem **125**
Livistona australis **88**
Livistona boninensis 89
Livistona chinensis 10,11,**89,90**,168
Livistona chinensis var. *subglobosa* 89
Livistona decipiens **91**
Livistona mariae **92**
Livistona robinsoniana 93
Livistona rotundifolia 4,**93**,168,170
Livistona saribus viii,10,**94**
Lodoicea maldavica 9
lontar palm **28**
Loureir's date palm **104**
lucubensis palm **69**
Lytocaryum weddellianum **95**
Lytocaryum weddellianum var. *cinerea* **95**
Macarthur palm **114**
macaw fat **70**
macaw palm **15,17**
macumba **15**
Magnesium (Mg) 161
Magnolia white scale 163,164
maharajah palm **63**
majestic palm **115**
majesty palm **115**
malio **115**
Manganese (Mn) 162
mangrove fan palm **87**
Manila palm **16**,143
Martius fan palm **140**
Martius windmill palm **140**
mat palm **53**
Mauritia flexuosa **96**,124
maya palm **72**
mazari palm **97,98**
mbocaya **15**
Mediterranean fan palm **48**
metallic palm **43**

Metamasius hemipterus . . . 163,164
metric conversion chart . . . 3
Mexican blue fan palm . . . **29**
Mexican fan palm . . . **149**
Mexican washingtonia . . . 148,**149**
miniature coconut palm . . . **95**
miniature date palm . . . **106**
miniature fishtail palm . . . **43**
miraguama palm . . . **54**
miriti. . . . **96**
Montgomery palm. . . . **143**
morete . . . **96**
moriche . . . **96**
mountain fishtail palm . . . **34**
mucaja . . . **15**
mule palm . . . 31
Myndus crudus . . . 167
Nannorrhops arabica . . . 97
Nannorrhops 'Iran Silver' . . . 97,98
Nannorrhops naudiniana . . . 97
Nannorrhops ritchiana . . . 9,**97,98**,168
Nannorrhops stocksiana . . . 97
Neanthe bella . . . **42**
needle palm . . . **117**
Neodypsis decaryi . . . 66
Neoveitchia storckii . . . **99**
Nicobar majestic palm . . . **121**
nicury . . . **132**
Nitrogen (N) . . . 161
Normanbya normanbyi . . . **100**
northern washingtonia . . . **148**
nutritional disorders . . . 161,162
oil palm . . . 70
old man palm . . . **53**
Opogona sacchari . . . 163
Opsiandra maya . . . 72
orange crownshaft palm . . . **22**
ouricuri . . . **132**
overtop palm . . . 134
Pacaya . . . **41,47**
pacayita . . . **41**
Pacific fan palm . . . **110**
palas paying . . . **85**
palem belang . . . **39**
palem tokek . . . **39**
palm aphid . . . 163,164
palm classifications . . . 10
palm conservation . . . 11
palm flowers . . . 9
palm fruits . . . 9
palm leaf skeletonizer . . . 163,164
palm leaves . . . 8
palm seeds . . . 9
palm stems . . . 8
palma amarga . . . **124**
palma cana . . . **123**
palma chilena . . . **80**
palma cimaronna . . . **72**
palma de guagara . . . **124**
palma de sombrero . . . **123**
palma de vaca . . . **124**
palma redonda . . . **124**
palmasito . . . **72**
palmetto palm . . . **127**
Palmetto weevil . . . 163,164
palmilla . . . **44**
palmito dulce . . . **47**
palmito palm . . . **71**
palmya palm . . . **28**
Panama hat palm . . . **123**
parlor palm . . . **42**
pata de gallo . . . **25**
pati . . . **131**
patioba . . . **131**
paurotis palm . . . **14**
peaberry palm . . . **137**
peach palm . . . **26**
pejibaye . . . **26**
pejivalle . . . **26**
pencil pointing . . . 168
Pestalotiopsis leaf spot . . . 165
petticoat palm . . . **59,148**
Phoenix canariensis . . . 100,**101,102**,108,157,163,164,166,168
Phoenix dactylifera . . . **103**,108,155,161,168
Phoenix dactylifera 'Deglet Noor' . . . 103
Phoenix dactylifera 'Medjool' . . . 103
Phoenix dactylifera 'Zahedi' . . . 103
Phoenix loureiri . . . **104**
Phoenix loureiri humilis . . . 104
Phoenix loureiri loureiri . . . 104
Phoenix reclinata . . . **105**,159,168
Phoenix roebelenii . . . 10,104,**106**,157,165
Phoenix rupicola . . . **107**
Phoenix sylvestris . . . **108**
Phytophthora bud rot . . . 166
picabben palm . . . **20**
piccabeen palm . . . **20**
pico . . . **25**
pigmy date palm . . . **106**
pinang merah . . . **22**
pinang palm . . . **63**
pinang yaki . . . **22**
Pinanga coronata . . . **109**
Pinanga kuhlii . . . 109
pindo palm . . . **31,133**
pink rot . . . 166
planting depth . . . 157
porcupine palm . . . **117**
Potassium (K) . . . 161
preto . . . **14**
princess palm . . . **64**
Pritchardia pacifica . . . **110**,168
Pritchardia thurstonii . . . 110,**111**,168
pruning . . . 158
Pseudophoenix sargentii . . . **112**
Pseudophoenix vinifera . . . *112*
Ptychosperma elegans . . . **113**
Ptychosperma macarthurii . . . **114**,168
Puerto Rican hat palm . . . **123**
pupunha . . . **26**
pygmy date palm . . . 95,104,**106**
Pythium rots . . . 166
queen palm . . . **133,134**
Queensland black palm . . . **100**
radicalis palm . . . **45**
Ravenea rivularis . . . **115**,163
reclinata palm . . . **105**
red feather palm . . . **50**

red latan palm **84**
red sealing wax palm **63**
red-leaf palm **50**
redneck palm **67**
reduplicate leaves 9
reed palm **46**
reed rhapis **120**
Reinhardtia gracilis **116**
Reinhardtia gracilis var. *gracilior* 116
Reinhardtia gracilis var. *gracilis* 116
Reinhardtia gracilis var. *rostrata* 116
Reinhardtia gracilis var. *tenuissima* 116
restinga palm **18**
Rhapidophyllum hystrix **117**
Rhapis excelsa **118,119**,120,162
Rhapis humilis **120**
Rhizoctonia root rots 166
Rhopaloblaste augusta **121**
ribbon palm **91**
roebelinii palm **106**
root ball size 156
root pruning 156
root systems 7
rootspine palm **62**
rotten sugar cane borer 163,164
round leaf fan palm **93**
Royal palm bug 163,164
royal palm **122**
Roystonea borinqueana 122
Roystonea elata 122
Roystonea oleracea 122
Roystonea princeps 122
Roystonea regia 10,11,**122**,158,159,168
ruffle palm **17**
ruffled fan palm **85**
Rynchophorus cruentatus 163
Sabal causiarum **123**
Sabal etonia 126
Sabal mauritiiformis **124**
Sabal mexicana 125,128
Sabal minor **125,126**
Sabal minor 'Louisiana' **125**,126
sabal palm **127,128**
Sabal palmetto 123,**127,128**,154,156,159,163
Sabal palmetto 'Lisa' **127**,128
Sabal x *texensis* 125
sagisi palm **73**
sago palm **38**
salt injury 168
satake palm **129**
Satakentia liukiuensis **129**
savannah palm **124**
saw palmetto **130**
scales 163
scrub palmetto **125**,126,**130**
sea thatch **138**
sealing wax palm **63**
seashore palm **18**
seed germination 10
seed propagation 154
Senegal date **105**
sentry palm **74**
serdang **93,94**
Serenoa repens **130**,154
Seychelles stilt palm **146**
short blue hesper **29**
silk top thatch **138**
silver date palm **108**
silver palm **51,52**
silver rootspine palm **62**
silver saw palm **14**
silver thatch **136,137**
silver thatch palm **51**
site preparation 157
skyduster **149**
slender lady palm **120**
snakeskin palm **39**
solitaire palm **113**,114
solitary fishtail palm **38**
sooty mold 165
southern washingtonia **149**
Sphaerodothus neowashingtoniae 165
spider mites 163
spindle palm **77**
spine palm **117**
spiny fiber palm **141**
spiny licuala **87**
Stigmina leaf spot 165
stilt palm **146**
striped palm **39**
sugar date palm **108**
sumuqué **131**
supports 157
swamp palmetto **125**
Syagrus amara 134
Syagrus botryophora **131**
Syagrus coronata **132**
Syagrus romanzoffiana 11,18,32,131,**133,134**,159,161,168
Syagrus romanzoffiana 'Australis' 133
Syagrus romanzoffiana 'Robusta' 133
Syagrus schizophylla **135**,168
tala palm **28**
talauriksha palm **28**
talipot palm **61**
tall Jamaican **55**
tar spot 165
taraw palm **94**
tasiste **14**
teddy bear palm **67**
tenera **41**
tepejilote **47**
Tetranychus urticae 163
Thai mountain giant **34**
thatch **52**
thatch leaf palm **74**
thatch palm **53,74,138**
Thielaviopsis trunk 166
thread palm **149**
thread scale 163
Thrinax excelsa **136**
Thrinax morrisii **137**
Thrinax parviflora 138
Thrinax radiata **138**
Thurston palm 110,**111**
tique **14**
toddy fishtail palm **38**
toddy palm **28**,38,**108**
Trachycarpus fortunei **139**,140,155,168,168,187

General Index

Trachycarpus martianus **140**
triangle palm **66**
Trithrinax brasiliensis **141**,**142**,168
Trithrinax campestris 141
trunk constrictions 167
trunk cracks 167
trunk splits 167
tufted fishtail palm **35**
unleito **99**
Vanuatu fan palm **85**
vegetative propagation 154
Veitchia arecina **143**,145,168
Veitchia joannis **144**,145
Veitchia mcdanielsii 143
Veitchia merrillii 16
Veitchia montgomeryana 143
Veitchia winin **145**
Verschaffeltia splendida **146**
voiavoi **104**
Wallich palm **147**
Wallichia disticha **147**
Washington palm **149**
Washingtonia filifera **148**,165,168
Washingtonia robusta vi,148,**149**,159,163,168
Washingtonian **149**
Weddell palm **95**
weeping cabbage palm **91**
white elephant palm **82**
wild date palm **107**,**108**
windmill palm **139**,140
window palm **116**
window pane palm **116**
wine palm **28**,**31**,**38**
winin palm **145**
Wodyetia bifurcata 11,100,**150**,163
xate **46**
Xylastodoris luteolus 163,164
yarey **57**,**58**,**123**
yarey hembra **57**
yareyon **57**
yayih **71**
yellow bamboo palm **68**
yellow latan palm 84
yuraguana de costa **51**
zebra fishtail palm **39**
Zombia antillarum 8,**151**
Zombia antillarum var. *gonsalezii* **151**
zombie palm **151**

Trachycarpus fortunei

Glossary

adventitious roots: roots originating from stem tissue rather than from other roots; all palm roots are adventitious
armed: bearing spines or teeth
bipinnately compound: a feather palm leaf that is twice-compound; that is, the primary leaflets themselves consist of system of smaller secondary leaflets
bract: a hood-like or leaf-like protective structure found at the base of an inflorescence
chlorosis (chlorotic, adj.): yellowing of plant leaves caused by disease or nutrient deficiency
costa: the extension of the leaf stem (petiole) into the blade on a costapalmate leaf
costapalmate: a fan palm leaf with an extension of the leaf stem (petiole) into the blade
clustering palm: a palm that branches at the base or below and produces several or numerous stems
crownshaft: a conspicuous neck-like structure formed by the tubular leaf bases of some feather-leaved palms that sheath each other very tightly around the stem
division: propagation of a clustering palm by splitting the clump
drupe: a fleshy, one-seeded fruit that does not open up at maturity, typical of many palm fruits
genus (plural: genera): a group of related species believed to be of common ancestry and defined by certain important shared characteristics that sets them apart from other species groups
hastula: a small, thin, more or less rounded protuberance of tissue located at the point where the petiole meets the blade on a fan palm leaf
induplicate: a palm leaf in which the leaflets or segments are folded upward, forming a "V"
inflorescence: the flower stalk of a plant
infructescence: the fruiting stalk of a plant
leaf base: the lowest and widest portion of the palm leaf stem or petiole that sheathes the stem
leaf blade: the upper, expanded portion of a palm leaf
leaf scar: the mark left behind on a palm trunk at a leaf's point of attachment after the leaf falls
leaf stem: the petiole of a palm leaf
necrosis (necrotic, adj.): death of plant tissue in which browning of blackening of the tissue occurs; frequently a symptom of disease, insect damage, nutrient deficiency, or some other type of physiological problem
node: the point on the stem at which a leaf is attached
palmate: a fan palm leaf lacking a costa
petiole: the stem of a palm leaf
pinnately compound: feather palm leaves that are only once-compound; that is, there is only a single series of leaflets
phloem: food conducting cells in plant tissue
rachis: the extension of the leaf stem (petiole) through the leaflets of a feather palm
reduplicate: a palm leaf in which the leaflets or segments are folded downward, forming an inverted "V"
rib: upraised vein on a palm leaf or leaflet
ring scar: the mark left behind on a palm trunk after a leaf that completely sheathes the stem falls off
root initiation zone: specialized area at the base of the palm stem from which roots are produced
secondary growth: the ability of plant stems and roots to produce new vascular tissue and increasing in diameter with age; this ability is lacking in palms
segment: the split portions of a fan palm leaf
spathe: a hood-like or boat-shaped bract
solitary palm: a palm that produces only one trunk or stem
subfamily: a subdivision of a plant family which unites genera that all share certain important characteristics and are believed to be of common descent
tribe: a group of closely related genera within a subfamily
unarmed: free of spines or teeth
vascular bundles: columns of water and food conducting cells within the stem of a palm
vascular tissues: the water and food conducting tissue of a plant
xylem: water conducting cells in plant tissue

A Selected Palm Bibliography

Blombery, A. and T. Rodd. 1988. *Palms of the World. Their Cultivation, Care and Landscape Use.* Angus & Robertson, New South Wales.

Boyer, K. 1992. *Palms and Cycads Beyond the Tropics.* Palm and Cycad Societies of Australia, Queensland.

Broschat, T. K. and A. W. Meerow. 2000. *Ornamental Palm Horticulture.* University Press of Florida, Gainesville.

Corner, E. J. H. 1966. *The Natural History of Palms.* Weidenfield and Nicholson, London.

Dranfield, J and H. Beentje. 1995. *The Palms of Madagascar.* Royal Botanic Gardens, Kew and International Palm Society, London.

Elliott, M. L., T. K. Broschat, J. Y. Uchida and G. W. Simone. 2004. *Diseases and Disorders of Ornamental Palms.* American Phytopathological Press, St. Paul.

Ellison, D. and A. Ellison. 2001. *Betrock's Cultivated Palms of the World.* Betrock Information Systems, Inc., Hollywood, FL.

Francko, D. A. 2003. *Palms Won't Grow Here and Other Myths.* Timber Press, Portland, OR.

Gibbons, M. 1993. *Palms.* Chartwell Books, Seacaucus, NJ.

Gibbons, M. 1993. *Palms: The New Compact Study Guide and Identifier.* Book Sales, London.

Gibbons, M. 2000. *Palms: The Illustrated Identifier to over 100 Palm Species.* Apple Press, East Sussex, UK.

Gibbons, M. 2003. *A Pocket Guide to Palms.* Chartwell Books, Secaucus, NJ.

Henderson, A. 1995. *The Palms of the Amazon.* Oxford University Press, New York.

Henderson, A., G. Galeano and R. Bernal. 1995. *Palms of the Americas.* Princeton University Press, Princeton, NJ.

Henderson, A. and F. Borchsenius (eds.). 1999. *Evolution, Variation and Classification of Palms.* New York Botanical Garden Press, Bronx.

Hodel, D. R. 1992. *Chamaedorea Palms.* International Palm Society, Lawrence, KS.

Hodel, D. R. (ed.). 1992. *The Palms and Cycads of Thailand.* Nong Nooch Tropical Garden and Allen Press, Lawrence, KS.

Hodel, D. R. and J. C. Pintaud. 1998. *The Palms of New Caledonia.* Nong Nooch Tropical Garden and Allen Press, Lawrence, KS.

Howard, F. W., D. Moore, R. Giblin-Davis and R. Abad. 2001. *Insects on Palms.* CABI Publishing, Cambridge, MA and Oxford, UK.

Jones, David L. 1984. *Palms in Australia.* Reed Books, New South Wales.

Jones, David L. 1985. *Palms in Colour.* Reed Books, New South Wales.

Jones, D. L. 1995. *Palms Throughout the World.* Smithsonian Institution Press, Washington DC.

Krempin, J. 1990. *Palms and Cycads Around the World.* Horwitz Grahame, Sydney.

Langlois, A. C. 1976. *Supplement to Palms of the World.* University of Florida Presses, Gainesville (1980 reprint published by Horticultural Books, Stuart, FL).

Leaser, D. 2004. *Palm Trees: a Story in Photographs.* Westwood Pacific Publishers.

Lorenzi, H., H. M. de Souza, J. T. de Medeiros Costa, L. S. C. de Cerqueira and E. Ferreira. 2004. *Palmeiras Brasileiras e Exóticas Cultivadas.* Instituto Plantarum de Estudos da Flora LTDA., Nova Odessa, Brazil.

Meerow, A. W. 2005. *Betrock's Cold Hardy Palms.* Betrock Information Systems, Inc., Hollywood, FL.

Meerow, A. W. 1992. *Betrock's Guide to Landscape Palms.* Betrock Information Systems, Inc., Hollywood, FL.

McCurrah, J. C. 1960. *Palms of the World.* Harper & Brothers, New York.

Riffle, R. L. and P. Craft. 2003. *An Encyclopedia of Cultivated Palms.* Timber Press, Portland, OR.

Stevenson, G. B. 1996. *Palms of Southern Florida.* University Press of Florida, Gainesville.

Tomlinson, P. B. 1990. *The Structural Biology of Palms.* Clarendon Press, Oxford

Uhl, N. W. and J. Dransfield. 1987. *Genera Palmarum.* Allen Press, Lawrence, KS.

About the Author

Dr. Alan W. Meerow was the former Professor and Palm and Tropical Ornamentals Specialist at the University of Florida's Fort Lauderdale Research & Education Center. He currently works as a geneticist for the Agricultural Research Service, and is a research collaborator at Fairchild Tropical Garden. He received his B. S. degree in botany and environmental horticulture from the University of California at Davis and his M.S. and Ph.D. from the University of Florida in horticultural science and botany. Dr. Meerow originated and taught the course Palm Production and Culture for many years in the University's Ft. Lauderdale Degree Program in Environmental Horticulture, and currently conducts research in various aspects of tropical horticulture and botany. He has been recognized by the Florida Nurserymen and Growers Association as Horticultural Writer of the Year in 1990, and Educator of the Year in 1991. In 2005, he received the Peter H. Raven Award of American Society of Plant Taxonomists for exceptional efforts at outreach to non-scientists. Dr. Meerow is an internationally recognized authority on the amaryllis family and has published numerous scientific papers on the taxonomy of that group. He has published over 200 scientific, extension, trade and popular magazine articles on plants. He is the author of Betrock's Guide to Landscape Palms, Betrock's Cold Hardy Palms *and, with Timothy K. Broschat,* Betrock's Reference Guide to Florida Landscape Plants *and* Ornamental Palm Horticulture *(University Press of Florida).*